全新版新世纪走遍美国
学习指导 4

Michael Berman

Janet Battiste

北京大学出版社
PEKING UNIVERSITY PRESS

北京市版权局著作权合同登记号　图字 01-2008-1460

图书在版编目(CIP)数据

全新版新世纪走遍美国. 学习指导 4/Michael. Berman 等编著.—北京：北京大学出版社，2008.11

ISBN 978-7-301-14380-3

Ⅰ. 全… Ⅱ. M… Ⅲ. 英语－听说教学－教材　Ⅳ. H319.9

中国版本图书馆 CIP 数据核字(2008)第 164900 号

Michael Berman　Janet Battiste
Connect with English, Instructor's Manual to accompany Video Comprehension Books 1—4
Connect with English, Instructor's Manual to accompany Conversation Books 1—4
Connect with English, Video Script 4
ISBN：0-07-292754-2
ISBN：0-07-292759-3
ISBN：0-07-365876-6
Copyright © 1998 by the WGBH Educational Foundation and the Corporation for Public Broadcasting. All rights reserved. Printed in the United States of America. Except as permitted under the United States Copyright Act of 1976, no part of this publication may be reproduced or distributed in any form or by any means, or stored in a data base or retrieval system, without the prior written permission of the publisher.
All rights reserved. This edition is authorized for sale in the People's Republic of China only, excluding Hong Kong, Macao SARs and Taiwan.
此书只限在中华人民共和国境内(不包括中国香港、澳门特别行政区及台湾地区)销售。未经出版者预先书面许可，不得以任何方式复制或抄袭本书的任何部分。
本书封面贴有 McGraw-Hill 公司防伪标签，无标签者不得销售。

书　　　名：	全新版新世纪走遍美国·学习指导 4
著作责任者：	Michael Berman　等编著
责 任 编 辑：	张建民
标 准 书 号：	ISBN 978-7-301-14380-3/H·2089
出 版 发 行：	北京大学出版社
地　　　址：	北京市海淀区成府路 205 号　100871
网　　　址：	http://www.pup.cn
电 子 信 箱：	zbing@pup.pku.edu.cn
电　　　话：	邮购部 62752015　发行部 62750672　编辑部 62755217　出版部 62754962
印 刷 者：	世界知识印刷厂
经 销 者：	新华书店
	889 毫米×1194 毫米　16 开本　9 印张　200 千字
	2008 年 11 月第 1 版　2008 年 11 月第 1 次印刷
定　　　价：	98.00 元(包括视频理解、会话练习、学习指导及光盘)

未经许可，不得以任何方式复制或抄袭本书之部分或全部内容。
版权所有，侵权必究
举报电话：(010)62752024　电子信箱：fd@pup.pku.edu.cn

Contents

Part 1 Guidebook for Video Comprehension Book ·············· 1–37

Introduction

37 Thanksgiving
38 Starting Over
39 The Pressure's On
40 Sharing Feelings
41 Unexpected Offers
42 The Audition

43 Dream Catcher
44 Gifts
45 True Love
46 Friendship
47 The Lost Boys
48 A Very Good Year

Part 2 Guidebook for Conversation Book ·············· 39–75

Introduction

37 Thanksgiving
38 Starting Over
39 The Pressure's On
40 Sharing Feelings
41 Unexpected Offers
42 The Audition

43 Dream Catcher
44 Gifts
45 True Love
46 Friendship
47 The Lost Boys
48 A Very Good Year

Part 3 Video Script ·············· 77–138

37 Thanksgiving
38 Starting Over
39 The Pressure's On
40 Sharing Feelings
41 Unexpected Offers
42 The Audition

43 Dream Catcher
44 Gifts
45 True Love
46 Friendship
47 The Lost Boys
48 A Very Good Year

Part 1

Guidebook for Video Comprehension Book

Introduction

What This Manual Can Do for You

This manual gives you the tools you need to use *Video Comprehension Books 1-4* in an effective and flexible way. This Introduction explains:

- what the *Video Comprehension Books* are, and how each *Video Comprehension Book* is organized;
- how to approach the variety of activity types found in the *Video Comprehension Books*;
- how to adjust the level and scope of these activities based on the abilities and interests of your students.

Following the Introduction, this manual devotes two pages to each individual chapter. These two-page spreads have four sections:

1. additional questions for every *What About You?* activity in the episode;
2. three expansion activities for each episode, using themes from the *What About You?* activities as springboards;
3. a synopsis of each episode, which provides the teacher with a quick reference to the events and characters in the story;
4. an answer key.

Finally, this manual contains a testing program which spans all four *Video Comprehension Books*. There is one test for every four chapters in the books, making for twelve tests in all.

Video Comprehension Books 1-4

There are four *Video Comprehension Books*, each with twelve chapters. Each chapter in the *Video Comprehension Books* corresponds to one episode in the **Connect with English** video. The books are divided as follows:

Book 1	Episodes 1-12
Book 2	Episodes 13-24
Book 3	Episodes 25-36
Book 4	Episodes 37-48

Each episode in the video has two basic segments: the actual story, which focuses on a young musician named Rebecca Casey, and her friends and family in Boston and San Francisco; and the *Viewpoints* segment, which features a Discussion Group of non-native English speakers from around the world. This group discusses and analyzes the story from different personal and cultural points of view.

The foundation of each *Video Comprehension Book* is its twelve core chapters, which help students understand the events and language in the story. In addition, Book 1 features a special *Meet the Discussion Group* chapter, and Books 2-4 feature a *Discussion Group Index*, which gives a short biography of the Discussion Group participants. Moreover, all four books feature a *Character Index*, which identifies all the main characters in the video and describes their relationships to

one another. Finally, in case students don't start at the beginning of the 48-episode story, Books 2-4 also feature review sections entitled *The Story So Far*. These succinct reviews summarize the main events of the previous episodes, and enable viewers to begin watching at any time in the course of the story.

The *Video Comprehension Books* are primarily designed for classroom use. As the activities in the books are based on repeated viewings of the video in the classroom, you will need access to a VCR and television, as well as the **Connect with English** video cassettes. Non-classroom use of these books is possible, however, if students are able to view the videos at home or in a laboratory environment. In this case, the teacher can have students watch the video on their own as an outside assignment and then go over the chapters in the books together in class.

GENERAL OVERVIEW AND PHILOSOPHY

The purpose of the *Video Comprehension Books* is to bring the challenging language and cultural nuances of the video within reach of all high-beginning through intermediate students. The systematic development of activities found in these books, while building listening comprehension skills and confidence, enables students at many levels to understand the essential language and events of the story.

The language level throughout the *Video Comprehension Books* has been kept purposefully low. Every attempt has been made to avoid complex structures although many opportunities for raising the language level have been included. For example, while the numbered activities in the book are receptive in nature, the *What About You?* activities offer students the chance to give more open responses in which they can express their views and opinions. The *Instructor's Manual* takes this a step further by providing additional *What About You?* questions and expansion activities at a variety of levels.

CHAPTER ORGANIZATION

Each 8-page chapter in the *Video Comprehension Books* has five principal sections which are briefly outlined below.

1. Preview/Before You Watch

This section is designed to help students understand the episode they are about to watch. Photo highlights and contextualized clues enable students to predict language and events they will see in the story.

2. Watch for Main Ideas

Here, students watch for global ideas as they view the entire episode for the first time. This section helps students to focus on the most important characters and events in the story. The *While You Watch* activity asks students to recognize or identify central people, places, things, or events. The *After You Watch* activities help solidify students' understanding of the story's main developments. All of the activities are receptive, in that they focus on students' understanding of the story rather than their ability to produce language. The *What About You?* activity at the end of this section asks students to make predictions about the characters and events in the story.

3. Watch for Details

This three-page section focuses students' attention on more detailed language, actions, and events of the story. Students complete the activities in this section as they rewatch each of the three parts of the episode, one at a time. In the *While You Watch* activities, students identify speakers, particular language, or completed actions. The *After You Watch* activities check students' finer understanding of the characters' actions, language, emotions, and motivations, as well as the subtle cultural nuances in the story.

4. Highlights

The *Culture* box provides an arena for cross-cultural comparison and discussion. Each chapter focuses on a different element of United States and Canadian culture found in the video. The corresponding *What About You?* activity then turns attention to the students' own cultural norms and opinions. In the *Expressions* activity, students work with key idioms, words, and phrases from the video.

5. Review and Discuss

This section always begins with the *Story Summary*, a cloze exercise which reviews the episode's main events. In the *Viewpoints* activity, students interpret a statement made in the *Discussion Group* portion of the video, then react to this statement in a corresponding *What About You?* activity.

For more information, refer to the *To the Teacher* and *Visual Tour* sections at the start of each *Video Comprehension Book*.

CLASSROOM MANAGEMENT

General Teaching Suggestions

1. *Know your materials.* It is important to preview and familiarize yourself with the **Connect with English** video episodes and *Video Comprehension Book* chapters before using them with a class. Since each episode/chapter contains a great variety of language, themes, and activity types, by previewing the material you will be much better equipped to adapt lesson plans to your particular class.

2. *Know your equipment!* Familiarize yourself as much as possible with your school's VCR and television before class time. Make sure the VCR works properly and that you can operate the fast forward, reverse, and pause buttons. Finally, note the VCR counter numbers at points in the video you wish to highlight or go back to. It is helpful to set the counter number at zero before you begin.

3. *Conduct previewing activities.* Always allow students to complete the *Preview/Before You Watch* section before watching the video. Similarly, have students preview the *While You Watch* activities in advance of watching the episode. It is important that students understand the listening task before they begin.

4. *Take full advantage of other prediction-based activities.* In addition to completing the *Preview/Before You Watch* page, utilize other ways to help students prepare to watch. Before watching the video, for instance, you can have students recount the previous episode. Ask students to try to guess the significance of the episode title. Before looking at the *Before You Watch* activity in the book, have students (in pairs or groups) make their own *Before You Watch* activity based on the *Preview* photographs. You can even show segments of the video *with the sound off* and have students predict the action and dialogue.

5. *Be creative!* Don't be afraid to adapt the activities to your specific class situation. For example, to give students more support in doing the activities, students can work together in pairs or small groups. If students are having trouble with *After You Watch* questions, they can preview these questions *before* they watch, thereby helping them to focus more directly on the targeted issues and language. And don't rule out one of the simplest ways to help your students: show the video segment again. This option is neither "cheating" nor is it counterproductive to students' listening comprehension skills; on the contrary, it provides more directed listening practice which will build their skills and confidence.

6. *Take full advantage of the Instructor's Manual!* You hold a wealth of information and ideas at your fingertips. Preview the additional *What About You?* questions and expansion activities at least a day before the class, if possible. Mark the questions you think will be most successful with your students. Most importantly, view the questions and expansion activities as suggestive rather than prescriptive; that is, change and adapt them to fit your needs.

Time

Each chapter in the *Video Comprehension Books* should take approximately two to three hours, which includes class time spent watching the video. For laboratory or home viewing situations, the amount will be considerably less. However, time spent on any given chapter can vary, depending on the ability of the students, the resonance of particular themes, and the amount of additional questions and expansion activities you elect to include. Some of the more involved expansion activities, for example, can easily add an hour or more to your lesson.

HOMEWORK, EVALUATION, AND TESTING

Homework

There are a wide variety of sources in the *Video Comprehension Books* for quality homework assignments.

- The *Expressions* and *Story Summary* activities can easily be assigned for homework. In addition, assigning the *Preview/Before You Watch* page for homework serves as a nice preparation for the coming episode.

- If your teaching situation does not require the use of the testing program in this manual, then these tests are an excellent source for homework assignments.

- The *What About You?* questions (including the additional questions in this manual) are ripe with homework opportunities. You can have students write short answers or paragraphs explaining their answers to the questions. You can even ask students to prepare their own *What About You?* questions.

- If students are watching the video in a language lab or at home, all numbered activities in the *Video Comprehension Books* can be assigned for homework. In language lab situations you may wish to allow students to do their homework in pairs or groups; this way, they will be able to discuss the episode and collectively work through any doubts or problems.

Evaluation and Testing
The testing program in this manual is an excellent means to evaluate students' comprehension of the **Connect With English** story line and characters, as well as the words and phrases covered in the *Expressions* activities. The tests feature a clear and familiar format, and can be graded quickly using the enclosed answer key.

As an alternative or supplement to the testing program, students may be asked to individually complete the *Watch for Main Ideas* and the *Watch for Details* sections of a chapter. Such a "test," administered once or twice per *Video Comprehension Book,* will be a good indication of the level of a student's listening comprehension skills and of his/her improvement.

Grading and assessment using any of the above methods of testing is, as always, a subjective endeavor. However, even for high-beginning students, because of the receptive nature of the activities, scores below 50% should certainly signal to both student and teacher that extra help is necessary.

The Connect with English Print Program

The **Connect with English** program contains many flexible print materials for a variety of instructional needs. In addition to the three core components — *Video Comprehension Books 1-4, Conversation Books 1-4,* and *Grammar Guides 1-4* — there is a diverse collection of supplemental materials that enhance and enrich the **Connect with English** experience.

CORE COMPONENTS

Video Comprehension Books 1-4
The *Video Comprehension Books* help students build listening comprehension skills and gain a clear understanding of the characters and story lines found in the **Connect with English** video series. Exercises include multiple choice, true/false, sentence completion, and cloze activities. Additional skills and topics that are covered in each book include reading, oral communication, and vocabulary development.

Using the video with the Video Comprehension Books: Depending on the time and length of the course, instructors may choose to show the **Connect with English** video during class, while simultaneously using the book. However, if repeated access to a television and VCR is not possible, teachers can have their students watch the video episodes in a library, language lab, or at home.

Conversation Books 1-4
Designed specifically for classroom use, the *Conversation Books* help students develop oral communication skills. Each chapter features a variety of communicative partner, group, team, and whole-class activities that provide a natural extension of the themes found in the corresponding video episodes. Icons indicating the difficulty of each activity allow teachers to adjust the level according to the needs of their students. An optional research project for each episode extends and expands the episode themes as students gather relevant data outside the classroom.

Using the video with the Conversation Books: It is not necessary to have classroom access to the video in order for students to complete the activities in the Conversation Books. While it is assumed that students will have seen the episode in its entirety at least one time, students' actual viewing can take place either in class, or in a library, language lab, or at home.

Grammar Guides 1-4
The *Grammar Guides* assist students in developing mastery of the grammatical structures and vocabulary items found throughout the **Connect with English** video. The topics presented in these four books follow a developmental scope and sequence. Grammatical structures are linked to specific episodes, providing students with contextualized examples. Exercises build from a receptive understanding of the grammar point, to language production through controlled exercises, and finally to *Power Practice* sections in which students write about more personalized, open-ended topics.

Using the video with the Grammar Guides: Students can use the *Grammar Guides* either before or after they watch the corresponding video episode, to either preview or review critical structures and grammatical topics. Students will welcome the carefully sequenced review of the language and its connection to the video through numerous examples and practice exercises.

SUPPLEMENTAL MATERIALS

Connections Readers
The 16 titles in this series of graded readers feature controlled vocabulary and grammar at four distinct levels of difficulty to help students read with understanding as well as enjoyment. The stories increase in complexity from level to level. The four Level One readers feature exactly the same story found in the video program, told in simplified English and extensively illustrated with color photos. The same basic story is expanded upon in Level Two, only with more reliance on narrative speech. Finally, the Level Three and Four readers dramatically expand the video story line, using the same characters from the video, but putting them in new situations.

Video Scripts 1-4
The scripts for the **Connect with English** video are available in four separate books, and can be used in conjunction with any of the other materials in the print package. Each script contains the exact dialogue from the video, as well as the stage directions used during the filming of the series. The scripts are useful for staging class role-plays, script readings, or even short plays. They also serve as a reference for teachers who wish to concentrate on specific language or grammatical patterns as they appear within the context of the language in the video episodes.

Home Viewer's Guide

Primarily designed for the self-study audience, the *Home Viewer's Guide* provides a comprehensive review of the entire 48 episode program. Each chapter contains video comprehension exercises, readings on United States and Canadian culture, and Behind the Scenes information about the filming of **Connect with English**. The *Home Viewer's Guide* comes in various bilingual editions including Spanish/English, Mandarin/English, Korean/English, and Thai/English.

Connect with English Soundtrack

The complete soundtrack from the **Connect with English** program is available on CD or audiocassette. It features 12 original songs in a wide range of musical genres including pop, country, jazz, blues, and rap.

FOR INSTRUCTORS

Video Comprehension Books 1-4 Instructor's Manual

This manual contains over 1000 additional *What About You?* questions and 100 expansion activities which help teachers expand the focus of the class to include speaking, critical thinking, interviews, projects, presentations, and writing assignments.

Conversation Books 1-4 Instructor's Manual

This manual contains specific teaching suggestions that enable instructors to adjust the level of every activity in each of the four books. Also included are oral proficiency checklists that instructors can use as an evaluative device in measuring students' communicative progress.

Grammar Guides 1-4 Instructor's Manual

Within this manual, teachers will find *Writing with Grammar* and *Communicating with Grammar* activities that provide additional practice with the grammar topics found in each episode. Also included is a detailed answer key.

Distance-Learning Faculty Guide

This guide contains useful information about how to use **Connect with English** materials in a distance-learning course, and also offers suggestions for how to establish new credit or non-credit distance-learning programs into any existing ESL/EFL curriculum.

Demonstration Video

This video contains actual classroom examples of how the **Connect with English** materials can be used in a variety of different instructional settings.

Course Options for Using the Connect with English Materials

The **Connect with English** print program is highly flexible and allows instructors to mix and match texts specifically according to their curriculum objectives and student needs. Multi-skills courses may include the use of all three core texts — the *Video Comprehension Books*, *Conversation Books*, and *Grammar Guides*. For courses with an emphasis on specific skills, many options are possible including those listed below. Of course, this list is by no means exhaustive, as the general design and nature of the entire **Connect with English** program lends itself to a variety of creative and useful classroom applications.

For courses with an emphasis on Listening Comprehension and/or Reading and Writing:

Of all the core texts, *Video Comprehension Books 1-4* provide the most complete practice in listening comprehension skills. For teachers who wish to incorporate even more reading practice into their course, the *Connections Readers* and the *Video Scripts* nicely supplement the *Video Comprehension Books*. They provide an additional source of reading material that ties in to the characters and events in the **Connect with English** story.

For courses with an emphasis on Conversation and Speaking:

Conversation Books 1-4 offer an abundance of practice in conversational skills. The *Conversation Books* pair nicely with the *Video Comprehension Books*, providing students with both communicative practice and a comprehensive review of the events in each episode.

For courses with an emphasis on Grammar:

Grammar Guides 1-4 provide a systematic presentation of the basic structures and grammatical features of American English. Each grammar topic is presented in clear and simple charts, and examples from the video episodes are used to highlight these key concepts. The *Grammar Guides* work well when combined with the *Video Comprehension Books*. They are also compatible with the *Connections Readers,* as they follow the same grammatical scope and sequence, thereby providing valuable recycling of the featured structures.

Thanksgiving

Additional WHAT ABOUT YOU? Questions

Page 1:
1. Are families in your country smaller than they used to be?
2. How many children do you want to have? Why?
3. What are some advantages to having several brothers and sisters?
4. Are there any television shows in your country about big families?

Page 3:
1. Why is it important for Kevin to go to college?
2. Do you think Kevin's father would be happy to know that Kevin is with Uncle Brendan?
3. What would make Rebecca feel better about going to San Francisco?

Page 5:
1. Have you ever taken a computer class? What kind?
2. Do you think you need to know a lot about computers in order to use one every day?
3. What is a community college? Are there community colleges in your country?

Page 6:
1. If you were Brendan, what would you have done in his situation with his girlfriend and his brother? What would you have said to Patrick? What would you have said to Margaret?
2. How do you think Rebecca's mother felt in that situation?
3. Do you ever learn new things about your parents' past? If so, can you think of any examples?

Page 7:
1. Thanksgiving is in part a harvest celebration. What harvest celebrations are there in other cultures?
2. On which holiday do you eat the most?
3. Are any of the family activities at the Caseys' Thanksgiving holiday similar to holiday activities in your country?

Page 8:
1. Are you a positive or a negative person? Do you see the glass as "half-full" or "half-empty"?
2. Do you always say "thank you" when someone helps you?
3. Do you think about your health? Do you think about your health even when you are healthy?

Expansion Activities

Page 1:
Divide students into groups. Have students survey their group members with the following questions:

1) When someone says "family" in your country, what family members do you think of?
2) What is the size of your family?
3) What is the average nuclear family size in your country (parents and children)?
4) Is your family the most important thing in your life?

Have one person report his/her group's results to the class. Compile the class's results on the board. Discuss the significance of nationality, ethnicity, religion, and gender in the results.

Page 5:
Conduct a brainstorming activity with the class. First, brainstorm ways that computers make your lives easier (directly or indirectly) on a daily basis. Then, create a second brainstorm list of ways that computers can make your lives more complicated. At the end of the brainstorming session, compare the two lists and discuss the students' general opinion of computers and how they affect their daily lives.

Page 7:
Divide students into research groups/pairs. See which group can find out the most about the following Thanksgiving words/names: Pilgrims, Wampanoag Indians, Squanto, Miles Standish, Plymouth Rock, and wigwams. Then, ask for volunteers to recount the story of Thanksgiving. Try to discuss the story from the point of view of both the Europeans and the Native Americans.

Synopsis of Episode 37

PART 1

Michael, his wife Peggy, and their two girls arrive at Brendan and Anne's house for Thanksgiving. Kevin plays outside with the girls as the adults prepare the meal. Later, the men watch football on television. Finally, they all sit down to eat dinner. Brendan says grace, thanking God for reuniting the family despite the misfortune of Patrick's death. Rebecca thanks everybody for welcoming them. Kevin announces his decision to stay at the farm. Michael raises a toast to his cousins.

PART 2

Rebecca agrees to sing for the family. She sings "'Tis a Gift to Be Simple." The next day, Kevin tells Rebecca he might take Michael's computer course, and admits that he likes being on the farm. He promises to stay in touch. They talk about some happy memories, as well as some sad ones. Rebecca remembers their mother all of a sudden, and asks Kevin why they don't talk about her anymore. Kevin barely remembers his mother. Rebecca sings him a lullaby that their mother used to sing to them when they were little. Rebecca and Kevin hug each other as she gets ready to leave the farm.

PART 3

Everybody loads Rebecca's things into the truck, and Brendan drives her to the airport. On the way, Rebecca asks him about the disagreement between him and her father. He pulls the truck over and explains. When Brendan went to the Korean War, he asked Patrick to look after his new girlfriend. But instead of watching her, Patrick married her. Brendan's girlfriend was Rebecca's mother. Rebecca says she's grateful that Brendan made it to the hospital before her father died, so the two brothers could resolve their differences. Brendan says he's sorry it took Patrick's illness to bring them together.

Answer Key

1. 1. dinner, 2. cousins, 3. teacher, 4. son, 5. question
2. c
3. 1. Anne, 2. Michael, 3. Brendan, 4. Erin and Katie
4. 1. True, 2. False, 3. True, 4. True, 5. False
5. 1, 3, 4
6. 1. Kevin, 2. Michael, 3. Rebecca, 4. Rebecca, 5. Rebecca
7. c
8. 1, 3, 4
9. a. 3, b. 2, c. 1, d. 5, e. 4
10. 3
11. 1. free, 2. down, 3. place, 4. love, 5. true, 6. bend, 7. come
12. 1. computer, 2. college, 3. field, 4. learn, 5. class
13. 1. B, 2. R, 3. B, 4. R, 5. B
14. 1. airport, 2. personal, 3. father, 4. letter, 5. sorry
15. 1. a, 2. c, 3. b
16. 1. a, 2. b, 3. a, 4. b
17. 1. meet, 2. wife, 3. dinner, 4. football, 5. says, 6. farm, 7. computer, 8. learn, 9. song, 10. airport, 11. tells
18. 1. True, 2. True

Starting Over

Additional WHAT ABOUT YOU? Questions

Page 1:
1. What have you had to start over?
2. What would you least like to start over?
3. If you could start this year over, what would you do differently?

Page 3:
1. Do most companies in your country give people time off when someone in their family dies?
2. Do you think it is fair that Rebecca loses her job?
3. Is Rebecca angry at Emma?
4. Have you ever missed a lot of school or work? What did you do?

Page 4:
1. Do you take a lot of photographs?
2. Which do you like better, color or black-and-white photographs?
3. Which is your favorite family photograph?
4. Do you need an expensive camera to take good pictures?

Page 6:
1. Do you worry about school?
2. In what ways is school important to you?
3. Do you balance school, family, and a job? Is this difficult for you?
4. Is it better for Rebecca that she lost her job at the after-school program?

Page 7:
1. Do you show your emotions?
2. If a man shows his emotions, what does that say about his personality?
3. Do men show more emotion today than they used to? If so, why?
4. Are men in some cultures more emotional than men in others?

Page 8:
1. Can you focus on school when you have other problems in your life?
2. What can Rebecca do to reduce stress?
3. What do you think Professor Thomas will say to Rebecca?
4. Do you think Rebecca should quit school this semester and start over next semester?

Expansion Activities

Page 1:
Have a class discussion based on question 3 (for page 1, above), but expand it to the following situation: If you could start your life over from any age or time period, when would it be, and why? Give students guidance by providing your own model answer as an example.

Page 4:
For this activity, have students bring newspapers and old magazines to class (scissors will be handy also). Divide students into groups, and have each group pick eight photographs from the newspapers and magazines to put into a "time capsule." Explain that the time capsules will be opened hundreds of years from now, so the photos should be chosen carefully to represent what each group feels is important about today's society. Each group presents its time capsule photos to the class and explains their significance.

Page 6:
Photocopy one or more pages of the want ads from an English-language newspaper, and distribute the copies to the students. Divide the students into pairs, and have them interview their partners using the following questions:

1) Which job would you want the most? Why?
2) Which job would you want the least? Why?
3) What is most important to you in a job?

Synopsis of Episode 38

PART 1

Alberto and a colleague at work receive their Christmas bonuses: two tickets to the opera. Alberto plans to take Rebecca. Rebecca returns to Nancy's house, where Nancy greets and comforts her. Rebecca asks about Edward. Nancy says Edward wants to move back to the house, but she says she just can't take care of him anymore.

PART 2

Rebecca calls her adviser, Professor Thomas. He offers to meet with her that day to talk about her studies. Before leaving, she tells Nancy she learned why Patrick and Brendan did not speak for 30 years. Nancy says she already knew about it, and that she had advised Rebecca's mother to marry Brendan, not Patrick. That's why Patrick didn't like her. But Nancy is glad to hear the two brothers made peace.

PART 3

Rebecca returns to the after-school program. Emma is glad to see her, but says she had to find someone else to take Rebecca's job. She says there might be an opening in the new year. She also says she'll put a notice on the bulletin board about Rebecca's guitar lessons. As Rebecca leaves, she passes by Ramón, who is coaching a group of children playing soccer. He is excited to see her, and happily goes to talk to her.

Answer Key

1. 1. a, 2. c, 3. a, 4. a, 5. b
2. 1, 3, 4, 5
3. a. 2, b. 4, c. 5, d. 3, e. 1
4. 1. True, 2. True, 3. False, 4. True, 5. False
5. 1. happy, 2. worried, 3. sad, 4. sad, 5. happy
6. 1, 4
7. 1. Christmas, 2. Rebecca, 3. father, 4. Edward, 5. come home, 6. schoolwork, 7. family
8. 1. R, 2. T, 3. R, 4. N, 5. R
9. 1. Professor Thomas, 2. 5:00, 3. worry, 4. Brendan, 5. Patrick
10. 1. b, 2. c
11. 1, 2, 5
12. 3, 4, 5
13. 1. b, 2. a, 3. a, 4. a
14. 1. tickets, 2. returns, 3. house, 4. father, 5. uncle, 6. calls, 7. meet, 8. courses, 9. marry, 10. talks, 11. filled, 12. sees
15. 1. Rebecca, 2. difficult

The Pressure's On

Additional WHAT ABOUT YOU? Questions

Page 1:
1. How do you greet people you haven't seen in a long time?
2. Do people shake hands in your country? When?
3. In your country, is it common to hug a good friend that you haven't seen in a long time?

Page 3:
1. What are some reasons that Rebecca should go to the opera with Alberto?
2. Do you like opera?
3. Have you ever gone to an opera?
4. Who is the most famous opera singer from your country?

Page 5:
1. Will this be a sad holiday for Rebecca?
2. Do you have any special strategies for studying for exams?
3. Should Rebecca study with other classmates?

Page 6:
1. Does Alberto understand Rebecca's situation?
2. Is Alberto selfish? Is he used to rejection?
3. If you were Rebecca, what would you do — take the exams or start over next semester?
4. Rebecca has a big challenge ahead of her — do you think she can make it through the semester?

Page 7:
1. Do you usually have holiday parties? If so, what food do you prepare?
2. Why are some people sad or depressed during the holidays?
3. What holiday would you most like to spend away on vacation?
4. Where would you like to volunteer to help out on a holiday?

Page 8:
1. Do you like to work hard?
2. Do younger people usually have the same attitude about work as their parents?
3. Do the most successful people work the hardest?
4. Why is it important to have a good balance between "work and play"?

Expansion Activities

Page 6:
In pairs, have students discuss the biggest challenge they have had in their lives. Then, as a class, find out which types of challenges are most common (academic, health-related, immigration-related, etc.). Discuss whether there are important differences between the challenges of men and women, or between those of different nationalities or age groups.

Page 7:
Divide students into groups. Explain that each group has won a free holiday vacation, and must decide on a place to go. Each group should come up with a list of reasons for choosing their vacation destination. For an alternate scenario, have each group decide on a holiday volunteer activity.

Page 8:
Have each student rank the three most important things in his/her life (for example: school, family, sports, etc.). Then, have each student try to find a classmate with a list that is the same as or similar to his/hers. Finally, discuss strategies that will help busy students find a balance between work/family obligations and time for relaxation and enjoyment.

Synopsis of Episode 39

PART 1

Rebecca and Ramón embrace. Alex hugs Rebecca too, before returning to his game. Ramón asks how she really is, and she confesses that she's not always so good. Ramón tells Rebecca that she must give herself time to grieve over her father's death. Rebecca tells him she lost her job, and he reminds her that he still wants her to give Alex and Vincent guitar lessons.

PART 2

Rebecca meets with Professor Thomas at the music school. He says he is worried about Rebecca's situation. She'll have to work extremely hard to pass her final exams. If she fails, she could lose her scholarship. Rebecca says she'd rather study hard than take incompletes and repeat the courses. Later, back at Nancy's house, Angela and Melaku welcome Rebecca home. They ask if she'll be able to catch up with her studies. She says yes. Angela tells Rebecca that she and Melaku won't be around for the holidays, so Rebecca will be alone at Christmas with Nancy.

PART 3

Alberto arrives at Nancy's house to visit Rebecca. He embraces her and welcomes her back, presenting her with tickets to the San Francisco Opera. Rebecca says she must study, but Alberto refuses to take no for an answer. She's less amused by his persistence this time. She tells Angela about Alberto's invitation. Angela is impressed with Alberto, and advises Rebecca to go out and have a great time. Rebecca isn't so sure; she seems overwhelmed by everything.

Answer Key

1. 1. letter, 2. important, 3. meet, 4. scholarship, 5. visits
2. a
3. 1, 2, 4
4. a. 3, b. 4, c. 2, d. 5, e. 1
5. 1. appointment, 2. take, 3. sorry, 4. tickets, 5. study
6. b
7. 1, 2, 3, 5
8. 1. b, 2. c, 3. b, 4. c, 5. a
9. 1, 2, 4, 5
10. 1. T, 2. R, 3. T, 4. A, 5. R, 6. A
11. 1. Professor Thomas, 2. Professor Thomas, 3. Rebecca, 4. Melaku, 5. Angela
12. 2, 3
13. 1. Opera, 2. Best, 3. nice, 4. enjoy, 5. plans, 6. school
14. a. 4, b. 5, c. 1, d. 3, e. 2
15. 1. True, 2. False, 3. True, 4. True, 5. False
16. 1. e, 2. c, 3. b, 4. a, 5. d
17. 1. happy, 2. team, 3. death, 4. lessons, 5. talk, 6. exams, 7. goes, 8. plans, 9. invites, 10. study, 11. tired, 12. room
18. 1. b, 2. b

Sharing Feelings

Additional WHAT ABOUT YOU? Questions

Page 1:
1. What are the advantages and disadvantages of studying alone/with others?
2. What is the biggest or most difficult exam you have ever taken? How did you study for it?

Page 3:
1. Have you ever gone on a trip with one of your brothers or sisters? If so, did you have fun together?
2. What is your favorite way to spend the holidays?
3. What holiday do you remember the most? How old were you?

Page 5:
1. What would you like to do on your next vacation?
2. Does Ramón wish he could go skiing with Alberto? Would the Mendoza brothers have a good time together?
3. Have you ever gone on vacation alone? If not, would you like to?

Page 6:
1. Do Alberto and Rebecca communicate well? Are they honest with each other?
2. Is Ramón a good person for Alberto to talk to about Rebecca? Why or why not?
3. Do you think you understand the opposite sex? Why or why not?

Page 7:
1. How has your relationship with your brothers/sisters changed?
2. Do you like the boyfriends/girlfriends of your brothers and sisters? If not, do you tell them?
3. Are brothers and sisters closer in some cultures than in others?
4. Is it important to your parents that you are close to your brothers and sisters?

Page 8:
1. How do you know you are in love?
2. Do most people find true love?
3. Do people usually find love when they are looking for it?
4. Is Alberto ready for a serious relationship? Is Ramón? Is Rebecca?

Expansion Activities

Page 3:
Divide students into pairs. Ask them to think of an important holiday season in their culture or country. Have students interview their partners using the following questions:
1) Where will you spend the holidays this year?
2) Where did you spend the holidays last year?
3) When you were a child, where did you spend the holidays?

Page 6:
Divide students into two groups — one consisting of the men in the class, the other of the women. Have them decide on group answers for the following gender survey questions. Also, have them try to guess the answers of the other group for each question. At the end, see which group was able to most accurately predict the answers of the other sex.
1) What do you want most in a girlfriend or boyfriend? (a. intelligence, b. good looks, c. money)
2) Who should pay for a first date? (a. the man, b. the woman, c. both)
3) What is most important in life? (a. friends, b. family, c. career)
4) How often should you be honest with a girlfriend/boyfriend? (a. always, b. usually, c. sometimes)
5) What is the most important room in a house? (a. bedroom, b. kitchen, c. family room)

Page 7:
Ask students to write about a particular relationship with a brother or sister. Lower-level students can write a short sentence or a paragraph, while higher-level students can write an essay. If students don't have any siblings, ask them to write about why they like or don't like being an "only" child.

Synopsis of Episode 40

PART 1

Bill finds Rebecca in the library, studying hard. He asks her to join him in the music lab so they can study together. He confesses that he doesn't want to be in school—he wants to be a rock and roll star. He's only in music school to satisfy his parents. He says he's going to an audition for a group called The Moles, and encourages Rebecca to come along. "Rock and roll is where the money is," he says. Rebecca says she's interested in making music, not money. Still, she agrees to sing backup for him at the audition if he'll help her study.

PART 2

Rebecca calls Alberto and tells him that she can't go to the opera. He's disappointed, and ends up going alone. After the opera, Alberto stops at the restaurant, where he and Ramón have a rare heart-to-heart conversation. Alberto asks Ramón to go on a skiing vacation with him. Ramón is flattered, but says he can't leave the restaurant or Alex during the holidays.

PART 3

Alberto starts to feel sorry for himself, and tells Ramón that Rebecca is starting to resist his "fatal charm." He says that she is more dedicated to her schoolwork than to him. Ramón explains that she probably just needs some understanding. They continue talking about women. Alberto expresses impatience with Rebecca; Ramón reminds him that he's always been impatient.

Answer Key

1. 1. studies, 2. opera, 3. working, 4. student
2. b
3. 1, 3
4. a. 2, b. 1, c. 3, d. 5, e. 6, f. 4
5. 1. Rebecca, 2. Ramón, 3. Alberto, 4. Bill
6. 1. the music school, 2. music, 3. parents, 4. an audition, 5. calls, 6. opera
7. 1, 2, 5
8. 1. studies, 2. music, 3. money, 4. will go, 5. rock group
9. b
10. 1, 3, 5
11. 1. a, 2. b, 3. b, 4. a
12. 1. R, 2. A, 3. R, 4. R, 5. A
13. 1. talking, 2. miss, 3. woman, 4. simple, 5. interested, 6. patient
14. b
15. 1. b, 2. d, 3. e, 4. a, 5. c
16. 1. library, 2. music, 3. exams, 4. future, 5. star, 6. audition, 7. calls, 8. says, 9. study, 10. alone, 11. restaurant, 12. wants, 13. interested, 14. patient
17. 1. False, 2. False

Unexpected Grief

Additional WHAT ABOUT YOU? Questions

Page 1:
1. How do you think Alberto feels in the photo above? How do you think Ramón feels?
2. If Alex doesn't want to go to Los Angeles, why does Ramón make him go?
3. In this episode, the Wangs receive an important letter. What do you think it says?

Page 3:
1. Do you ever have to choose who to spend the holidays with? If so, is it a difficult choice?
2. Do you ever go places you don't want to for the holidays?

Page 5:
1. Have you ever spent the holidays alone?
2. Have you ever worked during the holidays?
3. In this part of the episode, you see many people receiving gifts. In your country, is there a holiday for which you give gifts to other people?
4. If you get a present from someone, do you have to give him/her a present in return?

Page 6:
1. What would you do if you were Alberto?
2. Is Alberto surprised?
3. If you were Ramón, would you tell Alberto about what happened? Why or why not?
4. Does Ramón feel guilty?

Page 7:
1. What is the story of Christmas?
2. Which religions celebrate Christmas?
3. Is Christmas celebrated differently in different countries?
4. Do you celebrate holidays the same way your parents and grandparents did?

Page 8:
1. Why was Ramón's invitation such a surprise to Rebecca?
2. When was the last time someone surprised you? What was the surprise?
3. Have you ever had a bad surprise? If so, what was it?

Expansion Activities

Page 1:
Divide students into teams of six or eight for the Chain Letter Game. The object of this game is to be the first team to write a complete and correct sentence. The first person on each team writes a word on a piece of paper, which will be the first word of his/her group's sentence. Then, he/she passes it to the second person, who writes the second word of the sentence. No player can change another person's word; if he/she detects an error, he/she must simply start a new sentence on another line. As the teacher, you may leave the topic open or give a specific topic to write about, such as holidays.

Page 5:
Bring Christmas gift-giving to the classroom by playing Secret Santa! At random, give each student the name of another classmate; no student is to reveal which classmate's name he/she received. Over the next several class periods, each person brings in inexpensive (or hand-made) presents for the person to whom he/she was assigned; the presents should only have the recipient's name on them. Students are to place presents in a large bag or box as they enter the classroom. At the end of the class, presents are distributed. After the third round of this, students sit in a circle and try to guess the identity of their "Secret Santa."

Page 7:
In groups, have students discuss the commercialization of holidays such as Christmas. First, students should brainstorm examples of commercialization. Then, they should discuss which examples (or aspects of the examples) are positive, and which are negative. Finally, students should decide on how soon in the year stores and businesses should be permitted to advertise and commercialize for upcoming holidays. As a class, compare the groups' conclusions.

Synopsis of Episode 41

PART 1

Ramón puts Alex on the plane to Los Angeles. He promises to deliver Alex's Christmas presents to Vincent, Alberto, and Rebecca. Later that day, Mrs. Wang gives Vincent his present from Alex. Vincent is sad that Alex went to Los Angeles. Mr. Wang arrives home and shows his wife a letter offering him a job in Taiwan. Vincent secretly listens as his parents discuss their future. Mrs. Wang opposes a move to Taiwan; Mr. Wang is in favor of it. He still hasn't forgotten what happened at the picnic, and says Vincent will always be a foreigner in the United States.

PART 2

Ramón drops off Alex's present to Rebecca. She understands that Ramón is having a difficult time with Alex's absence, and she invites him in. He is surprised she isn't joining Alberto on his ski trip. They share some uneasy silences, before revealing that they'll each be alone at Christmas. He explains his annual participation in a "posada," in which he brings food to a community center for the less fortunate. She admires his Christmas spirit. As he gets up to leave, he asks if she'd like to spend Christmas with him. But before he finishes the invitation, he dismisses the idea and apologizes to her. Ramón leaves and Rebecca seems stunned by his invitation.

PART 3

Ramón drops off Alex's present to Alberto at Alberto's office. Alberto has a present for Alex, too. Alberto walks him to the door, where Ramón confesses his invitation to Rebecca. They both admit there is more to discuss concerning Rebecca, but they agree to talk about it later.

Answer Key

1. 1. False, 2. True, 3. True, 4. True, 5. True
2. 1, 3, 5
3. a. 1, b. 3, c. 5, d. 4, e. 2
4. 1. False, 2. False, 3. False, 4. True, 5. True
5. 1. b, 2. d, 3. a, 4. e, 5. c
6. 1. R, 2. R, 3. V, 4. W, 5. V, 6. W
7. 1. a, 2. b, 3. a, 4. a, 5. c
8. 1, 3, 4
9. 1. surprise, 2. Christmas, 3. Alex, 4. L.A., 5. difficult
10. 1. Alex, 2. Alex, 3. Alberto, 4. Ramón, 5. Ramón
11. 1. Christmas, 2. food, 3. Mexican, 4. house, 5. eat, 6. songs, 7. story
12. 2, 3, 4
13. 1. ski lodge, 2. can't, 3. bad, 4. talk to, 5. later
14. 1, 4
15. 1. now, 2. like, 3. deliver this, 4. rest
16. 1. airplane, 2. mother, 3. go, 4. present, 5. have, 6. parents, 7. moving, 8. house, 9. gives, 10. Christmas, 11. spend, 12. say, 13. unhappy, 14. talk
17. 1. b, 2. a

The Audition

Additional WHAT ABOUT YOU? Questions

Page 1:
1. Are you impatient?
2. How much of each day do you spend waiting?
3. Do you feel bad when you make someone wait? Do you do this often?

Page 3:
1. What do you think is The Moles' attitude toward Bill and Rebecca?
2. Was it a good idea for Rebecca to go to the audition? Why or why not?
3. If you were Rebecca, would you have left the audition early?

Page 4:
1. When you study for an exam, are you nervous?
2. Do you eat and sleep normally during exam weeks? Are you in a bad mood?
3. Do you agree with Nancy's opinion about Ramón?
4. Rebecca wants to ignore her love interests right now. Is this possible?

Page 6:
1. Do you like Rebecca's song?
2. What is Rebecca's song about?
3. Do you think The Moles will like Rebecca's song? Why or why not?

Page 7:
1. Which form of entertainment do you enjoy most often?
2. Which form of entertainment is your favorite?
3. If you could be an entertainer, which kind would you be? A singer? An artist?
4. Is it easy to be an entertainer? Do most entertainers make a lot of money?
5. Who are your favorite entertainers?

Page 8:
1. When you have to make the choice between work and a friend, which do you choose most often?
2. Is Rosalba right? Do you think Rebecca can "have it all" right now?
3. What advice would you give to Rebecca right now?

Expansion Activities

Page 1:
Divide students into pairs. Have them interview their partners using the following two questions:
1) What do you hate to wait for most?
2) What do you have to wait for most often?

Then, have each pair brainstorm ways to avoid waiting in common situations. Each pair should select their best ideas to present to the class.

Page 4:
Conduct a class discussion on exams.
1) Ask students which of the following kinds of exams they prefer. Which don't they like? Why?
   a) multiple choice   b) true/false   c) fill-in-the-blank   d) essay
2) Ask if students think final exams are necessary. If so, how should they be weighted in the overall course grade?
3) Ask if national standardized exams are fair. If not, what are the alternatives?

Page 7:
Divide students into groups to write and perform a short skit, play, or song. Give students one to two weeks to prepare. Remind students that their performances can be funny, sad, or dramatic. You can also give students the option of performing a non-original act. If possible, use your school's auditorium for the performances, and invite students from other classes to attend your "talent show."

Synopsis of Episode 42

PART 1

Nancy joins Rebecca, who is studying hard and drinking coffee. Nancy says she knows Rebecca has feelings in her heart for Ramón. Rebecca says she is interested in her studies right now, and can't think about romance with either brother. Later, Rebecca takes a final exam at school; it seems like a difficult test. Bill hands her a note reminding her about the audition.

PART 2

Rebecca and Bill show up at the audition. The Moles' lead singer can't see them at the moment, and makes them wait. They wait for a very long time. Rebecca wants to leave, but Bill convinces her to stay a little longer. Meanwhile, at the restaurant, Ramón admires a photo of himself and Rebecca from the retirement party.

PART 3

Finally, the band manager comes out and tells Bill and Rebecca that the band left. He asks them to leave their audition tapes. When they say they don't have any, the manager agrees to let them record their songs in the studio. The manager is uninterested as Bill plays his song. Then he asks Rebecca if she's auditioning. She almost says no, but Bill encourages her. She sings a song entitled "Dream Catcher." It's beautiful.

Answer Key

1. 1. c, 2. a, 3. b, 4. a
2. b
3. 1, 3
4. a. 2, b. 4, c. 1, d. 5, e. 3
5. 1. Nancy, 2. Rebecca, 3. Professor Thomas, 4. Rebecca, 5. The Moles, 6. the manager
6. 1. b, 2. c, 3. a
7. 1. N, 2. R, 3. N, 4. N, 5. R
8. 1. coffee, 2. father, 3. present, 4. schoolwork, 5. exam, 6. note
9. 2
10. 1. True, 2. False, 3. False, 4. True, 5. False, 6. False, 7. True, 8. False
11. c
12. 1. lights, 2. city, 3. dreams, 4. feel, 5. falling, 6. Everybody, 7. start, 8. needs, 9. bad, 10. me
13. 1. leave, 2. tapes, 3. his wife, 4. Bill and Rebecca, 5. Rebecca
14. 1. c, 2. a, 3. c, 4. b
15. 1. drink, 2. talk, 3. school, 4. study, 5. final, 6. audition, 7. wait, 8. band, 9. manager, 10. record, 11. sings, 12. listen, 13. phone, 14. guitar
16. 1. a, 2. a

Dream Catcher

Additional WHAT ABOUT YOU? Questions

Page 1:
1. Should Alberto tell Nancy why he is calling?
2. When you have something important to tell someone, do you prefer to call or pay a visit?
3. Have you ever missed an important telephone message? What happened?
4. Do you return all of your phone calls?

Page 3:
1. Why doesn't Rebecca want to call Alberto right away?
2. Do you think Rebecca knows why Alberto is calling?
3. Do you ever procrastinate?

Page 5:
1. Do you think Nancy is a smart woman?
2. Is it OK for Nancy to ask Rebecca about her relationships?
3. Does Rebecca mind that Nancy asks her personal questions?
4. Do you like it when someone asks you personal questions?

Page 6:
1. If you do what you love, will you always make enough money?
2. Bill thinks making money is very important. In what ways do you agree with him?
3. In what ways do you disagree with Bill?
4. Do you think most musicians are concerned with making money?

Page 7:
1. How many tests have you taken in one day?
2. How many days before a test do you begin to study?
3. What is the most important exam you have ever taken? How did you do?
4. Do you ever enjoy taking tests?

Page 8:
1. Do you think Bill and Rebecca will both "make it"? Do most musicians make it?
2. Do you know any musicians? Are they successful, or are they still trying to become successful?
3. Which kind of musicians make the most money?
4. Do you think music school will help Rebecca succeed in music?

Expansion Activities

Page 1:
Divide students into two teams for the *Telephone Game*. Have each team get in a line. Give a message to the two students at the front of the lines. (Give the same message to both teams. An example could be "The manager doesn't really care about Bill and Rebecca.") Each student whispers the message to the teammate behind him/her. The student at the end of the line for each team reveals to the class the message he/she received. The team who comes closest to the original message wins. Repeat the game with different messages.

Page 5:
Conduct a class discussion on personal questions. Ask students which of the following topics is impolite to ask someone about in their countries:

- age
- occupation
- salary
- marital status
- religion
- political party

Page 8:
Divide students into pairs or groups. Have each pair research the life of a famous musician of its choice, and make a biographical presentation to the class. Then, as a class, compare the presentations. What were the similarities between the musicians? How old were they when they became "famous"? What other jobs did the musicians have before they became famous? Were their parents musicians?

Synopsis of Episode 43

PART 1

At Nancy's house, Nancy answers the phone; it's Alberto. He says that it's important. He wants Rebecca to call him. Nancy takes down the message. The audition ends at the studio, and the manager gives Bill and Rebecca a copy of their tapes. "Don't call us, we'll call you," he says. Bill compliments Rebecca on her song, and offers to orchestrate it for her.

PART 2

Rebecca walks in the door and sees Nancy, who's up late. The two sit and share a box of chocolates while they talk about the day. Nancy asks about Rebecca's exams and gives Rebecca Alberto's message. Rebecca wonders whether it's too late to call him back. Nancy tells her to resolve the Mendoza brothers' situation. If she doesn't, history will repeat itself.

PART 3

Bill narrates the story of Rebecca's life. He tells of her hard work and preparation for her exams. He also tells how he took her to the audition to get her "nose out of the books." He admires her determination to get where she is and he likes her voice. But he also thinks she needs to think more about money and success too. Despite their differences, he thinks they'll both be successful.

Answer Key

1. 2, 4
2. c
3. 1, 2, 4
4. a. 1, b. 3, c. 2, d. 5, e. 4
5. 1. b, 2. d, 3. e, 4. c, 5. a
6. b
7. 1. M, 2. M, 3. B, 4. B, 5. R, 6. B
8. 1. Rebecca, 2. Nancy, 3. Rebecca, 4. the manager, 5. the manager, 6. Bill, 7. Bill
9. 1. negative, 2. doesn't think, 3. beautiful, 4. simple
10. 1, 2, 3
11. a. 4, b. 2, c. 5, d. 1, e. 3
12. 1. b, 2. b
13. 1, 2, 3, 6
14. 1, 3, 4
15. 1. b, 2. a, 3. b, 4. a
16. 1. c, 2. a, 3. e, 4. b, 5. d
17. 1. audition, 2. manager, 3. tapes, 4. help, 5. song, 6. calls, 7. home, 8. tells, 9. late, 10. serious, 11. exams, 12. wants, 13. voice, 14. different
18. 1. False, 2. True

Gifts

Additional WHAT ABOUT YOU? Questions

Page 1:
1. What is your favorite holiday?
2. Does everybody like holidays? If not, why?
3. In your country, are the highways dangerous during holidays?

Page 3:
1. Is Alberto sad?
2. Is Rebecca sad?
3. Why did Alberto break up with Rebecca?
4. What can you do when you want to forget about someone?

Page 4:
1. What kind of woman does Alberto want?
2. What kind of man does Rebecca want?
3. Will Alberto and Ramón's relationship become worse because of Rebecca?

Page 6:
1. What is the most important holiday in your country?
2. In your country, are there special cities or places to go for holidays?

3. Are all holidays in your country religious?
4. On which holidays in your country are the schools closed?
5. On which holidays are the schools open?

Page 7:
1. What volunteer work have you done? Did you enjoy it?
2. Is volunteerism a popular thing in your country?
3. Have you ever needed a volunteer for something?
4. Do you think Alberto ever volunteers like his brother Ramón does?
5. Do most volunteer jobs need training? Can some volunteer jobs be dangerous?

Page 8:
1. Is it easy for you to be friends with members of the opposite sex?
2. Do friends often become boyfriend and girlfriend?
3. Is it difficult for a man and a woman to stay friends after they have broken up? Why or why not?

Expansion Activities

Page 4:
Divide students into small groups for the *Newspaper Dating Game*. Bring in photocopies of the personal ads of an English-language newspaper, and distribute them to the groups. (Make sure both men and women appear on the personal ad pages.) Ask the groups to make three couples by matching three men with three women. Then, compare the groups' matches as a class.

Page 7:
Divide students into groups. Ask the groups to decide which situation in your community needs volunteers most, and which situation in the world needs them most. As an alternative for lower-level classes, brainstorm lists of possibilities before students work in groups.

Page 8:
In class, students watch one of the following three movies dealing with relationships between men and women: *When Harry Met Sally*, *Say Anything*, or *The Big Chill*. Have the students answer the following questions about the movie:

1) Are the main characters in the movie better as friends or as girlfriend-boyfriend?
2) Do the characters' attitudes toward their relationships change during the movie?
3) What is the movie's view on whether men and women can be friends? Do you agree with this point of view?

Synopsis of Episode 44

PART 1

Rebecca returns Alberto's phone call and leaves a message that she'll be in the studio for the next two days. He shows up at the studio, where they talk. They agree to be friends and they both seem happy about the decision. Alberto gives her a photo of Alex and Ramón that she had admired at the gallery opening several months earlier. She thanks him, and tells him that he inspired the song "Dream Catcher."

PART 2

As Alberto leaves the studio, he waits at the stairs, wondering if he has made the right decision about Rebecca. He sadly listens to her singing "Dream Catcher" back in the studio. He thinks of the good times they had together. Finally, he walks down the stairs. Before heading to the airport, Ramón and Alberto stop at Alberto's office to pick up his skis. Ramón presents Alberto with a new pair of goggles. Ramón is surprised Rebecca isn't going skiing with Alberto. At Nancy's house, Nancy sits in the kitchen with Rebecca, who is wrapping gifts. Nancy sees the picture of Ramón and Alex and asks about it. Nancy says that Alberto is trying to tell Rebecca something by giving her a picture of his brother.

PART 3

Ramón gives bonus checks to the restaurant staff, and asks them to help prepare the food that he will take to the community center on Christmas. Rebecca brings a box of food to the restaurant and puts it under the Christmas tree. Rebecca tells Ramón that she'd like to help at the community center. Later, Rebecca and Ramón go there together. People eat and sing Christmas carols. Rebecca and Ramón sing along with them. Afterwards, Rebecca and Ramón go back to the restaurant, where they have a glass of champagne. Ramón toasts to a very special Christmas. Then he calls Alex in Los Angeles. Alex also talks to Rebecca, and then he tells his father he's glad Rebecca's with him.

Answer Key

1. 1. False, 2. True, 3. True, 4. False, 5. True, 6. True
2. 1, 3, 4
3. 1. b, 2. a, 3. a, 4. b, 5. a
4. 1. b, 2. e, 3. d, 4. c, 5. a
5. 1, 2, 4
6. 1. A, 2. A, 3. R, 4. A, 5. R
7. a. 3, b. 5, c. 1, d. 4, e. 2
8. c
9. 1, 3, 4
10. 1. Ramón, 2. Alberto, 3. Rebecca, 4. Alberto
11. 1. b, 2. b
12. 1, 2, 3, 5
13. a. 4, b. 3, c. 1, d. 5, e. 2
14. 2, 3, 5
15. 1. What's happening?, 2. leave, 3. I don't like skiing., 4. think
16. 1. visits, 2. ski, 3. friends, 4. song, 5. good, 6. office, 7. airport, 8. gives, 9. presents, 10. photo, 11. food, 12. dinner, 13. drink, 14. calls
17. 1. b, 2. b

True Love

Additional WHAT ABOUT YOU? Questions

Page 1:
1. What is the best present you ever received?
2. What is the best present you ever gave someone?
3. Which do you like better, giving presents or receiving them?

Page 3:
1. Who will you spend New Year's Eve with this year?
2. What do you usually do on New Year's Eve?
3. When do you usually make plans for New Year's Eve?
4. Does everyone celebrate New Year's Eve on December 31st?

Page 4:
1. Have you ever seen an ekeko before?
2. Is there something like an ekeko in your culture?
3. Do you think the ekeko really works?
4. Are you superstitious? Do you believe in things like the ekeko?

Page 6:
1. What is the farthest you have ever traveled to visit someone in your family?
2. Do you like to have family members visit you?
3. Are there some family members you don't want to visit you?

Page 7:
1. Do you smoke?
2. Are there warning labels on cigarettes in your country?
3. Do different cultures have different opinions about smoking?
4. Have you ever tried to quit smoking?
5. What are some different ways to quit smoking? Which is the best?

Page 8:
1. What is a good age to get married?
2. Should the man be older than the woman in a married couple? If so, why?
3. What is a typical marriage ceremony like in your country?
4. In your country, do couples live together before they get married?

Expansion Activities

Page 1:
Divide the students into two groups. Tell each group that it has unlimited money to buy presents for the other group. Have students agree on a present for each member of the other group. At the end, each group tells what it would get each person in the other group.

Page 7:
Take a survey of smokers. To start, work as a class to decide on at least six questions to ask smokers (e.g., How long have you been smoking?, At what age did you start smoking?, Have you ever tried to quit?). Ask each student to interview three people, and bring results into class. (Lower-level students might work in pairs to complete the interviews.) As a class, compile the survey results in a chart on the board, and then ask students to write sentences describing those results. Students may need to be given sentence frames such as "The average person has smoked for ____ years."

Page 8:
Conduct a class discussion on the marriage customs of different cultures. Ask students to think about traditions, rituals, and beliefs involving fertility, luck, religion, friends of the bride/groom, family members, food, money, clothing, and parties.

Synopsis of Episode 45

PART 1

Rebecca and Ramón return to Nancy's house and open presents. Alex's gift to Rebecca is a clay statue of a woman playing baseball. It's entitled "Mighty Casey at the Bat." Rebecca's gift to Ramón is a recording of "Dream Catcher." Ramón's gift to Rebecca is an ekeko, a Peruvian good luck charm with symbols hanging from it: a diploma, representing her education; a symbol representing Kevin; and a guitar and a gold record, representing her dreams of musical success. They go to stoke the fire and are drawn to each other. They kiss passionately for the first time.

PART 2

Just at that moment, Nancy walks in. She has returned from the retirement home where she was visiting Uncle Edward. The three talk for a while about the day's events. Ramón gets up to leave, but before he goes, he invites Rebecca to join him at the restaurant on New Year's Eve. He has to work, but he says it will be a lot of fun. She accepts. At the door, they kiss again, even more passionately.

PART 3

Nancy already knows Rebecca and Ramón are in love. As Nancy and Rebecca sit by the fire, Rebecca admits that they are going to spend New Year's Eve together. She and Nancy exchange Christmas presents. Meanwhile, on the farm, Brendan and Anne are playing Scrabble with Kevin. Kevin tells them that he misses his sister, and then Brendan and Anne suggest that Kevin go to San Francisco to visit her. Later that night, Kevin calls Rebecca to tell her the good news: Brendan and Anne have given him a plane ticket to San Francisco.

Answer Key

1. 1. Rebecca, 2. Ramón, 3. Rebecca, 4. Rebecca, 5. Uncle Brendan and Aunt Anne
2. a
3. 1, 3, 4
4. a. 3, b. 4, c. 2, d. 1, e. 5
5. 1. True, 2. False, 3. True, 4. False
6. 1. Nancy, 2. Ramón, 3. Nancy and Rebecca, 4. Uncle Brendan and Aunt Anne, 5. Kevin, 6. Rebecca
7. 1, 2, 5
8. 2, 3
9. a. 5, b. 1, c. 3, d. 2, e. 4
10. 1. b, 2. a, 3. b, 4. c
11. 1. N, 2. N, 3. N, 4. R, 5. R
12. 1. surprises, 2. big, 3. yes, 4. Edward, 5. community center
13. 1. likes, 2. good, 3. happy, 4. happy
14. 1. news, 2. Uncle Brendan, 3. coming, 4. tomorrow, 5. town
15. a. 2, b. 4, c. 1, d. 5, e. 3
16. 1. Christmas, 2. wish, 3. miss, 4. visit, 5. long, 6. airplanes
17. 1. c, 2. a, 3. d, 4. b
18. 1. house, 2. give, 3. present, 4. tape, 5. song, 6. luck, 7. smoke, 8. kiss, 9. visit, 10. uncle, 11. spend, 12. game, 13. ticket, 14. phone, 15. see
19. 1. True, 2. False

Friendship

Additional WHAT ABOUT YOU? Questions

Page 1:

1. How late do you stay out on New Year's Eve?
2. Do you like to celebrate New Year's Eve with a lot of people or just a few?
3. What do you think Alex and Vincent are planning to do on New Year's Eve?

Page 3:

1. Is it a good idea for Bill to quit school? Was this a difficult decision for him?
2. How does Rebecca feel about Bill's decision?
3. What do you think is best for Vincent? For Alex? Where should they live?

Page 5:

1. Is $35.52 a lot of money for a young boy to have?
2. How did you get money when you were a child?
3. What did you spend your money on?
4. Did you ever have an "allowance"? What did you have to do to earn your allowance?

Page 6:

1. Is L.A. the best place for Bill to go?
2. What other cities are famous for music?

3. For success in a career, are personal contacts more important than education or ability?
4. Why doesn't Bill think music school is right for him?
5. What will Bill's parents think of his decision? Have your parents ever disagreed with any of your important decisions? How did you feel?

Page 7:

1. Have you ever had to move away from close friends or family?
2. How many times have you moved?
3. For whom is moving more difficult, children or adults? Why?
4. What is the most difficult thing about moving?
5. Do you think you will be living in the same city five years from now?

Page 8:

1. Have you ever moved to a new city because of a job?
2. Do you live in the same city as your parents?
3. Do you want your children to live in the same city as you?
4. Is it harder for families to stay together nowadays than before?

Expansion Activities

Page 5:

Have students bring in newspapers (English language, if possible) for this activity. Divide students into pairs. Explain that each pair has $35.52, just like Vincent and Alex (you can give your students a bigger budget if you want). By looking through newspaper advertisements and classifieds, have students choose how they will spend their money. (Have each group spend the money on an event rather than a thing.) Have each pair share its $35.52 adventure with the class.

Page 6:

Have students work in groups of three to complete a role-play in which Bill tells his parents that he is going to quit school and move to L.A. One student plays the role of Bill and the other two students are his parents. Have groups present their role-plays to the class. For lower-level classes, model a role-play with some of the class members, or provide helpful dialogue for each student to use in the role-play.

Page 7:

Divide students into groups. Have each group brainstorm things you need to do when you move to a new state or country (for example, arranging for a new telephone number, arranging for utilities, learning the new roads and highways, etc.). As a class, compare the groups' lists and write the different ideas on the board. Go through the most important items and have students explain how to do these things.

Synopsis of Episode 46

PART 1

Kevin is now in San Francisco. Rebecca shows him around the school music studio. He's impressed. He sits in a control room with the recording engineer, Jay. Ramón brings Alex home from the airport. They open Christmas presents together. Alex's gift from Rebecca is a baseball autographed by several Oakland A's. Ramón plays Rebecca's tape. The scene shifts to Rebecca in the studio, recording her song with Bill's new arrangements. He plays guitar, while other musicians play bass and piano. Kevin congratulates her on the song. He's glad to have seen it; they both admit they wish Dad had been there. Rebecca leaves a phone message for Ramón at the restaurant.

PART 2

Ramón brings Alex to Vincent's house. The boys haven't seen each other in a long time. They practice their guitars for a few minutes before Vincent tells Alex about his family's plans to move to Taiwan. They talk about living in different places and being separated, and try to think of a way in which they can stay together. They agree at least to spend New Year's Eve together, and spend all the money they have. Vincent has $35.52 in his piggy bank!

PART 3

At the studio, Bill and Jay finish mixing Rebecca's song. Jay leaves, and Kevin goes outside to get some air. Bill reveals that he's quitting school to go to L.A. for a job in the recording industry. Rebecca tells him that he's crazy to quit school, but he says he just has to follow his dreams.

Answer Key

1. 1. song, 2. dream, 3. visits, 4. happy, 5. presents, 6. house, 7. make
2. 1, 2, 3, 4
3. a. 3, b. 5, c. 1, d. 2, e. 4
4. 1, 2, 4
5. 1. surprised, 2. sad, 3. happy, 4. surprised, 5. excited
6. 1. a, 2. b, 3. b, 4. c, 5. a
7. 1. songs, 2. chance, 3. this, 4. you, 5. Dad, 6. Me too
8. 1. Jay, 2. Ramón, 3. Alex, 4. Alex, 5. Rebecca
9. 1, 2, 4, 6
10. 1. R, 2. R, 3. V, 4. A, 5. V
11. a. 2, b. 5, c. 1, d. 3, e. 4
12. b
13. 1, 3, 4
14. 1. False, 2. False, 3. True, 4. True
15. 1. Bill, 2. Rebecca, 3. Bill and Rebecca, 4. Bill and Rebecca
16. 1. d, 2. c, 3. b, 4. e, 5. a
17. 1. studio, 2. meets, 3. recording, 4. likes, 5. airport, 6. good, 7. present, 8. baseball, 9. play, 10. family, 11. plans, 12. money, 13. quit, 14. miss
18. 1. b, 2. b

The Lost Boys

Additional WHAT ABOUT YOU? Questions

Page 1:
1. When you were a child, when did your parents worry about you?
2. Do they worry about you now?
3. Have you ever gone ice skating?
4. Do you think ice skating is dangerous?
5. Will Mr. Wang look for Vincent and Alex at the skating rink?

Page 3:
1. If you were Alex or Vincent, what would your parents do?
2. Have your parents ever had to come get you at a hospital? If so, what happened?
3. How were you punished as a child?
4. Have you ever had a sports injury?

Page 5:
1. What are some popular places for children in your city? Have you ever gone to any of them?
2. Is Ramón more worried than he is angry?
3. At what age should children be allowed to go to an activity or an event on their own?

Page 7:
1. What is your favorite outdoor activity?
2. What is the most popular outdoor activity in your country?
3. Which is the most expensive outdoor activity? Which is the cheapest?
4. What outdoor activity would you like to try?

Page 8:
1. Did you always obey your parents? Can you remember a time when you didn't?
2. Would you punish Alex and Vincent? If so, what punishment would you give them?
3. Is it easy to raise children? How do you learn how to do this?

Expansion Activities

Page 3:
Divide students into pairs. Have them interview their partners using the following question: What crazy things did you do when you were a child? Then, have each student relate to the class one of his/her partner's crazy escapades. Which were the craziest in the class? Were they crazier than Alex and Vincent's skating adventure?

Page 7:
Divide students into teams for a game of charades. Have each team brainstorm a list of outdoor activities. Collect the lists. Then, the teams take turns sending a representative to the front of the class. Select an outdoor activity from the lists and write it on a piece of paper so that only the representative can see it. The representative has ten seconds to act out the activity (no words or sounds are permitted). If his/her team guesses the activity within the ten seconds, it gets a point. After all the students on all the teams have been representatives, the team with the most points wins.

Page 8:
Conduct a class discussion on parent-child relationships. Consider the following questions from as many different cultural perspectives as possible:

1) Who usually punishes the children, the mother or the father?
2) Can the father be a "friend" to his children?
3) What types of punishment are common in your country?
4) What is the best way to teach children to follow the rules?

Synopsis of Episode 47

PART 1

Vincent breaks into his piggy bank and leaves the house. He and Alex meet on a Chinatown street to go ice skating. Mrs. Wang notices the empty bank and calls Mr. Wang, who doesn't know where the boys are. She goes to the store, but Mr. Wang says not to worry — if Vincent is with Alex, they're fine. She checks the library, but they're not there either. Meanwhile, Rebecca introduces Kevin to Ramón at the restaurant. She and Kevin are about to leave when Mr. Wang shows up, looking for Vincent.

PART 2

Mr. Wang asks if Ramón has seen Vincent and Alex. He says he hasn't. Mr. Wang is going to drive around and look for them. Ramón, Rebecca, and Kevin go to Ramón's house; Alex isn't there. Meanwhile, Alex and Vincent are ice skating. Alex falls down and hurts his ankle. Back at Ramón's house, Kevin suggests the young boys may have gone somewhere to celebrate. Ramón finds a newspaper with an ad for a skating rink cut out. He and Rebecca go to the rink while Kevin stays by the phone. At the rink, the skate rental man says Alex was limping when the boys left an hour ago.

PART 3

Rebecca and Ramón drive around looking for the boys. Ramón is angry, but Rebecca tells him to try and understand how difficult Alex's life is right now. At the Mendozas' house, Kevin answers the phone. It's Ramón, checking for news. Kevin tells him Mr. Wang filed a missing person's report with the police. The baby-sitter, Monica, arrives. Kevin apologizes to her, saying Alex is missing. She agrees to wait there with him. Kevin talks to Mrs. Wang on the phone. She has heard from the boys; they're at the hospital. Kevin says he'll tell Ramón and Rebecca.

Answer Key

1. 1. c, 2. b, 3. a, 4. b, 5. c
2. 1, 2, 3, 4
3. a. 1, b. 4, c. 5, d. 3, e. 2
4. 1. excited, 2. worried, 3. look for boys, 4. angry at, 5. ankle, 6. baby-sitter
5. b
6. 1. V, 2. A, 3. R, 4. R, 5. V, 6. A
7. 1. True, 2. True, 3. True, 4. False, 5. False, 6. True, 7. False
8. 1. b, 2. a, 3. b, 4. b
9. 1, 4
10. a. 5, b. 2, c. 4, d. 3, e. 1
11. c
12. 1. the police, 2. at the door, 3. the baby-sitter, 4. friend, 5. hospital
13. 1. d, 2. b, 3. c, 4. a
14. 1. driving, 2. upset, 3. scare
15. 1. c, 2. b, 3. d, 4. a
16. 1. ice skating, 2. parents, 3. worried, 4. restaurant, 5. home, 6. finds, 7. bag, 8. phone, 9. falls, 10. photo, 11. hurt, 12. calls, 13. hospital
17. 1. False, 2. True

A Very Good Year

Additional WHAT ABOUT YOU? Questions

Page 1:
1. Do you think Ramón should have sold the restaurant? Was Alberto right?
2. Do you ever think that you have too much to manage?
3. Do you have a job, a child, and a personal life?
4. What parts of your life are most important to you?

Page 3:
1. Where do you think Alex should live — with his mother or father?
2. In your country, where do the children in divorced families usually live — with the mother or father?
3. Is Alex angry with his parents?
4. Have you ever had a day as emotional as Ramon's?

Page 5:
1. Why does Ramón feel guilty?
2. Are there times when you don't give people enough attention?
3. Should Ramón change something in his life? If so, what?

Page 6:
1. Is Alex really sorry for what he did?
2. What does it mean to be "grounded"? Do children get grounded in your country?
3. Does Alex think his punishment is fair? Do you?
4. When do you think Alex and Vincent realized they were doing something wrong?

Page 7:
1. Have you ever kept a New Year's resolution? What was it?
2. Have you ever been to a New Year's Eve celebration like the one in this episode?
3. What did you do on New Year's Eve when you were a child?
4. What do you do on New Year's Day?

Expansion Activities

Page 1:
Divide students into groups. Have each group think of possible ways for people to manage their time better. Then, discuss the groups' suggestions as a class.

Page 6:
Divide students into pairs or small groups. Have each pair write a description or a story about what one of the following people from the video will be doing in ten years:

- Rebecca
- Kevin
- Ramón
- Alex
- Alberto
- The Wangs
- Sandy
- Bill

Have the pairs present their descriptions/stories to the class.

Page 7:
Have your students make English class resolutions! For this activity, each student makes an English class resolution that he/she will try to follow for the rest of the course/semester. Help students with their individual resolutions. Here are some examples of good resolutions: "I will not speak my native language," "I will do all of my homework," and "I will speak English with my classmates." During the course, each time someone breaks his/her resolution, he/she will give 25 cents to "the class bank." You will hold this bank. At the end of the course, the students will vote on how to use this money. They can have a party, give the money to charity, etc.

Synopsis of Episode 48

PART 1

Rebecca and Ramón are still looking for Alex. They walk through the park and yell the boys' names, but no one responds. Meanwhile, at the hospital, Mr. and Mrs. Wang pick up Alex and Vincent. Alex is in a wheelchair. Mr. Wang is very angry with them. Vincent explains that he and Alex only did this because they knew they were going to be apart soon. Mrs. Wang reveals some news: she and Vincent will stay in San Francisco while Mr. Wang goes to Taiwan for a year. She'll need Vincent's help in the store. After this incident, Mr. Wang says, he is not so sure he can trust his son with such an important responsibility.

PART 2

Rebecca and Ramón are still walking through the park. Rebecca relates a story about a time when Kevin got lost. Ramón thinks maybe he should spend more time with Alex, or just let him live with his mother. Rebecca dissuades him, saying he's a good father. She gives him a hug as he starts to become emotional. She says he's capable of great love. They call home and find out Mr. Wang is bringing the boys home. They arrive at Ramón's house, where Monica is still there with Kevin.

PART 3

Mr. Wang brings Alex home. Alex apologizes to his father. Ramón hugs him, but he grounds him for a long time. The three parents forgive the boys, but tell them never to do such a thing again. Kevin walks Monica home. Ramón promises Alex that he'll do whatever it takes so Alex doesn't have to worry about where to live. Then the scene shifts to the New Year's Eve celebration at the Casa Mendoza restaurant. Everyone cheers and throws confetti at midnight. Rebecca and Ramón kiss. They agree that it's going to be a very good year.

Answer Key

1. 1. False, 2. True, 3. True, 4. False, 5. True
2. c
3. 1, 3, 4
4. 1. park, 2. Taiwan, 3. plans, 4. father, 5. home, 6. call, 7. talk, 8. the restaurant
5. 1. a, 2. c, 3. c, 4. a, 5. b
6. 1, 3, 4
7. 1. Yes, 2. Yes, 3. No, 4. Yes
8. 1. Taiwan, 2. Mom, 3. stay, 4. I, 5. Really, 6. one year
9. a. 3, b. 2, c. 5, d. 1, e. 4
10. 1. child, 2. friend, 3. father
11. 1. RM, 2. RC, 3. RM, 4. RM, 5. RC, 6. RC
12. 2, 3
13. 1. b, 2. a, 3. b, 4. b
14. 1, 2, 4
15. a. 5, b. 2, c. 3, d. 1, e. 4
16. 1. c, 2. a, 3. b, 4. d
17. 1. park, 2. find, 3. call, 4. hospital, 5. angry, 6. ran, 7. move, 8. spend, 9. says, 10. house, 11. baby-sitter, 12. happy, 13. restaurant, 14. party

Test 10: Episodes 37-40

NAME _____ DATE _____

1 Identify these places. Use the words in the box to complete the sentences. (5 points)

| the farm | Nancy's house | ✓San Francisco |
| school | the restaurant | Professor Thomas's office |

1. Rebecca is happy to be back in _____San Francisco_____.
2. Rebecca is living at _____.
3. Kevin is still living on _____.
4. Rebecca has a lot of work to do at _____.
5. Rebecca has a meeting in _____.
6. Ramón and Alberto talk at _____.

2 How much do you remember about episodes 37–40? Put the sentences in order from 1 to 5. (4 points)

a. __1__ The Caseys eat Thanksgiving dinner.
b. ____ Rebecca arrives in San Francisco.
c. ____ Alberto visits Rebecca at Nancy's house.
d. ____ Alberto goes to the opera.
e. ____ Brendan tells Rebecca a family secret.

3 Check (✓) *True* or *False* for each sentence below. (7 points)

	True	False
1. Kevin is moving back to Boston.	____	✓
2. Rebecca's father married Brendan's girlfriend.	____	____
3. Michael teaches a history class.	____	____
4. Rebecca is going to take her final exams.	____	____
5. Rebecca gets her old job at the after-school program.	____	____
6. Rebecca goes to the opera with Alberto.	____	____
7. Bill asks Rebecca to go to an audition.	____	____
8. Alberto wants more attention from Rebecca.	____	____

④ **Who says these sentences? Circle the answers. (5 points)**

1. "Kevin has decided to put up with us, so his sister can go back to college in San Francisco." Michael / (Brendan)

2. "Things were never the same between your father and me." Brendan / Anne

3. "If you don't pass, you risk losing your partial scholarship." Nancy / Professor Thomas

4. "I had to replace you." Alberto / Emma

5. "Money isn't all that important to me." Rebecca / Bill

6. "I'm considering a ski vacation in Aspen." Ramón / Alberto

⑤ **Complete the sentences in the paragraph below. Circle the answers. (6 points)**

Rebecca loses her friends /(job) at the after-school program. She is worried / excited about
                     (1)   (2)
school. She needs to pass her audition / exams to keep her scholarship / job . Ramón / Alberto
                                (3)   (4)   (5)
wants Rebecca to take a break from studying. He wants her to go to the opera / a restaurant , but
                                                                        (6)
Rebecca needs to study. He is happy / disappointed .
                              (7)

⑥ **Match the underlined words from the story with their meanings. Check (✓) the answers. (3 points)**

1. Rebecca: "My father passed away."
   ✓ a. died
   ___ b. left

2. Kevin: "Have a terrific life in San Francisco."
   Rebecca: "Thanks. I'll give it a shot."
   ___ a. be sad
   ___ b. try

3. Ramón: "So, where are you off to?"
   ___ a. going
   ___ b. living

4. Alberto: "I thought I'd just drop by."
   ___ a. go out
   ___ b. visit

Test 11: Episodes 41-44

NAME _____ DATE _____

① Identify these places. Use the words in the box to complete the sentences. (4 points)

the community center   Los Angeles   the restaurant   ✔the studio   Taiwan

1. Bill and Rebecca have to wait at _____the studio_____.
2. Alex is in _____ for Christmas.
3. Mr. Wang gets a job offer in _____.
4. Ramón and Rebecca volunteer at _____.
5. Ramón and Rebecca call Alex from _____.

② How much do you remember about episodes 41–44? Put the sentences in order from 1 to 6. (5 points)

a. ____ Rebecca and Ramón serve food at the community center.
b. __1__ Alex leaves San Francisco.
c. ____ Alberto and Rebecca agree to be friends.
d. ____ Ramón talks to Alex on Christmas Day.
e. ____ Alberto leaves to go skiing.
f. ____ Ramón invites Rebecca for Christmas.

③ Answer the questions below. Check (✓) Yes or No. (7 points)

	Yes	No
1. Does Vincent hear his parents talk about Taiwan?	✓	
2. Do Mr. and Mrs. Wang agree about Taiwan?		
3. Does Alex celebrate Christmas with his mother?		
4. Does Rebecca record a song at the audition?		
5. Does Rebecca study a lot?		
6. Do Alberto and Rebecca argue about their relationship?		
7. Do Ramón and Alberto fight about Rebecca?		
8. Does Rebecca spend Christmas alone?		

④ **Circle the answers to the questions below. (5 points)**

1. Who wants to leave the audition early?   (Rebecca) / Bill
2. Who sings the song "Dream Catcher"?   Rebecca / Bill
3. Who gives Rebecca advice about the Mendoza brothers?   Bill / Nancy
4. Who visits Rebecca at the music studio?   Alberto / Nancy
5. Who gives Rebecca a photograph?   Ramón / Alberto
6. Who thinks Rebecca needs to relax a little?   Bill / the manager

⑤ **Complete the sentences in the paragraph below. Circle the answers. (6 points)**

Rebecca and Bill go to an (audition) / a concert. It was Bill's / Rebecca's idea. They wait to play
                                    (1)   (2)

for The Moles / The Goggles, but the band breaks up / leaves. The manager / Professor Thomas lets
               (3)   (4)   (5)

Bill and Rebecca record their songs. Alberto gives Rebecca a photo of a guitar player / Ramón and Alex.
                                                                                                (6)

Nancy thinks that Alberto is trying to tell Rebecca something / win Rebecca's love.
                                                                      (7)

⑥ **Match the underlined words from the story with their meanings. Check (✓) the answers. (3 points)**

1. Alex: "Give Vincent, Rebecca, and Uncle Alberto their presents."
Ramón: "Don't worry. I'll do it right away."
   ✓ a. very soon
   ___ b. later

2. Rebecca: "Would you care for anything to drink?"
   ___ a. like
   ___ b. get

3. The manager: "He's tied up right now. Wait outside."
   ___ a. busy
   ___ b. not here

4. Bill: "I think Rebecca is very cool."
   ___ a. tired
   ___ b. nice

Test 12: Episodes 45-48

NAME _____ DATE _____

1) Identify these places. Use the words in the box to complete the sentences. (5 points)

| the hospital | the restaurant | the skating rink |
| ✔Nancy's house | San Francisco | Taiwan |

1. Ramón and Rebecca give each other presents in __Nancy's house__.
2. Kevin visits Rebecca in _____.
3. Alex and Vincent go to _____.
4. Mr. Wang picks up the boys at _____.
5. Mr. Wang is going to work in _____.
6. There is a New Year's Eve party at _____.

2) How much do you remember about episodes 45–48? Put the sentences in order from 1 to 6. (5 points)

a. ____ Kevin tells Rebecca he is coming to visit her in San Francisco.
b. ____ Rebecca and Ramón dance on New Year's Eve.
c. ____ Mr. Wang, Ramón, and Rebecca look for Alex and Vincent.
d. ____ Rebecca records her song, "Dream Catcher."
e. _1_ Rebecca, Ramón, and Nancy talk on Christmas day.
f. ____ The boys go ice skating.

3) Check (✓) the sentences below that are not true. (6 points)

1. _✓_ Ramón and Alberto buy Kevin a ticket to San Francisco.
2. ____ Nancy gives Rebecca an ekeko.
3. ____ Bill is going to Los Angeles.
4. ____ Kevin thinks Rebecca needs more singing practice.
5. ____ Alex hurts his ankle at the skating rink.
6. ____ Vincent has to go to Taiwan.
7. ____ Ramón wants Alex to be happy.

④ **Who says these sentences? Circle the answers. (4 points)**

1. "Everybody needs a dream catcher. . ." Ramón / (Rebecca)
2. "It's a big night at the restaurant. . . Why don't you come and be my guest?" Alex / Ramón
3. "Next year, I'll be in Taiwan, and you'll be in L.A." Mrs. Wang / Vincent
4. "I have some friends in the record industry, and they say if I'm there, they'll get me a job." Rebecca / Bill
5. "I can't do it—manage a restaurant, Alex, and a personal life." Ramón / Alberto

⑤ **Complete the sentences in the paragraph below. Circle the answers. (7 points)**

Alex and Vincent go skating. They tell / (don't tell) their parents. Mr. Wang goes to the
(1)

police station / skating rink . Ramón and Rebecca look in the park / restaurant . Kevin waits at
(2)   (3)

Ramón's house with a police officer / the baby-sitter . Finally, the Wangs find the boys at the
(4)

hospital / library . Ramón punishes / doesn't punish Alex. But he says Alex can go to
(5)   (6)

Los Angeles / the restaurant to celebrate New Year's Eve. At the party, Ramón tells Rebecca that it's
(7)

going to be a very good / difficult year.
(8)

⑥ **Match the underlined words from the story with their meanings. Check (✔) the answers. (3 points)**

1. Vincent: "They want to go back to Taiwan."
   Alex: "What a drag."
   ____ a. That's far.
   ✔ b. That's terrible.

2. Vincent: "This is going to be an awesome New Year!"
   ____ a. quiet
   ____ b. great

3. Ramón: "Maybe he took a short cut through the park."
   ____ a. a faster way
   ____ b. a friend

4. Rebecca: "Maybe he. . . lost track of time."
   ____ a. forgot about the time
   ____ b. lost his watch

TESTING PROGRAM ANSWER KEY

Test 10: Episodes 37-40
1. **1.** San Francisco, **2.** Nancy's house, **3.** the farm, **4.** school, **5.** Professor Thomas' office, **6.** the restaurant
2. **a.** 1, **b.** 3, **c.** 4, **d.** 5, **e.** 2
3. **1.** False, **2.** True, **3.** False, **4.** True, **5.** False, **6.** False, **7.** True, **8.** True
4. **1.** Brendan, **2.** Brendan, **3.** Professor Thomas, **4.** Emma, **5.** Rebecca, **6.** Alberto
5. **1.** job, **2.** worried, **3.** exams, **4.** scholarship, **5.** Alberto, **6.** the opera, **7.** disappointed
6. **1.** a, **2.** b, **3.** a, **4.** b

Test 11: Episodes 41-44
1. **1.** the studio, **2.** Los Angeles, **3.** Taiwan, **4.** the community center, **5.** the restaurant
2. **a.** 5, **b.** 1, **c.** 3, **d.** 6, **e.** 4, **f.** 2
3. **1.** Yes, **2.** No, **3.** Yes, **4.** Yes, **5.** Yes, **6.** No, **7.** No, **8.** No
4. **1.** Rebecca, **2.** Rebecca, **3.** Nancy, **4.** Alberto, **5.** Alberto, **6.** Bill
5. **1.** audition, **2.** Bill's, **3.** The Moles, **4.** leaves, **5.** The manager, **6.** Ramón and Alex, **7.** tell Rebecca something
6. **1.** a, **2.** a, **3.** a, **4.** b

Test 12: Episodes 45-48
1. **1.** Nancy's house, **2.** San Francisco, **3.** the skating rink, **4.** the hospital, **5.** Taiwan, **6.** the restaurant
2. **a.** 2, **b.** 6, **c.** 5, **d.** 3, **e.** 1, **f.** 4
3. 1, 2, 4, 6
4. **1.** Rebecca, **2.** Ramón, **3.** Vincent, **4.** Bill, **5.** Ramón
5. **1.** don't tell, **2.** police station, **3.** park, **4.** the babysitter, **5.** hospital, **6.** punishes, **7.** the restaurant, **8.** good
6. **1.** b, **2.** b, **3.** a, **4.** a

Part 2

Guidebook for Conversation Book

INTRODUCTION

What This Manual Can Do for You

This manual provides essential information on how *Conversation Books 1–4* can be successfully used to help your students improve their oral communication skills in English. This manual tells you:

- what the *Conversation Books* are and what each *Conversation Book* contains;
- how the *Conversation Books* are organized and why they are organized this way;
- the language focus of each activity in the *Conversation Books;*
- how to adjust the level of each activity to match the abilities of your students;

This introduction includes these topics: **a general overview and philosophy** of the books, **chapter organization, classroom management,** and **homework, evaluation and testing.** It is recommended that you read through each of these brief topics, since they will explain the pedagogical principles on which these books are based, including the thematic organization.

In addition, this manual devotes two pages to each individual episode in the section titled *Classroom Teaching Suggestions.* The information you will find there includes:

1. **communicative objectives and language focus** for each activity in the *Conversation Books;*
2. specific suggestions for **how to change the level of the activities** to make them easier for students of lower language proficiency or more challenging for students of higher language proficiency;
3. an **answer key,** for those activities that have definite, right answers.

Finally, the manual has a **testing program,** with oral checklists that cover the main communicative objectives in the books. There is one oral checklist for every four chapters in the books, making twelve checklists in all.

Conversation Books 1–4

There are four *Conversation Books,* each with 12 chapters. Each *Conversation Book* chapter relates to a video episode. Here is how the books are divided:

Book 1	Episodes 1-12
Book 2	Episodes 13-24
Book 3	Episodes 25-36
Book 4	Episodes 37-48

The *Conversation Books* are specifically designed for classroom use. While it is not necessary to have a television and VCR in the classroom, students should watch the corresponding video episode at least once before they attempt the activities in the book. You may assign students to watch the episodes at home, in the library, or in a language lab. Class time can then be spent on completing the activities in the *Conversation Books.*

GENERAL OVERVIEW AND PHILOSOPHY

The purpose of the four *Conversation Books* is to help students develop oral communication skills using the themes found in the **Connect with English** video episodes as a springboard for discussion.

A variety of activities encourages conversation, including role-plays, interviews, surveys, discussions, games, and information gaps. These activities involve the use of common language skills and functions, such as asking for information, expressing opinions, apologizing, congratulating, and so on. (The primary language skills for each activity in the *Conversation Books* are outlined in the *Classroom Teaching Suggestions* section of this manual.)

Using the *Conversation Books,* students engage in natural, authentic conversation. Because the activities are based on themes and issues that arise out of the video episodes, they provide a stimulus — and a natural context — for the exchange of ideas, opinions, and knowledge. For example, in Episode 1, Rebecca talks about her dream of going to music school. The related theme in the *Conversation Book* is called *Pursuing Your Dreams,* and discussion and interview activities encourage students to share their dreams for the future.

The activities in the *Conversation Books* vary in configuration — many are for pairs; a large number are for small or large groups; some are for the entire class. Some activities also involve writing — from simple tasks such as recording one's choices in a list to more sophisticated ones such as writing a paragraph consisting of information gathered from an interview. In this way, the books help promote proficiency not only in speaking and listening, but also in writing and reading.

FLEXIBLE LEVELING

Conversation Books 1–4 are suitable for students at high-beginning through intermediate levels of language proficiency. While the language level and difficulty of the activities have been carefully controlled, the activities in the *Conversation Books* do call for different degrees of language production from students. Some activities may simply require students to ask and answer *yes/no* questions provided in a survey or to make choices from a list or a series of pictures. Others may require more sophisticated use of language, such as arguing one side of an issue or engaging in a multiple-exchange role-play. In other words, the activities vary from ones in which the responses are more controlled to ones that involve free production of English.

To make the material suitable for classes at different levels, the activities can be adjusted to be more or less challenging. In the same way, the material can be adjusted to suit the needs of multilevel classes in which students vary in their language ability.

Special icons are used to identify the difficulty level of each activity in the *Conversation Books*. These icons help teachers tailor the activities for the needs of students at different levels of language proficiency.

▲ Arrows pointing up indicate that the difficulty of an activity can be increased.

▼ Arrows pointing down indicate the difficulty of an activity can be simplified.

⇕ Arrows pointing in both directions indicate that the difficulty level of an activity can be either increased or simplified.

Detailed teaching suggestions for modifying each activity are found in the *Classroom Teaching Suggestions* section of this manual.

CHAPTER ORGANIZATION

Each chapter in the *Conversation Books* is six pages long. In addition, each chapter has a related project found in the Appendices. Here is a summary of the organization of a typical chapter:

• Pages 1–4 COMMUNICATIVE ACTIVITIES

The first four pages of each chapter contain a variety of communicative activities that are based on relevant and important themes derived from the correspondng video episode.

• Pages 5–6 TWO-PAGE ACTIVITY

Pages 5 and 6 of every chapter contain an extended theme that is covered in a two-page activity. These two-page activities alternate among the following:

Games: Games involve students in situations in which they need to use natural language to achieve a specific objective. In many cases, students are directly involved in the creation of game cards or questions. An Appendix in the back of the book also contains game pieces or markers that can be cut out and used as needed.

Information Gaps: For information gaps (controlled pair activities), the material for Student A is on page 5 and the material for Student B is on page 6. Students need to exchange the information they each have in order to complete the activity successfully.

Songs: The song activities are based on the songs that appear within the **Connect with English** story. The songs are also featured on the soundtrack CD or audiocassette.

• Appendix OPTIONAL PROJECT

An optional project for each episode is located in the Appendix. These projects require students to get information outside of class — either through books and other reference sources or through fieldwork, including interviewing people other than their classmates.

*(For more information, refer to the **To the Teacher** and **Visual Tour** sections at the start of each Conversation Book.)*

It is important to note that the activities in an episode are independent. They can be done in any order — so, for example, the two-page game may be the first activity that the class does in a chapter. Occasionally, one or two activities are linked, in which case they should be done in combination. For example, in the first activity, students might be asked to complete a survey. In the following activity they must analyze and report the survey results.

Each activity in the *Conversation Books* is clearly identified by an activity bar, which contains the following information:

- the activity number (by sequence in a chapter);
- the classroom configuration (partner, group, team, class);
- the activity type (e.g., survey, interview, discussion).

There are generally two *What About You?* activities in each chapter. These are a series of two to four questions that prompt students to examine and discuss how a particular theme relates to their lives. The *What About You?* questions can be used as the springboard for whole-class discussions or for students to answer in groups or in pairs. They can even be used for written assignments. These questions are most appropriate for students at higher levels of language proficiency since they often stimulate sophisticated discussions.

Another regular activity type in the *Conversation Books* is called *Ways to Say It*. In these activities, students are introduced to common phrases in English and are provided with situations as prompts to use the phrases in more controlled speaking activities.

PROJECT ACTIVITIES

The project activities are optional and are found in the Appendices located at the back of each of the *Conversation Books*. Project pages contain research-oriented activities or community surveys and polls based on important themes from each episode. The projects reinforce the communicative nature of the books and invite students to expand their learning and conversation beyond the classroom.

For research projects, encourage the use of English-language sources. If possible, see that the students have access to books that are written at a simple level of English and that are well illustrated (these can often be found in the children's section of libraries or bookstores). For fieldwork projects, if the materials are being used in a non-English-speaking environment, students can do the research in the local language but report the results in English. Note that the *Classroom Teaching Suggestions* section of this Instructor's Manual contains many ideas for simplifying the project activities.

CLASSROOM MANAGEMENT

Conversation Books 1–4 are extremely flexible. They can serve as the main text for any course that emphasizes oral communication skills. They can also be used in conjunction with other books in the **Connect with English** print program to create a more comprehensive course that focuses on a wider range of skills. See the section titled **Connect with English** Print Program for more information.

GROUPING

Activities in the *Conversation Books* are designed for a variety of classroom configurations: partner, group, team, class. The type of classroom configuration for each activity is suggested in the corresponding activity bar. Spaces to the right of the activity bars allow students to indicate partner's name, group number, and team number. This makes it easier for students and teachers to keep track of student collaborations. Group and team numbers are also useful when different groups are asked to compare and contrast survey or discussion results with one another.

There are several ways to assign students to pairs, groups, or teams, and you will want to use a variety of approaches:

- A simple way to assign students is to have them count off — even numbers go to one team or group and odd to another.
- Write numbers or letters on small pieces of paper and have students draw them at random. Students are assigned to a team/group according to the number or letter they draw.
- In certain cases, you may want to group students by language proficiency level. For example, a student at a higher proficiency level can be paired with a student at a lower proficiency level. This way the lower-level student can benefit from help from the higher-level student. The same arrangement can be pursued with groups.
- Finally, you might consider grouping students of similar proficiencies. The *Classroom Teaching Suggestions* section of this manual provides alternate activities that can be assigned to different groups within a class according to their ability.

TIMING

The time length for any activity can vary, depending on how much time is devoted to preparation and how much follow-up is done. The *Classroom Teaching Suggestions* section gives a time that typically would be needed for each activity. However, this can be increased if suggested activities in that section are used. Also, the time may be extended if teacher/student modeling is done before students do the activity in their pairs or groups or if follow-up and extension activities are done.

In some cases, students may be particularly interested in a topic and may want to discuss it further. Such student participation and involvement should be encouraged. In other cases, where students are less interested in a topic, you may want to move to another activity on a different theme.

SEQUENCING THE ORDER OF ACTIVITIES

As previously mentioned, any and all of the activities in a chapter can be assigned. In general, all activities are independent of one another—that is, activities can be done in any sequence, or certain activities can be omitted. However, there are some cases where students use information gathered in one activity in a follow-up activity on the same theme.

You may want to consider reviewing and assigning the optional project as students begin work in a unit. This way, by the time the activities in the main chapter are completed, students will be ready to report on their research or fieldwork. Also consider having students play any of the two-page games at the start of each chapter. If this is done, students can play the game several times throughout the course of the chapter.

HOMEWORK, EVALUATION, AND TESTING

HOMEWORK

Most of the activities in the *Conversation Books* are designed as pair and group work, rather than independent work. However, they can be extended in various ways to provide independent work that can be done as homework. Here are some general suggestions:

- Students can answer the *What About You?* questions in writing. They can write short sentences, simple paragraphs, or longer essays.
- Students can write about their personal experiences on any theme once they have completed the related activities in that chapter. For example, after students have finished activities related to the theme of *Best Friends*, they can write about how they met their best friend.
- Students can complete related vocabulary activities. An example of this would be in Activity 1 of Episode 2. Here, students can list and categorize foods in addition to those already provided.
- Students can write word webs related to a theme (see Episode 2, page 3).
- Students can write short summaries of various things such as class debates, interviews, survey results, or even the events in the video episode.

EVALUATION

Given the oral nature of these books, an effective way to judge student achievement and progress is by on-going classroom observation. One way to do this is to have a list of student names next to which to you can make comments as you observe students working in class. You may want to do this once or twice a week. (A reproducible *Notes* section for this purpose can be found at the end of this manual.)

It is also useful for students to do self-evaluations in which they analyze what they have learned. For example, at the end of each episode, students can complete the following sentences:

In this episode, two things I learned are _____.

Now I can _____.

The most interesting thing for me in this episode was _____.

TESTING

In addition to the general suggestions for evaluation mentioned above, twelve oral evaluation checklists are also included in this manual. These oral checklists test the language proficiencies that students have practiced throughout the chapters in the *Conversation Books*. There is one checklist for every four episodes (Episodes 1–4, 5–8, 8–12, etc.).

The oral checklists provide a series of situations that naturally engage students in conversation and elicit the language functions covered in the **Connect with English** episodes. Students will be talking about the themes and situations that have become familiar to them through watching the video episodes and completing the related activities in each chapter. The open-ended answer style allows students of varying proficiencies to demonstrate their individual understanding of the language function and theme.

The oral checklists are relatively short and can be done before, during, or after class. Scores are based on your assessment of a student's proficiency, fluency, and depth of response for each objective. As more objectives are covered, the checklists can provide a general picture both of a student's proficiency as well as a student's progress in using English. (See the introduction to the oral evaluation checklists for more information about scoring.) The checklists can be used as a basis for grading, and can also be placed in a student's portfolio to show progress and work performed.

The Connect with English Print Program

CORE COMPONENTS

The **Connect with English** program contains many flexible print materials for a variety of instructional needs. In addition to the three core components — Video Comprehension Books 1–4, Conversation Books 1–4, and Grammar Guides 1–4 — there is a diverse collection of supplemental materials that enhance and enrich the **Connect with English** experience.

VIDEO COMPREHENSION BOOKS 1–4

The Video Comprehension Books help students build listening comprehension skills and gain a clear understanding of the characters and story lines found in the **Connect with English** video series. Recognition skills related to facial expressions, body language, and cultural nuances are also emphasized in the exercises which include multiple choice, true/false, sentence completion, and cloze activities. Special What About You? activities invite students to share their own opinions and ideas as they relate to the events in the video episode. Additional skills and topics that are covered in each book include reading, oral communication, and vocabulary development.

Using the video with the Video Comprehension Books: Depending on the time and length of the course, instructors may choose to show the **Connect with English** video during class, while simultaneously using the book. However, if repeated access to a television and VCR is not possible, teachers can have their students watch the video episodes in a library, language lab, or at home. Class time can then be used for discussion and review of the activities in the book.

CONVERSATION BOOKS 1–4

Designed specifically for classroom use, the Conversation Books help students develop oral communication skills. Each chapter features a variety of communicative partner, group, team, and whole-class activities that provide a natural extension of the themes found in the corresponding video episodes. Activity types vary in each chapter, but generally include an assortment of role-plays, discussions, interviews, surveys, games, information gaps, and questionnaires. Icons indicating the difficulty of each activity allow teachers to adjust the level according to the needs of his/her students. An optional research project for each episode is found in an Appendix at the back of the book. These projects serve to extend and expand the relevant themes of each chapter as they engage students' interest and involvement in gathering relevant data outside the classroom.

Using the video with the Conversation Books: It is not necessary to have classroom access to the video in order for students to complete the activities in the Conversation Books. The activities in these books are based on important themes from the **Connect with English** story. Students are never asked to recall specific information from the corresponding video episode. Instead, they are asked to react, interact, and talk about the story themes and how these themes relate to their own lives. While it is assumed that students will have seen the episode in its entirety at least one time, students' actual viewing can take place either in class, or in a library, language lab, or at home.

GRAMMAR GUIDES 1–4

The Grammar Guides assist students in developing mastery of the grammatical structures and vocabulary items found throughout the **Connect with English** video. The topics presented in these four books follow a developmental scope and sequence. Grammatical structures are linked to specific episodes, providing students with contextualized examples. Exercises build from a receptive understanding of the grammar point, to language production through controlled exercises, and finally to Power Practice sections in which students write about more personalized, open-ended topics.

Using the video with the Grammar Guides: Students can use the Grammar Guides either before or after they watch the corresponding video episode, to either preview or review critical structures and grammatical topics. Lower-level students will find the Grammar Guides a valuable resource tool they can rely on to help them internalize the authentic language of the video. More advanced students will welcome the carefully sequenced review of the language and its connection to the video through numerous examples and practice exercises.

SUPPLEMENTAL MATERIALS

CONNECTIONS READERS

The 16 titles in this series of graded readers feature controlled vocabulary and grammar at four distinct levels of difficulty to help students read with understanding as well as enjoyment. (The structures used in the four levels of these readers correspond with the scope and sequence presented in the Grammar Guides.) The stories increase in complexity from level to level. The four Level One readers feature exactly the same story found in the video program, told in simplified English and extensively illustrated with color photos. The same basic story is expanded upon in Level Two, only with more reliance on narrative speech. Finally, the Level Three and Four readers dramatically expand the video story line, using the same characters from the video, but putting them in new situations.

VIDEO SCRIPTS 1–4

The scripts for the **Connect with English** video are available in four separate books, and can be used in conjunction with any of the other materials in the print package. Each script contains the exact dialogue from the video, as well as the stage directions used during the filming of the series. Lines are numbered sequentially throughout the episodes, providing an easy reference for both students and teachers. The *Video Scripts* can be used before, during, or after viewing each episode, for previewing, scanning, and discussion purposes. The scripts are extremely helpful in staging class role-plays, script readings, or even short plays. The scripts also serve as a reference for teachers who wish to concentrate on specific language or grammatical patterns as they appear within the context of the natural language in the video episodes.

HOME VIEWER'S GUIDE

Primarily designed for the self-study audience, the *Home Viewer's Guide* provides a comprehensive review of the entire 48-episode program. Each chapter contains video comprehension exercises, readings on United States' and Canadian culture, and *Behind the Scenes* information about the filming of **Connect with English**. The *Home Viewer's Guide* comes in various bilingual editions including Spanish/English, Mandarin/English, Korean/English, and Thai/English.

CONNECT WITH ENGLISH SOUNDTRACK

The complete soundtrack from the **Connect with English** program is available on CD or audiocassette. It features 12 original songs in a wide range of musical genres including pop, country, jazz, blues, and rap.

FOR INSTRUCTORS

VIDEO COMPREHENSION BOOKS 1–4
INSTRUCTOR'S MANUAL

Over 1000 additional *What About You?* questions and 100 expansion activities provide an abundance of extra options for teachers to choose from. These questions and activities help teachers expand the focus of the class to include speaking, critical thinking, interviews, projects, presentations, and writing assignments. In addition, the range of activities supplied in this manual allows teachers to easily adjust the level of their class to meet students' individual needs. Finally, twelve tests and an answer key provide a comprehensive review of all 48 episodes.

CONVERSATION BOOKS 1–4 INSTRUCTOR'S MANUAL

This manual contains specific teaching suggestions that enable instructors to adjust the level of every activity each of the four books. Also included are oral proficiency checklists that instructors can use as an evaluative device in measuring students' communicative progress.

GRAMMAR GUIDES 1–4 INSTRUCTOR'S MANUAL

Within this manual, teachers will find *Writing with Grammar* and *Communicating with Grammar* activities that provide additional practice with the grammar topics found in each episode. Also included is a detailed answer key.

DISTANCE-LEARNING FACULTY GUIDE

This guide contains useful information about how to use **Connect with English** materials in a distance-learning course, and also offers suggestions for how to establish new credit or non-credit distance-learning programs into any existing ESL/EFL curriculum.

DEMONSTRATION VIDEO

This video contains actual classroom examples of how the **Connect with English** materials can be used in a variety of different instructional settings.

Course options for using the *Connect with English* materials

The **Connect with English** print program is highly flexible and allows instructors to mix and match texts specifically according to their curriculum objectives and student needs. Multi-skills courses may include the use of all three core texts - the *Video Comprehension Books, Conversation Books,* and *Grammar Guides.* For courses with an emphasis on specific skills, many options are possible including those listed below. Of course, this list is by no means exhaustive, as the general design and nature of the entire **Connect with English** program lends itself to a variety of creative and useful classroom applications.

FOR COURSES WITH AN EMPHASIS ON LISTENING COMPREHENSION AND/OR READING AND WRITING:

Of all the core texts, *Video Comprehension Books 1–4* provide the most complete practice in listening comprehension skills. Special *Before You Watch, While You Watch,* and *After You Watch* activities help students understand the general as well as detailed events from the video story. Multiple choice and cloze activities provide practice in reading, and the many *What About You?* questions can be used as writing assignments.

For teachers who wish to incorporate even more reading practice into their course, the *Connections Readers* nicely supplement the *Video Comprehension Books.* They provide an additional source of reading material that ties in directly to the characters and events in the **Connect with English** story. The *Video Scripts* also are valuable components to use for a focus on reading skills. The scripts contain the actual dialogue of each episode, and can provide a great amount of support for students who need help in following the story.

FOR COURSES WITH AN EMPHASIS ON CONVERSATION AND SPEAKING:

Conversation Books 1–4 offer an abundance of practice in conversational skills. Each book contains a variety of partner, group, team, and whole-class activities based on important themes from each episode. Students using these books will also practice reading, writing, listening, and vocabulary skills. The *Conversation Books* pair nicely with the *Video Comprehension Books,* providing students with both communicative practice and a comprehensive review of the events in each episode.

FOR COURSES WITH AN EMPHASIS ON GRAMMAR:

Grammar Guides 1–4 provide a systematic presentation of the basic structures and grammatical features of American English. Each grammar topic is presented in clear and simple charts, and examples from the video episodes are used to highlight these key concepts. The *Grammar Guides* work well when combined with the *Video Comprehension Books* for a complete review of story highlights and an emphasis on grammatical features. In addition, the *Connections Readers* use the same grammatical scope and sequence as the *Grammar Guides,* thereby providing valuable recycling of the featured structures.

CLASSROOM TEACHING SUGGESTIONS

This section provides useful material for using the *Conversation Books* in the classroom.

For each activity, there is:
- a description of the principal language functions (skills) students will demonstrate;
- estimated time required to complete the activity;
- suggestions for adjusting the activity for students of lower and higher language proficiency.

The teaching suggestions on the following pages correspond to the icons found in activity bar preceding each activity in the *Conversation Books*:

▲ *Up:* Arrows pointing up indicate suggestions for how the difficulty or an activity can be **increased**.

▼ *Down:* Arrows pointing down indicate suggestions for how the difficulty of an activity can be **simplified**.

◆ *Up and Down:* Arrows pointing in both directions indicate suggestions for how the difficulty of an activity can either be **increased or simplified**.

Some activities have additional classroom tips which include such things as suggestions for materials needed or extra follow-up work related to the activity. For those activities with definite answers, an Answer Key is also provided.

EPISODE 37
THANKSGIVING

THEME Family Holidays

1 | CLASS | BRAINSTORM

Language Focus: Talking about personal experiences, discussing customs/culture
Time: 5-10 minutes

ADJUSTING THE LEVEL
Up: Have students each write a paragraph about what his/her family usually does on a particular holiday. Ask them to consider these topics:
- what people wear
- what people eat
- what games people play
- who does the work of preparing and cleaning up for the get-together

Have students share their paragraphs in small groups.

2 | PARTNER | INTERVIEW

Language Focus: Talking about personal experiences, discussing customs/culture, interviewing
Time: 10 minutes

ADJUSTING THE LEVEL
Up: Have students work in groups and compare answers. Have them try to answer these questions:
- Are there any differences in activities according to the countries people are from? If so, what are they?
- Are there more similarities or differences in the lists?

3 | GROUP | DISCUSSION

Language Focus: Reading descriptions to solve a puzzle
Time: 10-15 minutes
Answer Key: Answers will vary, but check for the following: Cousin Jane is not near Dad (she doesn't like smoke); Grandpa Joe is not near Cousin Peter (he doesn't like little children); Mom isn't near Aunt Betty (she doesn't like her); Aunt Betty is across from Cousin Jane.

ADJUSTING THE LEVEL
Down: Illustrate a strategy for helping to solve the puzzle by connecting related pairs of items.
   EXAMPLE
   Dad smokes.
   Cousin Jane doesn't like smoke.
   Conclusion: We shouldn't put Dad near Jane.

THEME Family Secrets

4 | PARTNER | ROLE-PLAY

Language Focus: Telling stories
Time: 20-30 minutes

ADJUSTING THE LEVEL
Down: First, have students review the family secret that Rebecca found out from Uncle Brendan.
Then, with the class, brainstorm some possible reasons or scenarios for one or more of the family secrets in the activity:
   EXAMPLE
   First situation
   - The man was your mother's first boyfriend. They were going to get married. But then your mother met your father, and she knew he was the right man for her right away. She broke off the engagement.
   - The man in the picture is your uncle, your mother's brother. You just have never seen a picture of him when he looked so young.

With the class, write a brief role-play based on one of the situations.

Up: After students do the activity, have them each think of a family secret and write a story in a paragraph or in narrative form. It can be based on a secret from real life, the activity, or a book or film, or it can be made up by the student.

THEME Thanksgiving Day

5 | PARTNER | MAKING GUESSES

Language Focus: Talking about historical events, making guesses
Time: 10 minutes
Answer Key: 1. 1621, 2. 1789, 3. 1863, 4. 1939

ADJUSTING THE LEVEL
Down: Draw a time line on the board or prepare an overhead. The year 1492 should be at one end of the time line and the current year at the other end. Ask students what the significance of 1492 is (the first Europeans came to the Americas). Mark 1789 on the line and explain that the first president of the United States took office in that year. Invite students to tell any other important dates they know in the history of the United States and mark them on the time line.

6 | PARTNER | STORYTELLING

Language Focus: Talking about past events, retelling a story
Time: 15-20 minutes

ADJUSTING THE LEVEL
Down: Guide students through the reading. Ask them to answer these questions after they read each paragraph:
Paragraph 1: Who were Pilgrims? Why did they come to North America?

Paragraph 2: How did the Pilgrims get to North America?
Paragraph 3: What problem did the Pilgrims have when they arrived in North America?
Paragraph 4: What did the Pilgrims have to learn? Who helped them?
Paragraph 5: Why did the Pilgrims celebrate the first Thanksgiving? How did they celebrate it?
Paragraph 6: How did Thanksgiving become a holiday in the United States?

For Part D, help students find the dates in the story. Show them how to calculate the differences and come up with a score, using one pair's answers as an example.

Up: Encourage students to retell the story without looking back at the text in the book. Or, have students make a time line about the story of the Thanksgiving holiday.

GAME Thanksgiving Football

| 7 | TEAM | GAME |

Language Focus: Asking and answering questions, writing information questions, retelling events from a story
Classroom Tip: Explain a typical football field by copying the game board onto the board or an overhead. Explain that, in football, one team tries to get to one of the goal lines to score a touchdown and the other team tries to get to the other goal line. Using sample questions, demonstrate how teams move up and down the field toward the goal lines.
Time: 15-20 minutes

ADJUSTING THE LEVEL

Down: Review how to form *Who, What, When,* and *Where* questions, mentioning the use of *do/does/did* and the inversion of *be*. To help students form questions, write a list of five or six possible answers on the board, and have the class orally brainstorm questions for the answers.

EXAMPLE
A: Guitar lessons.
Q: What does Rebecca give to Alex and Vincent?
A: Oysters.
Q: What did the Caseys eat at the restaurant?

Up: Have students play the game again. However, this time students should write definitions of words in English from the video for other students to guess.

EXAMPLE
• This is a kind of shellfish. People eat them raw. (oysters)
• This a popular sport in the United States. People watch this sport on Thanksgiving Day. (football)

PROJECT   APPENDIX 1

Computer Classes

| 1 | GROUP | RESEARCH |

Language Focus: Talking about school courses, talking about computers, using interview skills
Time: 5-10 minutes (In addition, students do fieldwork outside of class.)

ADJUSTING THE LEVEL

Down: Before students do the activity, have volunteers talk about common types of computer courses available in schools and describe what the courses teach. Make a list of the courses on the board.

Up: Encourage students to get more information about the courses, such as prerequisites/requirements for entrance, availability of computers at school, number of students in a class, textbooks, and so on.

| 2 | GROUP | SURVEY |

Language Focus: Using interview skills, making generalizations
Classroom Tip: Have groups compare answers and, with the class, come up with a profile of a typical student for your school and what the school should teach.
Time: 10-15 minutes (In addition, students do fieldwork outside of class.)

ADJUSTING THE LEVEL

Down: Review the list of courses from Activity 1. Make sure that students understand what the courses teach by having volunteers explain their contents.

EPISODE 38
STARTING OVER

THEME Christmas Bonuses

1 | GROUP | SURVEY

Language Focus: Discussing gifts, stating preferences, interview skills
Time: 5-10 minutes

ADJUSTING THE LEVEL
Up: As students do the survey, have them also ask why the person wants a particular Christmas bonus, using the question *Why do you want that bonus?*

2 | GROUP | COMPARISON

Language Focus: Discussing gifts, describing personal experiences
Time: 10 minutes

ADJUSTING THE LEVEL
Up: Have groups report overall results to the class in either a pie graph or a bar graph.

3 | GROUP | DISCUSSION

Language Focus: Giving opinions, negotiating
Time: 15-20 minutes

ADJUSTING THE LEVEL
Down: Before students do the activity in their groups, discuss the items as a class. Make a chart listing the positive and negative aspects of each choice.
  EXAMPLE
  Full-time employees who did great work

Positive	Negative
Rewards those who deserve it	• We have to figure out who did good work. • The people not getting bonuses will be upset.

Up: Have students work in groups of five or six and do a role-play of a meeting of the board of directors. Different students should take different positions.
  EXAMPLE
  •One person doesn't want any bonuses given.
  •One person thinks everyone should have bonuses.
  •One person is the chairperson who will decide on what Christmas bonus will be given.

THEME Giving Advice

4 | PARTNER | WAYS TO SAY IT

Language Focus: Giving advice
Time: 10-15 minutes

ADJUSTING THE LEVEL
Down: Before students do the activity, brainstorm a list of possible solutions for each problem.
  EXAMPLE
  Problem: I feel very stressed and anxious.
  Solutions: do less work, get help in your work, set priorities (do the important things first), relax, do something you like to do, listen to music, play a sport, exercise

Up: Have students do a role-play in groups of three — the first student states a problem and the other two students give advice. However, the two students giving the advice don't agree on the best thing to do. Have groups share their role-plays.

5 | GROUP | DISCUSSION

Language Focus: Giving advice
Time: 15 minutes

ADJUSTING THE LEVEL
Down: As a class, brainstorm two pieces of advice for each problem. In the groups, students can choose between the two pieces of advice to give Harry or think of some advice of their own.

THEME Losing a Job

6 | GROUP | DEBATE

Language Focus: Giving opinions, talking about work issues
Time: 15 minutes

ADJUSTING THE LEVEL
Down: To prepare students to do the activity, have students think of things that Rebecca and Emma could say about the situation and the job.
  EXAMPLE
  Rebecca: I really need a job. When I left, it was an emergency. I didn't know when I would be back. I am good at the job. The children like me.

  Emma: I had to hire someone else. There was no one to work with Rebecca's group of children at that time. It was unfair to the parents. They pay for our program, and they want their children to play and learn. It was unfair to the other workers in the program, too: they had to do Rebecca's job, as well as their own.

Up: Have students do a follow-up debate relating to work issues that they suggest; for example, the types of benefits that all employees should get.

7 | PARTNER | DISCUSSION

Language Focus: Reading want ads, discussing job requirements, giving opinions
Time: 10-15 minutes

ADJUSTING THE LEVEL
Down: Tell students to analyze the jobs according to these criteria:
- Does Rebecca have the right experience for the job?
- Are the hours good for Rebecca?
- Will the job help her in her future career?

Up: Present actual help-wanted ads to students and see if they can find a good job for Rebecca. You might want to obtain pages from help-wanted ads and put them on overheads.

INFORMATION GAP
Decorating a Christmas Tree

8 | PARTNER | INFORMATION GAP

Language Focus: Describing locations, asking for and giving information
Time: 10-15 minutes

ADJUSTING THE LEVEL
Down: Before students do the activity, draw a Christmas tree on the board or on an overhead. Draw ornaments similar to those in the activity. Describe the placement of a few of the ornaments on the tree, and then invite volunteers to do the same. Write the following words on the board to help students in their descriptions:
- above
- below
- next to
- to the right of
- to the left of
- between
- at/near the bottom of
- at/near the top of
- in the middle of

Up: Have students do a similar follow-up activity. Each student draws a Christmas tree with ornaments. Then he/she makes a copy of it, leaving out some of the ornaments. Students then give the copy to their partner, and the pair work together to fill in the missing ornaments.

PROJECT   APPENDIX 2
Sports for Children

1 | PARTNER | SURVEY

Language Focus: Discussing sports, using interview skills
Time: 10-20 minutes (In addition, students do fieldwork outside of class.)

ADJUSTING THE LEVEL
Down: To prepare students for the activity, have students discuss the sports that children play in their country and the benefits of each for children.

Up: In addition to interviews with children and parents, have students interview people who work with children and sports, such as gym teachers in schools or people who run after-school programs. When students report results, have them debate whether the opinions of these people should count more in making decisions about the sports program than the opinions of children or parents.

EPISODE 39

THE PRESSURE'S ON

THEME Managing Priorities

1 | GROUP | DISCUSSION

Language Focus: Discussing everyday activities, giving reasons
Time: 15-20 minutes

ADJUSTING THE LEVEL
Down: To simplify the activity, have groups first do the following:
- List the three most important things for Rebecca to do
- List the three least important things for Rebecca to do

Then have them use these decisions to help them choose the six items for their lists.

Up: Have each group write up a schedule for Rebecca's Tuesday night and present it the class, explaining reasons for choices. The group should include any phone calls she should make. Have the class vote on the best schedule.

THEME Stress

2 | PARTNER | INTERVIEW

Language Focus: Talking about personal experiences
Time: 5-10 minutes

ADJUSTING THE LEVEL
Up: Have students continue the interview. Students are to think of a particularly stressful time in their lives. Partners ask each other the following questions:
- What was the most stressful time in your life?
- What caused all the stress?
- What finally happened to change your situation?

Alternatively, during the interview, have partners ask follow-up questions such as these:
- Why does school cause you stress?
- Why does your family cause you stress?

3 | PARTNER | STRESS TEST

Language Focus: Discussing everyday events, discussing personal experiences
Time: 10 minutes

ADJUSTING THE LEVEL
Down: Before students do the activity, have them make up sentences with *often, sometimes,* and *never,* using information from Activity 2. Write sentence frames such as the following on the board to guide students:

I _____ feel stress because of school.
I _____ feel stress because of my car.

Up: Before students do the activity, have them predict how they think they will score. After they do the activity, have them discuss results — and any surprises — with their partners.

4 | GROUP | SURVEY

Language Focus: Discussing everyday activities, sharing personal experiences
Time: 10-15 minutes

ADJUSTING THE LEVEL
Down: Before students do the activity, have the class brainstorm a list of common ways in which people relieve stress. Write the list on the board.

Up: As a follow-up activity, write the following letter on the board or on an overhead. Have each student write a letter in response, giving advice about how to deal with stress.

EXAMPLE
Dear Miss Advice,
I often feel stressed. I work eight hours a day. I go to school three nights a week to learn English. I am worried about doing a good job at work. I am worried about doing a good job at school. I am always working and worrying.

Post students' letters. Have the class vote on some of the best responses.

THEME Being Direct

5 | PARTNER | WAYS TO SAY IT

Language Focus: Giving direct answers to problem situations, discussing problem situations
Time: 10-15 minutes

ADJUSTING THE LEVEL
Down: Go over the expressions in the box. Then present situations like those in Activity 5 and have students give frank answers, using the expressions in the box.

EXAMPLE
T: Do you mind if I smoke in here?
Ss: To be perfectly honest, I wish you wouldn't.

Other questions:
- Is it all right if I leave class early?
- Can I turn on the rock and roll radio station?
- Can I borrow your dictionary?
- Does my dog bother you?

Up: Have students develop role-plays of at least six exchanges for one or two of the situations in Activity 5, or for one of their own.

| 6 | PARTNER | DISCUSSION |

Language Focus: Discussing everyday situations, giving opinions, discussing customs/culture
Time: 10 minutes

ADJUSTING THE LEVEL
Down: Before students do the activity, discuss the situations as a class. After students do the activity, have them discuss the reasons for their answers.

Present some situations when it is OK to be direct in American culture and have students discuss any differences with what is done in their countries:
- People can refuse to grant permission for someone to smoke.
- People can refuse to answer personal questions, such as *How old are you?* or *How much money do you make?*
- Friends can often say whether or not they like something that a friend is thinking of buying.
- Teachers can tell students when they are not performing well. They usually do this in a private meeting with the student.

GAME Studying for Exams

| 7 | GROUP | GAME |

Language Focus: Talking about school, talking about everyday activities
Time: 20-30 minutes (Students can play the game several times during the episode.)

ADJUSTING THE LEVEL
Down: Have students brainstorm study tips as a class. Students can use the list of tips as they prepare the game cards.

Up: After students play the game, have each group come up with a list of the five best study tips and a list of five things not to do when studying. Groups should present and explain their lists, answering any questions from the class. Have the class vote on the best set of tips.

PROJECT   APPENDIX 3

Opera

| 1 | PARTNER | RESEARCH |

Language Focus: Using sources to get information, summarizing a story
Classroom Tip: Provide information on one or more musical works. The explanations found on CDs would be a possible source, as would music encyclopedias.
Time: 10 minutes (In addition, students do research outside of class.)

ADJUSTING THE LEVEL
Down: Do the activity with the class. Select a musical work. You can play parts of it and display material from various sources, such as a CD jacket or an encyclopedia. With the class, model the activity. Help students find the information needed to complete the chart in the activity.

| 2 | CLASS | STORYTELLING |

Language Focus: Telling stories, making oral presentations
Time: 20-30 minutes

ADJUSTING THE LEVEL
Down: Have pairs of students give their presentations to one another before they give it the class. The pairs should ask questions of one another, asking about anything that was not clear or indicating any other information that they would like to have.

Up: Encourage students to give more detail about the characters in the opera and about the composer.

EPISODE 40
SHARING FEELINGS

THEME
Things That Are Important to You

1 | GROUP | RANKING

Language Focus: Giving opinions, expressing preferences
Classroom Tip: After the activity is finished, have groups report results, telling their top three answers. Find the most common answers given by the class.
Time: 10-15 minutes

ADJUSTING THE LEVEL
Down: After students do the activity, help them summarize results by writing the following sentence frames on the board and having students complete them:
   To most students in my group, _____ is important.
   To many students in my group, _____ is important.
   To some students in my group, _____ is important.
   To only a few students in my group, _____ is important.

Up: Before students do the activity, have individual students write what they think the group's answers will be. Have students report the survey results for their group in a suitable form, such as in a line or bar graph or in a simple paragraph. Have groups discuss similarities/differences.

2 | PARTNER | INTERVIEW

Language Focus: Giving opinions, interviewing
Time: 5-10 minutes

ADJUSTING THE LEVEL
Down: Before students do the activity, have the class brainstorm other things that they think are important in people's lives.
   EXAMPLE
   • being in good health
   • having a special talent

Up: Have students write a paragraph in which they tell about three things that are important in their lives right now. Have students share paragraphs with their partners.

THEME Being Patient or Impatient

3 | CLASS | BRAINSTORM

Language Focus: Discussing everyday experiences
Time: 5-10 minutes

ADJUSTING THE LEVEL
Down: Before doing the activity as a class, have students work in pairs and try to answer the following questions: *Think back over the last week. In what situations have you waited? How long did you wait?* Have students share their lists of situations as they brainstorm as a class.

4 | GROUP | SURVEY

Language Focus: Talking about everyday experiences, giving personal opinions, interviewing
Time: 5-10 minutes

ADJUSTING THE LEVEL
Up: Have students work in pairs and interview a partner about a time he or she had a long wait and what happened. For example, it might have been waiting to hear the results of exams, waiting for a vacation to come, waiting for someone to meet him/her, or waiting to get an official document like a visa. Guide students with these questions:
   • What was the situation when you were impatient?
   • When did it happen?
   • How long did you have to wait?
   • How did you feel while waiting?
   • When did the wait finally end?
Students report their partner's experiences to another pair.

5 | GROUP | DISCUSSION

Language Focus: Discussing everyday experiences
Time: 10 minutes

ADJUSTING THE LEVEL
Down: Introduce the activity by telling of personal experiences when it was good to be patient (when waiting for someone or something important, such as an important visitor or a job interview), and impatient (when someone who was sick needed help and wasn't getting it, or when someone promised to do something important right away and didn't do it).

Discuss how people in the United States show how they are impatient by physical gestures (tapping feet or sighing), or by complaining in a loud voice. Discuss any cultural differences that students may have noticed as to how and when people in different cultures show impatience.

THEME Making Money

6 | PARTNER | BRAINSTORM

Language Focus: Discussing everyday experiences, giving information
Classroom Tip: Pair students of higher and lower language proficiency.
Time: 15 minutes

ADJUSTING THE LEVEL
Down: With the class, discuss ways people make money other than employment.
1. Explain the pictures at the right (a business, investments in the stock market, an invention) and how people can make money from them.
2. Encourage students to think of how people they know have been successful in earning money. Share any examples that you know about.

Make a class list of ways to make money and write it on the board before students do the activity. Remember to remind students to give specific examples and details as they work with their partners.

7	TEAM	GAME	

Language Focus: Negotiating, giving reasons
Classroom Tip: Before students play the game, make sure that no two teams have chosen the same or very similar ideas.
Time: 15 minutes

ADJUSTING THE LEVEL
Down: Before students put their five ideas on the board, have them present them to the class.

Up: Before students play the game, have individual students come up with a list of the five items they would choose. Have students present their lists and tell why they want the items, trying to persuade the other members of their team. The team makes its choices after listening to all the presentations.

INFORMATION GAP
Rock and Roll Music

8	PARTNER	INFORMATION GAP	

Language Focus: Reading reviews, using the vocabulary of music, asking for and giving information
Classroom Tip: Begin with a discussion about rock and roll and about some of the more famous bands and musicians from this musical style. You might want to have some CD covers or pictures of rock and roll groups available to show the class.
Time: 15 minutes

ADJUSTING THE LEVEL
Down: To prepare students for the activity, have them brainstorm words related to music in the following categories:
- Musical instruments
- Musical styles
- Names of CDs they know in English

Also review words for expressing opinions:
- Adjectives: *great, fantastic, wonderful*
- Verbs: *I like this. / I recommend this.*

Invite volunteers to tell about one or two of their favorite albums, incorporating the language.

PROJECT APPENDIX 4

Using the Library

1	GROUP	RESEARCH	

Language Focus: Getting information, summarizing information
Time: 5-10 minutes (In addition, students do fieldwork outside of class.)

ADJUSTING THE LEVEL
Down: Do the activity as a class field trip. You might want to have a librarian present some of the information, but have students do items 7 and 8 on their own.

Up: Have students add other interesting information that they find out about the library.

2	PARTNER	RESEARCH	

Language Focus: Using various sources to get information
Time: 5-10 minutes (In addition, students do research outside of class.)

ADJUSTING THE LEVEL
Down: Before students do the activity, as a class, brainstorm likely places/sources where students can find the answer to each item.

Up: Have each pair make up five similar questions to give to another pair. Of course, the pair has to have an actual source for each answer (written on a separate piece of paper)!

As an alternate, make up a list of ten questions that would interest the students. (Make sure sources with the answers are available to students.) Have a "treasure hunt." The first pair to find all the answers and give the sources is the winner!

EPISODE 41

UNEXPECTED OFFERS

THEME Moving to a Different Country

| 1 | GROUP | BRAINSTORM |

Language Focus: Discussing personal experiences, making generalizations
Time: 10 minutes

ADJUSTING THE LEVEL

Down: Before students do the activity, have them discuss any personal experiences they have had moving to a new country by asking the following questions:
- When you moved to a new country, what changes did you have to make?
- What things were different to you or new to you in the country you moved to?

After experiences are presented, ask students to find any similarities.

Up: Have students work in pairs and interview each other about any experiences they have had moving to or visiting another country.
- What things in the new country surprised you?
- What things were hard for you to do?
- What problems did you have when you first arrived?
- What things did you have to learn?
- What did you miss about your country?
- What did you like about the other country?

Students report their partner's answers/story to another pair.

| 2 | PARTNER | INTERVIEW |

Language Focus: Making comparisons, interviewing
Time: 5-10 minutes

ADJUSTING THE LEVEL

Up: Have students get together with their groups from Activity 1 and predict the class's top three answers to Activity 2. As a class, tally the answers (to Activity 2) and ask groups to compare their predictions with the actual results.

THEME Invitations

| 3 | PARTNER | WAYS TO SAY IT |

Language Focus: Inviting, accepting or refusing invitations
Time: 10-15 minutes

ADJUSTING THE LEVEL

Down: Review the language in the boxes. Prepare two sets of cards. One set has invitations; the other set has cards with either the words *yes/accept* or the words *no/refuse*. Have students work in pairs. Partners should not choose from the same set. The pairs act out a role-play according to the information on the cards.

EXAMPLE
Invitation cards: go to lunch together, work on a project together, come to a party at my house, go out for dinner
A: (card = go to lunch together) Would you like to go to lunch?
B: (card = yes/accept) Yes. I'd like that.

Have pairs repeat the activity several times.

Up: Have students prepare role-plays of invitations for people in the video. Here are some ideas:
- Rebecca asks Bill to study in the library.
- Bill asks Rebecca to go for a coffee after the audition.
- Alberto asks Rebecca to go to the opera with him.
- Nancy asks Rebecca to go to the retirement home with her to visit Edward.
- Rebecca asks Angela to go to lunch at a café with her.

| 4 | PARTNER | MATCHING |

Language Focus: Reading invitations, understanding customs/culture
Time: 5-10 minutes
Answer Key: 1. d (✔), 2. b, 3. c (✔), 4. a (✔), 5. e, 6. f

ADJUSTING THE LEVEL

Up: Have students work in small groups and discuss situations in which they send written invitations in their countries. Tell them to discuss the information they put on invitations. Encourage them to compare and contrast their customs with U.S. customs for sending written invitations. Finally, have students come up with a summary of what they learned from one another and share the results with the class.

THEME The Christmas Spirit

| 5 | CLASS | DISCUSSION |

Language Focus: Discussing customs/culture
Time: 10-15 minutes

ADJUSTING THE LEVEL

Down: Discuss some of the customs associated with Christmas in the United States:
- giving gifts to friends (clothing, games, jewelry, and so on)
- giving food and clothing to those who need it
- giving to charities (for example, donations of toys or clothing)

As a lead-in to the class activity, ask students if they know of any other holidays or periods with any of these customs or with similar customs.

| 6 | GROUP | PRESENTATION |

Language Focus: Persuading others, giving reasons
Time: 20-30 minutes

ADJUSTING THE LEVEL

Down: Have students discuss the work of each of the groups on the list. Choose one (preferably one not being used by any of the student groups) and model the activity: discuss the nature of the charity, the good things it does, and reasons people should contribute to it. Write the information on the board. Then model how to give a presentation incorporating this information.

GAME Giving Christmas Presents

| 7 | TEAM | GAME |

Language Focus: Discussing gifts, using vocabulary for gifts
Time: 15 minutes
Answer Key: Each person's present begins with the same letter as the person's first/last name and it has the same number of letters as the person's first name: Saul Sills, skis; Susanna Sills, sweater; Sally Sills, snake; Samuel Sills, skates; Carson Chills, camera; Cindy Chills, clock; Caroline Chills, computer; Cal Chills, cat; Brian Bills, books; Brenda Bills, blouse; Ben Bills, bat; Beatrice Bills, baseball; Tom Tills, tie; Thalia Tills, ticket; Teddy Tills, train; Tallulah Tills, tricycle.

ADJUSTING THE LEVEL

Down: Before students do the activity, have them look at the objects on the page for one minute. Then have students work in pairs and list as many of the objects as they can remember.

Up: After students play the game, have them write a paragraph about the gift they would most like to receive and why. Post the paragraphs in the classroom and invite other students to guess who wrote each paragraph.

PROJECT   APPENDIX 5

Vacations

| 1 | PARTNER | RESEARCH |

Language Focus: Using various sources to get information
Classroom Tip: Have available travel-related information, such as brochures or guidebooks. For variety, make sure that each group chooses a different place to report on.
Time: 10 minutes (In addition, students do research outside of class.)

ADJUSTING THE LEVEL

Down: Model doing the activity for a place to which you would like to go. If possible, have available travel brochures or guidebooks with information to answer the questions, and help students to find the answers.

| 2 | PARTNER | PRESENTATION |

Language Focus: Describing places, making oral presentations, expressing personal preferences
Time: 20-30 minutes

ADJUSTING THE LEVEL

Down: Have pairs give their presentations to other pairs. Have pairs ask about anything they don't understand and say whether they feel they have enough information to decide if they want to visit the place.

Up: As students listen to the presentations, have them write one interesting fact from each presentation. After the presentations, have students work in small groups and share their lists.

EPISODE 42

THE AUDITION

THEME **Waiting**

1 | CLASS | BRAINSTORM

Language Focus: Discussing everyday situations
Time: 10 minutes

ADJUSTING THE LEVEL

Down: Have students discuss the situations in the pictures for the activity. Have them answer these questions:
- What is each person waiting for?
- What would you do in similar situations?

Up: Before students do the activity as a class, have students work in pairs and make their own lists of everyday situations in which people wait.

2 | GROUP | SURVEY

Language Focus: Giving opinions
Time: 10-15 minutes

ADJUSTING THE LEVEL

Up: As a follow-up, have students rank the list by how often (very often, sometimes, never) they personally wait in each of the situations. Have them try to find out if there is a connection between how often they wait and what they hate waiting for.

3 | PARTNER | INTERVIEW

Language Focus: Getting information
Time: 5-10 minutes

ADJUSTING THE LEVEL

Down: Have students do a follow-up activity. Have them make a list of three situations in which they waited a long time and give the times. Have students share their lists in small groups.

Up: Have students work in small groups and discuss differences and similarities in cultures they know about relating to time. Have them answer these questions:
- Do people wait a lot? In what situations do people commonly wait and expect to wait?
- Are people usually on time for business appointments? for school? for social events?
- Are there situations where people seldom wait in one country and where people commonly do in another?

Have groups share conclusions and examples from their discussion as a class.

4 | CLASS | DATA ANALYSIS

Language Focus: Making comparisons, giving personal reactions
Time: 10-15 minutes

ADJUSTING THE LEVEL

Down: Supply language for the class to discuss results by writing the following sentence frames on the board:

The class average to wait for _____ is _____ minutes.
I would wait longer than that.
I wouldn't wait longer than _____ minutes for that.

Have students work in small groups and rank the importance of waiting for the items in Activity 3 and any others they would like to add. Have groups present their answers to the class.

Up: Before the activity, have pairs predict the average waiting time. After the activity, find the pair that was closest to the class average. (Pairs should find the difference between their guess and the class average for each item and then add all the numbers.) The pair with the lowest number wins.

THEME **The Importance of Education**

5 | CLASS | DISCUSSION

Language Focus: Giving personal opinions
Time: 10-15 minutes

ADJUSTING THE LEVEL

Up: Choose one of the five items. Have students raise their hands according to the answer they gave for that item. Students with the same answer form groups. Each group comes up with reasons and examples from real life to support its opinion and shares the information with the class. Do this with two or three items.

6 | GROUP | ROLE-PLAY

Language Focus: Giving opinions, persuading
Time: 15 minutes

ADJUSTING THE LEVEL

Down: Before students do the activity, have them list reasons that the child and parents can give and write them on the board. Then model how to do the role-play with volunteers, first playing the child and then a parent.

7 | GROUP | PRESENTATION

Language Focus: Giving opinions, persuading
Time: 20-30 minutes

ADJUSTING THE LEVEL

Down: Before students do the activity, have them answer this question as a class: *Why do you want to learn English?*

THEME An Audition

8 | CLASS | GAME

Language Focus: Engaging in everyday conversations
Time: 20-30 minutes

ADJUSTING THE LEVEL

Down: Before students do the activity, brainstorm a list of good situations from the video to use in their auditions.
   Then, with a volunteer, model the conversation between Rebecca and Alberto at the gallery. Take these positions:
- At first, Rebecca is nervous being at a gallery. Give Rebecca's response to seeing the picture of Alex and Ramón. Give Rebecca's response to seeing her picture.
- Alberto wants Rebecca to see his photographs, but he wants her to be surprised.

   Have students consider these questions as they prepare their role-plays:
- What does my character want to say?
- What is my character feeling?
- What is going to happen at the end?

SONG Dream Catcher

9 | PARTNER | SONG

Language Focus: Interpreting a song, understanding figurative meanings
Time: 15 minutes
Answer Key: 1. b, 2. c, 3. b, 4. c, 5. The singer wants the dream catcher to catch her., 6. The person who is a "dream catcher" can help another person when things are going badly.

ADJUSTING THE LEVEL

Down: Review the meaning of a dream catcher. It is a Native American object made of string and feathers. The Native American legend says that a dream catcher stops bad dreams but lets good dreams go through.
   Go over the words of the song with students. Discuss these questions as a class:
- What problem does the singer have?
- What does she want? Why?

10 | GROUP | DRAWING

Language Focus: Describing a scene, describing art
Classroom Tip: Have art supplies such as paper, paint, crayons, markers, and colored pencils available, or ask students to bring them in.
Time: 15-20 minutes

ADJUSTING THE LEVEL

Down: To simplify the activity, discuss the question in Part A as a class. Then have students work in pairs. You might want to pair students who have more artistic ability with those who are less artistic. Circulate as students are drawing and ask them what they are drawing and why.

Up: Have students do the same activity for another song that they know in English. In their presentations, have students both play the song and explain their pictures.

11 | TEAM | GAME

Language Focus: Talking about music
Time: 10 minutes

ADJUSTING THE LEVEL

Down: Before students do the activity, play one or two sad songs or blues songs in English. Explain what the lyrics are saying and discuss any new vocabulary. Ask the students their opinions of the song.

Up: After students do the activity, have them tell about the contents and lyrics of some of the songs. Then ask teams to choose a song from the list for a presentation. In the presentation, they should summarize the lyrics of the song and, if possible, play it for the class.

PROJECT   APPENDIX 6

Dedication

1 | PARTNER | RESEARCH

Language Focus: Using various sources to get information, reporting information, giving oral presentations
Classroom Tip: If possible, have simple English-language biographies or encyclopedias available.
Time: 20-30 minutes (In addition, students do research outside of class.)

ADJUSTING THE LEVEL

Down: Choose a person for whom you have material available, or have the class choose a person they admire and obtain materials about him or her. With the class, go through the sources to obtain the information. Then, with the class, paraphrase the information needed to answer the questions and write the answers on the board.

EPISODE 43

DREAM CATCHER

THEME Success

1 | PARTNER | RANKING

Language Focus: Giving personal opinions, interviewing
Classroom Tip: After students do the activity, have them report their answers to obtain overall results — i.e., the items that are ranked "Very important" on most lists.
Time: 10 minutes

ADJUSTING THE LEVEL

Up: Ask students to come up with a list of two or three things that typically mean "success" in their home countries/cultures.
   Have students work in groups and share their lists. They should discuss these questions:
   - What things do most people in my country think are important for success? What things do people in the United States think are important for success?
   - What are the differences between the two countries in the ways people think about success? What are the similarities?

THEME Talent

2 | CLASS | BINGO

Language Focus: Discussing abilities, giving personal information, interviewing
Classroom Tip: After students do the activity, go over each item in the squares, have students raise their hands if they can do it, and make a tally of how many students can do each item.
Time: 15 minutes

ADJUSTING THE LEVEL

Down: Before students do the activity, have them work in pairs and tell what talents on the board they each have. For this lead-in activity, try to pair students of higher and lower language proficiency. Have students count the number of things they each can do. Find the student with the highest total. Go over any unfamiliar vocabulary before starting the activity.

Up: Have the students work in groups and make a list of 19 items to put on their own bingo cards. Have each student write up a card, using the same 19 items. Have students exchange cards with another group to use in a follow-up game.

3 | GROUP | ROLE-PLAY

Language Focus: Discussing personal abilities, persuading others
Time: 20 minutes

ADJUSTING THE LEVEL

Down: Before students do the activity, as a class, brainstorm abilities that might be useful on the spaceship and why. Write lists like the following on the board.
   EXAMPLE
   tell jokes:
   People on the spaceship will need to laugh. They are in a very stressful situation.
   perform first aid:
   People on the ship and the new planet will need medical attention.
   know how to program a computer:
   We will need to write new computer programs to solve new problems.

THEME Having Confidence

4 | GROUP | BRAINSTORM

Language Focus: Giving reasons, giving personal opinions, talking about occupations
Time: 10 minutes

ADJUSTING THE LEVEL

Down: Before students do the activity, have them brainstorm reasons why the following people need confidence:
   - teachers
   - TV reporters
   - athletes

Up: As students do the activity, have them list two reasons why each group needs confidence.

5 | GROUP | INTERVIEW

Language Focus: Giving opinions, interviewing
Classroom Tip: After students do the activity, take a tally to see how many students think each item is true or false.
Time: 10-15 minutes

ADJUSTING THE LEVEL

Down: Before students do the activity, have them ask you for your opinions. Explain your answers by giving examples.
   After students do the activity, choose one of the five items. Have students raise their hands according to the answer they gave for that item. Students with the same answer should form groups. Each group comes up with reasons and examples from real life to support its opinion and shares the information with the class. Do this with two or three items.

| 6 | TEAM | GAME |

Language Focus: Using English vocabulary words, spelling
Time: 10 minutes

ADJUSTING THE LEVEL
Down: Encourage students to use a dictionary to check the spellings of words.

Up: Have students both write the words and explain why the words are included. They should use a separate piece of paper for their sentences.
- EXAMPLE
  - college — Rebecca is going to the San Francisco College of Music.
  - opera tickets — Alberto gets opera tickets as a Christmas bonus.
  - Nancy — Nancy is Rebecca's godmother.

INFORMATION GAP Taking a Message

| 7 | PARTNER | INFORMATION GAP |

Language Focus: Using telephone language, asking for and giving information, taking notes
Time: 10-15 minutes

ADJUSTING THE LEVEL
Down: Model doing the activity. Copy the message pad on the board or on an overhead. Ask students to copy it on a piece of paper. You give the following message. Students are to ask questions to get the information they need to fill out the form. Each student should fill out his/her own form. Then go over the answers together.
- EXAMPLE
  You had plans to meet your friend, Anita, at a restaurant after work today. You need to stay longer at work today. You will still meet her — but one half-hour later. You will meet her at the restaurant at 6:30, not at 6:00.

Up: Have pairs take all of the messages, using a separate piece of paper.
Then have the pairs make up their own message. Tell them to think of messages they have taken or given recently. Each pair then prepares a role-play in which one gives the message to the other. The pair presents it to a group. The members of the group listen carefully and take down the message they hear on separate pieces of paper.

PROJECT   APPENDIX 7

Chocolates

| 1 | PARTNER | RESEARCH |

Language Focus: Using sources to get information
Time: 5-10 minutes (In addition, students do research outside of class.)

ADJUSTING THE LEVEL
Down: You may want to present students with sources that supply the information and put them on overheads or read them to the students. The students take notes to answer the questions.

Up: Have the class brainstorm two or three questions to add to the list of questions and try to answer them in their research.
- EXAMPLE
  - What kinds of chocolate are popular in _____?
  - How is chocolate made?
  - What countries produce the most cocoa beans?

| 2 | GROUP | SURVEY |

Language Focus: Discussing culture/customs, using interview skills, reporting information
Time: 15-20 minutes (In addition, students do fieldwork outside of class.)

ADJUSTING THE LEVEL
Down: Have volunteers tell about special uses of candy in their countries. Use the information given to illustrate how to fill out the chart in the activity.

EPISODE 44

GIFTS

THEME The Community Center

1 | GROUP | DISCUSSION

Language Focus: Discussing community needs, negotiating
Time: 10-15 minutes

ADJUSTING THE LEVEL

Up: Have each group write two or three sentences about why it made the choices it did. Have the groups answer these questions:
- Why is this item important to help the community?
- Why is it important for a community center to provide this service?

2 | CLASS | POLL

Language Focus: Discussing community needs, presenting choices
Time: 10 minutes

ADJUSTING THE LEVEL

Up: Have students also tell why they made the choices they did, using their answers from the Adjusting the Level — *Up* suggestions in Activity 1. Then have students discuss the following items:
- In their countries, which of the services on the list are often provided by government?
- Which are provided by religious groups?
- Which are provided by private charity groups?

Point out that in the United States, private groups often provide these services.

3 | PARTNER | PUZZLE

Language Focus: Using food vocabulary, reading information to solve a puzzle
Time: 15 minutes
Answer Key: 1st floor, Meal B; 2nd floor, Meal D; 3rd floor, Meal C; 4th floor, Meal A; 5th floor, Meal E

ADJUSTING THE LEVEL

Down: Before students do the activity, have them group the following food items into the correct categories in the chart: chicken, beef, hamburger, cheese, ice cream, soda, cake.

Meat: _____
Dairy Products: _____
Sweets: _____

Show one way of solving the puzzle:
EXAMPLE
The person who can't eat beef lives on the first floor, so that person shouldn't get meals D and E. The vegetarian lives on the 4th floor. He lives below the person who can't eat milk products. The person who can't eat milk products is on the top floor. That person shouldn't get Meal A or Meal D.

Up: Have students explain their answers.
EXAMPLE
From the first and fourth clues, we know that the vegetarian lives on the 4th floor. So Meal A goes to him. All the other meals have meat. The person who can't eat sweets lives below the vegetarian, so he lives on the 3rd floor. He gets Meal C because he wants chicken. Meal B has chicken but it has sweets, . . . and so on.

THEME Breaking Up

4 | GROUP | OPINION SURVEY

Language Focus: Giving opinions, interviewing
Time: 10-15 minutes

ADJUSTING THE LEVEL

Up: Extend the interview by having students ask the following questions:
- Why do you think people can be friends after they break up?
- Why do you think it is easy/hard for people to be friends after they break up?

Have students give reasons for their answers.
EXAMPLE
Reasons you can be friends: You really like the other person. You may have a lot of interests in common. You know a lot about the person.
Reasons it is hard to be friends: It may make you jealous to see the person with someone else.

5 | PARTNER | DATA ANALYSIS

Language Focus: Making generalizations, making comparisons
Classroom Tip: After the activity is finished, have groups report results and add up the votes to find overall results for the class.
Time: 10 minutes

ADJUSTING THE LEVEL

Down: After pairs complete the activity, have them say which of the following statements are true and which are false, according to the information they have from their groups.

1. More than half the women think that people can be friends after they break up.
2. More than half the men think that people can be friends after they break up.
3. Less than half the women think that people can be friends after they break up.
4. Less than half the men think that people can be friends after they break up.

5. Less than half of the men and women think that people can be friends after they break up.
6. More than half of the men and women think that people can friends after they break up.

Up: After pairs do the activity, have them work in their groups from Activity 4 to report group results in graph form, such as in bar or circle graphs. Have groups compare graphs.

THEME Inspirations

6	PARTNER	WRITING	

Language Focus: Writing a paragraph, discussing personal experiences, interviewing
Time: 20-30 minutes

ADJUSTING THE LEVEL
Down: With the class, brainstorm personal inspirations. Encourage volunteers to share inspirations like those suggested in the directions for the activity, or by other situations; for example, they saw someone doing something well — taking pictures, or swimming — and they wanted to do the same thing themselves.
   Then model the activity. Have students ask you the questions and have volunteers write your answers on the board. Then, as a class, write a paragraph that incorporates your answer.

GAME Skiing

7	TEAM	GAME	

Language Focus: Reviewing vocabulary, spelling words
Classroom Tip: Before teams play the game, model the guessing activity by choosing a few words, writing blanks on the board, and asking students to guess letters to figure out the words (for example, *college, audition, restaurant, architect*).
Time: 20-30 minutes (The game can be played several times during the episode.)

ADJUSTING THE LEVEL
Down: Give students this tip for playing the game. They should write down the letters of the English alphabet. As guesses of letters are made, they can cross the letters out.

Up: The students must both guess the words and tell how they relate to the *Connect with English* video. Teams have to give at least two sentences for each word. The teacher is the judge of correct sentences.
   EXAMPLE
   Ramón gives Alberto a nice pair of goggles. Alberto can use the goggles on his ski trip.

PROJECT   APPENDIX 8

Helping People in the Community

1	GROUP	RESEARCH	

Language Focus: Using various sources to get information, using interview skills
Time: 20-30 minutes (In addition, students do research and fieldwork outside of class.)

ADJUSTING THE LEVEL
Down: You may want to model the activity by talking about a service organization or by providing information about it on an overhead. Students can answer the questions in Part B in writing.
   To further simplify the activity, you might want to provide students with names, addresses, and phone numbers of local organizations which they can research.

Up: Have two groups work together. Each group writes an article for a school newspaper about the organization that the other group researched in Part A. Have each group post its article.

EPISODE 45
TRUE LOVE

THEME An Ekeko

1 | PARTNER | INTERVIEW

Language Focus: Talking about personal experiences and wishes, interviewing
Time: 10-15 minutes

ADJUSTING THE LEVEL
Down: Before students do the activity, discuss as a class the possible meaning of each of the items pictured in Activity 1.
   EXAMPLE
   • diploma — a degree in computers
   • ring — marriage
   • passport — travel
   • pen — writing something that is published
   • star — becoming famous
   • heart — finding someone to love

As a class, brainstorm a list of wishes and possible ekeko items to go with each wish.

Up: Have individual students write a paragraph in which they explain their choices of ekeko items. Have pairs share their paragraphs.

2 | TEAM | GAME

Language Focus: Describing things
Time: 20-30 minutes

ADJUSTING THE LEVEL
Down: Model how to do the activity with the items presented.
   EXAMPLES
   guitar
   Player A: It's a musical instrument. It has strings. Rebecca has one.
   Player B: It's a guitar.

   tennis racket
   Player A: It's used to play a sport. It has strings.
   Player B: It's a soccer net.
   Player A: No, you use it to hit a ball.

3 | CLASS | DISCUSSION

Language Focus: Describing items, describing personal experiences and wishes
Time: 20-30 minutes

ADJUSTING THE LEVEL
Down: Have students give their explanations of the ekekos in groups of three before they give them to the class. The others in the group ask questions about things that they don't understand and they give any help with needed vocabulary.

Up: Have students work in pairs and write an article for a school newspaper article describing the ekeko activity that the class did. They should report on the most common and most unusual items.

THEME Exchanging Christmas Presents

4 | PARTNER | WAYS TO SAY IT

Language Focus: Expressing appreciation and thanks
Time: 10 minutes

ADJUSTING THE LEVEL
Down: Go over the expressions in the box. Then have each student write the name of a gift that he or she would like on a piece of paper, as well as his or her name. Students take turns drawing a paper at random and presenting the "gift" (the paper) to the student whose name is on the paper. The second student thanks the first for the "gift."

Up: Have the students work in pairs and do role-plays of various characters in the video as they receive gifts. The pairs perform their role-plays, with the class trying to guess the characters and the gift. Here are some suggestions of situations to role-play:
   • Rebecca — receiving car or necklace from her Dad
   • Rebecca — receiving the photograph from Alberto
   • Uncle Brendan — receiving the ring from Rebecca
   • Ramón — receiving the tape from Rebecca

5 | GROUP | DISCUSSION

Language Focus: Talking about likes and interests, describing people
Time: 20-30 minutes

ADJUSTING THE LEVEL
Up: Have the students think of a funny present and a serious present for each person, as they do the activity. An example of a funny present would be a chocolate soccer ball, for someone who likes chocolate and soccer.

THEME Falling in Love

6 | PARTNER | DISCUSSION

Language Focus: Discussing reasons, discussing personal characteristics
Classroom Tip: Have partners report their choices to the class. List the two most common reasons that students have given for why each of the characters — Ramón and Rebecca — is falling in love.
Time: 5-10 minutes

ADJUSTING THE LEVEL
Up: Have pairs present their choices and their reasons for their choices to the class. Have the class find the four most popular choices for both Ramón and Rebecca. With the class, make a list of information from the video to support each reason. Then have the class vote for the two best reasons for each character.

| 7 | GROUP | DISCUSSION | ▲ |

Language Focus: Giving personal opinions, discussing reasons for actions
Time: 10-15 minutes

ADJUSTING THE LEVEL
Up: Have the groups write reasons for their opinions, in addition to their choices.
   EXAMPLE
   Kindness: We think kindness is a good reason to fall in love. A kind person will be a good spouse. You will be able to count on the person to help you and understand your problems.
   Fame: We don't think that fame is a good reason to fall in love. In fact, it might be difficult to have a famous person as a husband or wife. You can't have a normal home life because fans will want to know everything you do.

INFORMATION GAP **Planning a Trip**

| 8 | PARTNER | INFORMATION GAP | ▼ |

Language Focus: Asking for and giving information, reading about travel, reading descriptions of places
Time: 15 minutes

ADJUSTING THE LEVEL
Down: Have Student As and Student Bs work in separate groups. Student As work on page 5 and Student Bs work on page 6. Groups work on completing the following chart for each of the three tours on their page:

Places the tour goes	
Things you do with the tour group	
How long the tour is	
Cost of the tour What is included in the cost	

Students can refer to the charts as they do the information gap activity.

PROJECT APPENDIX 9

Legends

| 1 | GROUP | RESEARCH | ▼ |

Language Focus: Reading legends, summarizing a story in writing
Classroom Tip: Have available books about legends. Illustrated books and books for children might provide material written at a language level appropriate for students.
Time: 10 minutes (In addition, students do research outside of class. You may want to allow class time for groups to write their summaries of legends.)

ADJUSTING THE LEVEL
Down: Model how to do the activity by reading a legend aloud or presenting it on an overhead and having students summarize it as a class.
   Here are some questions that students can answer in their summaries:
   • Who are the characters?
   • What are the magical events?
   • What happens at the end?
   • What does the legend explain?

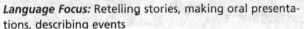

Language Focus: Retelling stories, making oral presentations, describing events
Classroom Tip: Have materials for making posters available, including large sheets of paper and colored pencils, markers, or crayons.
Time: 20-30 minutes (You may want to allow class time for groups to prepare their posters and descriptions.)

ADJUSTING THE LEVEL
Down: Have groups present a description of what they plan to draw to another group before they put it on their poster. The other group asks questions about things they don't understand or things they would like more information about.

Up: Have students discuss legends from their countries that are similar to the legends they heard about in class.

EPISODE 46

FRIENDSHIP

THEME Being Impressed

1 | PARTNER | RANKING

Language Focus: Giving opinions, talking about things that impress people, interviewing
Time: 10-15 minutes

ADJUSTING THE LEVEL
Up: Have students write a separate paragraph for each of the two things on the list of things that impress them the most and tell why. Have students share their paragraphs in small groups.

2 | CLASS | BRAINSTORM

Language Focus: Talking about personal knowledge and experiences
Time: 5-10 minutes

ADJUSTING THE LEVEL
Down: Have students think about the kinds of things they do to impress people and the kinds of things that impress them. Discuss these questions as a class:
- Has anyone impressed you in the last week? What happened?
- Think of people you know who impress you. Why do they impress you?

Up: Have students do the activity in pairs and then share their lists with the class.

3 | PARTNER | COMPARISON

Language Focus: Talking about personal knowledge and experiences, giving opinions
Time: 10 minutes

ADJUSTING THE LEVEL
Up: Have each pair prepare a role-play in which one partner tries to impress the other by doing the items on their lists. Have pairs present their role-plays in small groups.

THEME Collecting Autographs

4 | GROUP | DISCUSSION

Language Focus: Making generalizations, describing groups of people
Time: 10 minutes

ADJUSTING THE LEVEL
Down: Do the activity as a class. Some other possible groups are actors, writers, political leaders, and TV personalities. Help students with spellings of proper names.

Up: Have students each write a paragraph about the person whose autograph they would most like to have and tell why. Post students' paragraphs and invite other students to read the paragraphs and write their reactions next to them.

5 | CLASS | GAME

Language Focus: Talking about personal experiences
Classroom Tip: After the game, have the ten students whose items are on the board tell their stories. Provide help as necessary.
Time: 10 minutes

ADJUSTING THE LEVEL
Down: Have students work in pairs. They should help each other decide on the most interesting experience each has had. They then help their partners write about their experiences.

After you have written the items for the activity on the board, explain them. Model how to ask an appropriate question for several items on the board.

EXAMPLE
see a famous actor
Did you ever see a famous actor?

Up: After the class plays the game, have the ten students whose items are on the board tell their stories, as suggested above. Have students who are listening write a summary of the experience that they think is the most interesting and share their summary with a partner.

THEME Sharing Good News

6 | PARTNER | WAYS TO SAY IT

Language Focus: Telling good news, reacting to good news
Time: 10-15 minutes

ADJUSTING THE LEVEL
Down: Before students do the activity, write the expressions on the board. Also, write a list of good-news items like the following:
1. I just got a new job.
2. I just found a nice apartment.
3. I got an A in my English class.
4. I just sold my old car at a good price.
5. I just got engaged to my girlfriend/boyfriend.

Tell the good news and have individual students respond to it. Then have individual students give the news, while other students respond to it.

Up: Have students think of some real piece of good news that they have had lately and tell it in groups. The other students in the group should respond appropriately to the news.

| 7 | GROUP | GAME |

Language Focus: Giving good news, reacting to good news
Time: 15 minutes

ADJUSTING THE LEVEL
Down: Before students do the activity, brainstorm a list of 10 to 15 pieces of good news as a class. These items can then be used in the activity.

Up: As students do the activity, they should vary both the news and the responses. Before this, brainstorm a list of positive reactions as a class, such as *That's wonderful! / That's fantastic. / You're so lucky. / I am happy for you. / Get out of here!*

GAME The Music Business

| 8 | TEAM | GAME |

Language Focus: Asking questions, talking about music, writing questions
Time: 30-40 minutes

ADJUSTING THE LEVEL
Down: Model writing several questions with the class. Then invite students to suggest the names of songs and singers to incorporate in the questions.

Up: Students can vary the questions. They can ask about singers, lyrics, and so on.

> EXAMPLE
> Who were the members of the Beatles?
> a. Paul McCartney, John Lennon, Ringo Starr, George Harrison
> b. Paul McCartney, John Lennon, Yoko Ono, Ringo Starr
> c. John Lennon, Mick Jagger, Paul McCartney, Ringo Starr

PROJECT   APPENDIX 10

Languages

| 1 | GROUP | RESEARCH |

Language Focus: Using various sources to get information, using language names
Time: 5-10 minutes (In addition, students do research outside of class.)

ADJUSTING THE LEVEL
Up: Have students in each group write three additional facts that they find out about languages and share them with another group.

| 2 | TEAM | GAME |

Language Focus: Using language names, using interview skills
Time: 20 minutes

ADJUSTING THE LEVEL
Down: Allow students to interview other students in class and people outside of class. Write the following questions on the board to guide them as they do the activity:
- What languages do you speak?
- What languages do you know at least a few words from?
- Can you show me how to write "hello" in that language?
- Can you tell me how to say it?

EPISODE 47
THE LOST BOYS

THEME Changing Plans

1 | PARTNER | INTERVIEW

Language Focus: Talking about everyday situations, interviewing
Time: 10-15 minutes

ADJUSTING THE LEVEL

Down: Discuss the situations as a class before students give their answers. Have volunteers tell their answers and why.

Up: Before students do the activity, have them discuss times when they changed their plans during the last month. Have them tell why. With the class, make a list of reasons why people change plans:
- The weather is bad.
- Something else more important comes up (a relative is sick).
- At the last moment you don't feel like going out.

Have students discuss times when it is good to change plans and times when it isn't.

THEME Baby-sitting

2 | GROUP | WRITING INSTRUCTIONS

Language Focus: Writing instructions
Time: 10-15 minutes
Answer Key: Answers will vary. Here are some likely answers: John shouldn't eat chocolates. Give John an apple to eat. Put John to bed at 9:00. Give John his medicine before you put him to bed. You can eat the ice cream in the refrigerator. John can watch videos, or he can draw, or he can read books.

ADJUSTING THE LEVEL

Down: Before students do the activity, present the language for giving instructions:
EXAMPLE
You / The child should _____.
You / The child shouldn't _____.
You can _____.
Don't _____.
Please _____.

With the class, brainstorm a list of common instructions for baby-sitting.
EXAMPLE
- Please put John to bed at 9:00.
- John shouldn't watch TV.
- You can eat the food in the refrigerator.
- You should give John his medicine.

THEME Children and Money

3 | PARTNER | PUZZLE

Language Focus: Talking about types of money
Time: 10-20 minutes
Answer Key:
1. 3 quarters + 2 pennies
2. 3 quarters + 3 nickels + 5 pennies,
   or 2 quarters + 4 dimes + 5 pennies,
   or 2 quarters + 9 nickels,
   or 8 dimes + 3 nickels,
   or 1 quarter + 4 dimes + 6 nickels
3. 1 quarter + 2 dimes + 1 nickel + 3 pennies
4. 1 half-dollar + 1 dime + 1 nickel + 1 penny

Bonus question:
3. 1 quarter + 2 dimes + 1 nickel + 1 penny
4. 1 quarter + 1 dime + 3 nickels + 1 penny
5. 1 quarter + 5 nickels + 1 penny
6. 5 dimes + 1 penny
7. 4 dimes + 2 nickels + 1 penny
8. 3 dimes + 4 nickels + 1 penny
9. 2 dimes + 6 nickels + 1 penny
10. 1 dime + 8 nickels + 1 penny
11. 10 nickels + 1 penny

ADJUSTING THE LEVEL

Down: Go over the coins and their value. Do a sample item with the class and show how to solve it.
EXAMPLE
26 cents, 2 coins

It must be a quarter and a penny.
25 cents + 1 cent = 26 cents
1 quarter + 1 penny = 2 coins

Up: Have pairs write problems like those on the page and have other pairs solve them.

4 | PARTNER | INTERVIEW

Language Focus: Talking about customs/culture, talking about personal experiences
Time: 10 minutes

ADJUSTING THE LEVEL

Up: Have pairs come up with a list of three good rules for parents to follow when they give money to their children.

EXAMPLE
- Children should earn the money they get by doing chores.
- Children should get an allowance every week. It should not be more than ____.
- Children should be encouraged to save money.
- Children should be able to spend their allowance on anything they want.

Pairs should share their lists.

5 | PARTNER | ROLE-PLAY

Language Focus: Giving reasons, persuading
Time: 15-20 minutes

ADJUSTING THE LEVEL

Down: Brainstorm reasons that either child or parent might give in order to persuade the other.
Child:
- I want to buy a computer. I can use the computer for games, but the computer can help me with my schoolwork, too.
- I know that you need to clean the garage. I'll help you clean it and keep it clean.

Parent:
- I need to save money to buy a car for the family.
- You have bought several expensive things and then not used them very much.

Model doing the activity as a class, taking first the role of the parent and then that of the child.

INFORMATION GAP
Missing Person's Report

6 | PARTNER | INFORMATION GAP

Language Focus: Describing a person, asking for and giving information
Time: 15-20 minutes

ADJUSTING THE LEVEL

Down: With the class, brainstorm a list of words to describe people. Write the list on the board.

EXAMPLE
Height: tall, short, medium
Weight: Heavy, thin, average
Hair: long, short, curly
Hair color: blond, black, red, brown
Clothing: jeans, white shirt, athletic shoes, tie, green jacket

Then show a picture of a person (such as one from a magazine) and work with the class to fill out a missing person's report on the person in the picture. Use the chart in the activity as a model.

PROJECT   APPENDIX 11

Ice Skating

1 | PARTNER | RESEARCH

Language Focus: Using sources to get information, talking about sports
Time: 5-10 minutes (In addition, students do research outside of class.)

ADJUSTING THE LEVEL

Down: To simplify the activity, you might find an encyclopedia article or an almanac that has the answers to the questions. Have the pairs try to find the answers.

Up: Have students find the answers to additional questions, either ones that interest them or ones like the following.

EXAMPLE
- What is ice dancing?
- How is figure skating organized at the Olympics?
- How is figure skating scored at the Olympics?

2 | PARTNER | RESEARCH

Language Focus: Getting information, talking about sports
Time: 20 minutes (In addition, students do research outside of class.)

ADJUSTING THE LEVEL

Down: For Activity B, show how to calculate the speeds over the various distances by the formula:

distance traveled ÷ time = the speed (rate) of travel

Have students discover who travels the fastest by determining the rate traveled in various sports for each distance.

EPISODE 48
A VERY GOOD YEAR

THEME New Year's Resolutions

1 | PARTNER | INTERVIEW

Language Focus: Talking about personal intentions, interviewing
Time: 10 minutes

ADJUSTING THE LEVEL

Up: Have students write a paragraph on one of the following topics:
- A New Year's Resolution I Kept
- A New Year's Resolution I Didn't Keep
- Why I Don't Make New Year's Resolutions

Have students share their paragraphs in small groups.

2 | CLASS | GAME

Language Focus: Talking about personal intentions, explaining guesses
Time: 10 minutes

ADJUSTING THE LEVEL

Up: After students do the activity, have them discuss why some answers were easy or hard for them. For example, there may have been several people with the same resolution, which made it hard to guess. Or they may know some students well enough to be certain of their resolutions, which made it easy to guess.

Then have students vote on the "winners" in the following categories of resolutions:
- The one hardest to keep
- The one easiest to keep
- The silliest one
- The one I really would like to make and keep

3 | CLASS | DISCUSSION

Language Focus: Discussing personal intentions, discussing study tips
Time: 20 minutes

ADJUSTING THE LEVEL

Down: Before students do the activity, have the class brainstorm some good tips for learning English, such as listening to videotapes or audiotapes, writing summaries of films they see in English, and so on.

Up: After students do the activity, have them each write a list of good tips for learning English. Have them work in groups of three and come up with a master list of ten good tips. Then have the groups pool tips and come up with a master list for the class. Post the list somewhere in the classroom for everyone to see.

THEME Trust

4 | PARTNER | TRUST TEST

Language Focus: Giving personal information, discussing personal qualities, interviewing
Time: 10-15 minutes

ADJUSTING THE LEVEL

Down: Give a dictionary definition of trust: to believe that someone is honest and will not hurt you or cheat you. Discuss with students situations where it might not be a good idea to trust someone; for example, when someone you don't know asks you for a favor.

Up: Extend the activity by having pairs answer this question for each situation: *Is it a good idea to trust the person in Situation 1?* Have pairs form small groups and compare answers and defend the ones they have given.

THEME Parenting

5 | PARTNER | SURVEY

Language Focus: Giving opinions, discussing personal experiences, interviewing
Time: 10-15 minutes

ADJUSTING THE LEVEL

Up: As students do Part A of the activity, have them write reasons for their examples.

EXAMPLE
I don't want to give my child $20 for a video because that is expensive. He/she may watch it once and never watch it again.

Then gather class results into two groups. For each item, find the answers given by those students who have children versus the answers given by students who do not have children. Have students try to analyze and explain any similarities or differences.

6 | CLASS | DEBATE

Language Focus: Giving reasons
Time: 20-25 minutes

ADJUSTING THE LEVEL

Down: Have students discuss whether they think their parents were too strict with them and give reasons. (An alternate idea would be to have students discuss whether they think that parents in the United States are too strict or too relaxed with their children.)

As a class, discuss the example in the video:
- What did Alex and Vincent do that was wrong?
- How is Ramón going to punish Alex?
- Do you think that Ramón is too strict with Alex?
- Ramón lets Alex go the New Year's party. Do you think that Ramón is too lenient with Alex?

GAME Grounding

| 7 | TEAM | GAME |

Language Focus: Discussing people's behavior, making judgments about people's behavior, using vocabulary for common activities
Time: 20-30 minutes

ADJUSTING THE LEVEL
Down: Before students start the activity, check that they understand key vocabulary by asking them to complete the following matching activity:

1. cheat   a. leave home
2. lie   b. take something that is not yours
3. run away   c. not tell the truth
4. spill   d. when liquid pours out of a container by accident
5. steal   e. do something dishonest to win or gain something

Up: Have students play the game again with a list of at least ten bad behaviors that they brainstorm as a class.

EXAMPLE
- not obeying you when you tell the child to clean his/her room or do an important chore
- saying something mean to a relative
- not attending a family party
- not doing his/her homework
- taking money you give him/her to buy groceries and spending it on something for himself/herself

PROJECT   APPENDIX 12

New Year's Eve

| 1 | PARTNER | RESEARCH |

Language Focus: Talking about customs/culture, getting information from sources, using interview skills
Classroom Tip: You might have information about New Year's celebrations available in the classroom, particularly materials that are at the appropriate language level.
Time: 10 minutes (In addition, students do research outside of class.)

ADJUSTING THE LEVEL
Down: Before students do the activity, have them give the information for one or two cultures they know. Write a master list of answers on the board.

| 2 | CLASS | PRESENTATION |

Language Focus: Talking about customs/culture, making oral presentations
Time: 20-30 minutes

ADJUSTING THE LEVEL
Down: Before each pair gives its presentation to the class, it should present it to another pair, who will ask questions about anything that is unclear.

Up: Have students discuss similarities and differences among the New Year's celebrations.

ORAL EVALUATION CHECKLISTS

This section contains checklists which can be used to assess students' mastery of the language proficiency objectives promoted by the activities in the *Conversation Books*. There are 12 checklists in all — one for every four episodes in the *Conversation Books*.

How to Use the Checklists

The checklists should be administered after students have viewed the corresponding four video episodes and have completed the activities in the *Conversation Books*. The themes and language objectives that are being tested are conveniently listed on each checklist.

1. **Make a copy of the checklist for each student.** This way you can keep individual evaluations and notes on each student's performance.

2. **Administer the checklists during one-on-one sessions.** These can take place outside the classroom or in the classroom as other students engage in other activities such as group work. Administration time generally should not exceed 5-10 minutes per student. In addition, you may want to skip the proficiencies/themes that were not covered in class.

3. **For each objective, read the script in italic type aloud to the student.** In some cases, you will be asked to engage students in role-plays. In such cases, suggestions for role-play openers and language are given.

4. **Circle the score that you think best represents the student's mastery of each objective.** These scores range from 0 to 3, and represent the students' ability to respond and perform each language objective.

Using the Scores

The scores can be used to get a general picture of student progress. If a student's scores are mostly 0 and 1, this indicates that he or she may not have gained mastery of this particular objective. If a student's scores are consistently 2 and 3, this, on the other hand, indicates that he or she is making good progress.

You can use the scores on the checklists, together with your observations of a student's performance/proficiency in class and written homework, to give the student a grade for the class. These scores can also aid in grouping students according to language proficiency.

ORAL EVALUATION CHECKLIST   EPISODES 37-40

STUDENT NAME _____

KEY: 0 = does not meet the objective   1 = meets the objective with difficulty
        2 = meets the objective adequately   3 = meets the objective with ease

OBJECTIVES   SCORE/NOTES

1. Talking about Personal Experiences — Family Holidays
Theme: Family Holiday — Episode 37

Answer this question:
What does your family do for family holidays? Describe four things.   0   1   2   3

2. Giving Advice
Themes: Giving Advice — Episode 38; Studying for Exams — Episode 39
Role-Plays
We are going to do three role-plays. I am going to tell you some problems.
You give me advice.
Part 1:   0   1   2   3
- I have a really bad cold. I have felt sick for two days.
- I need to find a new apartment. I need a place closer to school.

Part 2:   0   1   2   3
In this role-play, I am friend of yours from school. Give me at least three pieces
of advice for my problem: I am having trouble in school. My grades are not good.
I don't do well on tests. What can I do to get better grades on my exams?

3. Talking about Priorities
Theme: Managing Priorities — Episode 39

Answer these questions: 0   1   2   3
- What are some things that you have to do at home this week?
- Now tell me, which are the most important? What are you going to do first? Last?

4. Talking about Personal Experiences — Stress
Theme: Stress — Episode 39

Part 1: Answer this question: 0   1   2   3
- What three things give you the most stress?
- Do you think that you have a lot of stress in your life? Why or why not?

Part 2: Answer this question: 0   1   2   3
What do you do to relieve stress?

5. Expressing Personal Opinions — Important Things
Theme: Things That Are Important to You — Episode 40

Answer these questions:
To some people, being rich or being famous is important. What things   0   1   2   3
are important to you? Why?

6. Giving Information, Expressing Opinions — Making Money
Theme: Making Money — Episode 40

Answer these questions:
Part 1: What are some ways to make money?   0   1   2   3
Part 2: What do you think are the best ways to make money?   0   1   2   3

ORAL EVALUATION CHECKLIST — EPISODES 41-44

STUDENT NAME _____

KEY: 0 = does not meet the objective   1 = meets the objective with difficulty
        2 = meets the objective adequately   3 = meets the objective with ease

OBJECTIVES   **SCORE/NOTES**

1. Giving Invitations, Accepting and Refusing Invitations
Theme: Invitations — Episode 41

Role-Plays: *We are going to do two role-plays.*   0 1 2 3
Part 1: *In this role-play, I am a friend of yours. I am going to ask you out.
You accept the invitation. Would you like to go to the jazz concert on
Friday night? I have an extra free ticket.*
Part 2: *In this role-play, you invite me to get a coffee after class.*   0 1 2 3
You want to talk about the class assignment.
Note: Accept the invitation.

2. Expressing Personal Opinions, Talking about Personal Experiences — Waiting
Theme: Waiting — Episode 42

Answer these questions:
Part 1: *In what situations do you really hate to wait? Tell me two situations.*   0 1 2 3
Part 2: *What is the longest you ever waited for something? Tell me about it.* 0 1 2 3

3. Expressing Personal Opinions — Education
Theme: Importance of Education — Episode 42

Why do you think it is important to learn English? Tell me two reasons.   0 1 2 3

4. Talking about Talents and Abilities
Theme: Talent — Episode 43

Role-Play   0 1 2 3
*We are going to do a role-play. You are applying for a special job. The job requires
a person who can do many different things or who has special talents. Tell me about
the talents you have. Try to persuade me to give you the job.*
Note: Keep questioning the student to elicit information. Also, ask why the
talents are important.

5. Talking on the Phone, Taking Messages
Theme: Taking Messages — Episode 43

Role-Play   0 1 2 3
*We are going to do a role-play. I am going to call you on the phone. I want to talk
to your roommate, Jane, who is not in. You take the message. You can ask me
to repeat anything that you don't understand.*
Note: Provide students with a form like that in Episode 43, page 5.
*Hello. This is _____. Is Jane there? . . . Can I leave a message? I want her to meet me
at the café near school at 8:00 tomorrow morning so that we can study together.
She should call me at 788-2992.*
Note: Check that students fill in the key information.

6. Talking about Personal Experiences — Inspirations
Theme: Inspirations — Episode 44

Answer this question: *Did a person or thing ever "inspire" you to do something?* 0 1 2 3
Tell me about it.

ORAL EVALUATION CHECKLIST — EPISODES 45-48

STUDENT NAME _____

KEY: 0 = does not meet the objective   1 = meets the objective with difficulty
     2 = meets the objective adequately   3 = meets the objective with ease

OBJECTIVES   SCORE/NOTES

1. Talking about Personal Dreams and Plans
Theme: An Ekeko — Episode 45

Ramón gives Rebecca an ekeko. You put things that tell about your dreams on an ekeko.   0 1 2 3
Answer these questions:
- What items would you put on your ekeko?
- What do they mean to you?

2. Expressing Preferences, Expressing Opinions, Expressing Thanks — Gifts
Theme: Exchanging Christmas Gifts — Episode 45

Part 1: (Show Episode 41, page 5.) You can get any gift on this page. What gift do   0 1 2 3
you want? Tell me why.
Part 2: Now we are going to do a role-play. I have a gift for you. Here it is. Open it now.   0 1 2 3
Note: Use any classroom prop or a picture of an item for the gift.
Part 3: Now you are going to give gifts to family and friends. Think of three people   0 1 2 3
you know. What gifts would you give to these people? Tell me why.

3. Talking about Personal Experiences — Being Impressed
Theme: Being Impressed — Episode 46

To impress someone, people sometimes talk about important things they have done.   0 1 2 3
What do you usually do to impress new friends?

4. Sharing Good News
Theme: Sharing Good News — Episode 46

Part 1: Please respond to my statements. I have some good news.   0 1 2 3
- I just won a new stereo in a contest.
- I just got a promotion at work. I am going to have a better job.
Part 2: Role-Play   0 1 2 3
Now we are going to do a role-play. Tell me about some good news that you have.
It can be something that really happened if you want.
Note: Respond appropriately with phrases from the book.

5. Describing Someone
Theme: A Missing Person's Report — Episode 47

Role-Play   0 1 2 3
We are going to do a role-play. (Show students a picture of a person from
a newspaper or magazine.) This person is missing. You need to describe this person
to the police over the phone. I am a police officer. Tell me as much about the person
as you can. Tell what the person looks like. Tell what the person is wearing.

6. Talking about Personal Habits/Preferences — New Year's Resolutions
Theme: New Year's Resolutions — Episode 48

Answer these questions: 0 1 2 3
- What will your New Year's resolutions be for next year?
- Will you keep your resolutions? Why or why not?

Part 3

Video Script

EPISODE 37

Thanksgiving

PART 1

1 OUTSIDE THE FARMHOUSE—DAY

2 *Michael's car drives up and stops at Great Brook Farm. Michael, Peggy, and their girls get out. There is much greeting*
3 *and hugging and introducing.*

4 **MICHAEL** Hi, Mom.

5 **ANNE** How ya doin'?

6 **MICHAEL** Good. How are you? (*to Brendan*) Hi, Dad, good to see ya. (*turning to his cousins*) You must
7 be cousin Kevin. Hi. I'm Michael. Rebecca, nice to meet you.

8 *Michael puts out his hand, and Kevin and he shake hands.*

9 **BRENDAN** And this is Peggy . . . and this is Erin . . . and this is Katie!

10 *Michael and Peggy's children are introduced to Rebecca and Kevin. The children are delighted to meet their new cousins.*

11 **MICHAEL** And these kids are hungry!

12 *They all laugh and begin entering the house.*

13 FARMHOUSE, KITCHEN

14 *All the adults help prepare the Thanksgiving dinner, which includes vegetables, fruit, the turkey, potatoes, rolls, and*
15 *pies. Peggy cuts vegetables, and Anne checks the turkey.*

16 **REBECCA** Anne, I'm gonna check on the squash.

17 **ANNE** Mm-hm. Check on those green beans too, OK?

18 **MICHAEL** Mom, where are the girls?

19 **ANNE** They're outside playing with Kevin.

20 OUTSIDE THE FARMHOUSE

21 *Kevin plays soccer with Michael's young daughters.*

22 FARMHOUSE

23 *Hallway. Brendan and Anne have a quiet conversation.*

24 *Living room. Kevin, Brendan, and Michael are watching a football game on TV.*

25 **BRENDAN** (*disgusted with the game*) Bah . . .

26 **KEVIN** That's a tough league . . .

27 **MICHAEL** They used to be able to win . . .

28 **BRENDAN** Yes . . .

29 **MICHAEL** Remember those days?

30 **REBECCA** What's the score?

31	MICHAEL	Green Bay 21, 'da Bears,' 17. Hey, I understand my, uh, dad has you working the cow
32		barn already, shoveling cow manure. Welcome to the Casey farm.
33	BRENDAN	He's doing a darn good job.
34	MICHAEL	(*leaning over to Kevin*) Hold out for health benefits.
35	BRENDAN	(*pointing to Michael*) Yeah, he never worked the barn. Wanted to do computers as soon as
36		possible.

37 *They all laugh.*

38 FARMHOUSE, DINING ROOM

39 *The family is seated at the Thanksgiving table. Anne carries in the turkey.*

40	PEGGY	Oh, that looks wonderful.
41	ERIN	How much does it weigh?
42	PEGGY	That's about twenty pounds!
43	ERIN	(*speaking to her sister*) That's almost heavier than you!

44 *Everyone laughs.*

45 *The Thanksgiving feast. Brendan sits at the head of the table, Anne at the foot, the others along the sides. They all join*
46 *hands for the prayer of thanks.*

47	BRENDAN	(*with bowed head*) I would like to say a word of thanks before we enjoy this feast. Recently,
48		You have taken away one of our family members, Patrick . . . But, in return, You have
49		brought us Kevin and Rebecca. Thank You for reuniting our family and for this delicious
50		meal we are about to share with our grandchildren and our children. Amen.

51 *There are murmurs of approval.*

52	REBECCA	I'd also like to say a word of thanks. I wanna thank all of you for being so kind and
53		welcoming at a time when we needed it most.
54	ANNE	Before we begin eating, I would like to say that we have a very special reason for being
55		thankful today.
56	KEVIN	Uncle Brendan and Aunt Anne have agreed to let me stay and help out on the farm.
57	BRENDAN	Kevin has decided to put up with us . . . so that his sister can go back to college in San
58		Francisco.
59	REBECCA	Oh . . . Kevin! Thank you!

60 *Rebecca hugs Kevin.*

61	MICHAEL	(*to Rebecca*) Give us a hug . . . that's great!

62 *Rebecca hugs Michael.*

63	MICHAEL	I would like to propose a toast to our new cousins from Boston to welcome them . . . And
64		although I could go on and on . . . and have, I think I will turn it over to our darling
65		daughter Kate, who is never at a loss for words . . . Honey, would you like to lead us in a
66		little Thanksgiving prayer?
67	KATE	Yes . . . Good bread, good meat, Good lord . . . Let's eat!

68 *Laughter and applause. The meal and conversation begin.*

PART 2

69 FARMHOUSE

70 *The family is sitting together.*

71	PEGGY	Anne tells me that you're going to the San Francisco College of Music.
72	REBECCA	I was . . . until my father passed away.
73	ANNE	Well, now you can go ahead with your plans.
74	PEGGY	So, you're a musician?
75	REBECCA	I really hope to write music and, maybe, perform.
76	PEGGY	(*to Anne*) So, Anne, do we have a star in the family?
77	ANNE	We might. But I've never heard Rebecca sing. (*addressing Rebecca*) But Brendan tells me
78		you have a beautiful voice. Would you sing for us?
79	PEGGY	Oh, please do.

80 *With a little persuasion, Rebecca agrees and goes to get her guitar.*

81	REBECCA	OK, lemme get my guitar.

82 *She exits the room. Michael and Kevin are talking in another part of the room.*

83	KEVIN	Your dad tells me you teach a computer course.
84	MICHAEL	Yeah. I teach at the community college in town.
85	KEVIN	I'm into computers.
86	MICHAEL	Good for you. It's a great field—something new happening all the time.
87	KEVIN	Oh, yeah, there's a lot to learn.
88	MICHAEL	Oh yeah. Hey, maybe you could enroll in my class . . .
89	KEVIN	Why not? I'll be staying here for a while.
90	MICHAEL	Good.

91 *Rebecca walks by with her guitar.*

92	KEVIN	Maybe she'll sing . . .
93	MICHAEL	Let's go.

94 *Rebecca enters and the room waits in anticipation.*

95	REBECCA	You'll have to excuse me. I'm a little rusty. Uh . . . lemme see . . . I'll sing an old folk
96		song, a Shaker song. It's called ' 'Tis a Gift to Be Simple.'

97 *She begins to play the guitar and then to sing. Anne and Brendan listen to Rebecca, surprised and impressed. The two*
98 *children are mesmerized. Kevin seems very proud of his sister's singing.*

99	REBECCA	(*singing*) 'Tis a gift to be simple, 'tis a gift to be free,
100		'Tis a gift to come down where we ought to be.
101		And when we are in the place just right,
102		We'll be in the valley of love and delight . . .
103		When true simplicity is gained,
104		To bow and to bend we will not be ashamed.

105   To turn, to turn will be our delight,
106   'Til by turning, turning, we come 'round right . . .

107 *FARM, AT THE POND—DAY*

108 *Kevin and Rebecca are walking alone near the pond, saying goodbye.*

109 **KEVIN**   I talked to Michael about his computer classes. They start up again after the first of the
110   year.

111 **REBECCA**   The insurance money should be in by that time. You'll have no trouble paying for the
112   course.

113 **KEVIN**   Yeah. Kind of hard to imagine, huh? Me being on a farm . . .

114 **REBECCA**   You seem to like it . . .

115 **KEVIN**   I do . . . it's kind of weird.

116 *FARMHOUSE BARN*

117 *They walk near the barn.*

118 **REBECCA**   It's been quite a year.

119 **KEVIN**   Yeah. I had a dream about Dad.

120 **REBECCA**   Oh?

121 **KEVIN**   I was this little kid . . . and I was holding onto this blanket . . .

122 **REBECCA**   You had a blanket . . . You carried it around with you all the time . . . You called it your
123   'blankie.'

124 **KEVIN**   I don't remember.

125 **REBECCA**   Mom used to use all kinds of tricks to pry it away from you so she could wash it.

126 **KEVIN**   I don't remember it at all.

127 *FARMHOUSE BARN*

128 *Kevin rolls something into the barn. They enter. Rebecca waits in the doorway.*

129 **REBECCA**   It all slips away so fast . . . . the memories . . .

130 **KEVIN**   I guess so . . .

131 **REBECCA**   Promise me you'll take care of yourself . . .

132 **KEVIN**   Hey, Sis . . . I'm not a kid anymore.

133 **REBECCA**   I'm sorry.

134 *Rebecca talks quietly but with intensity to her brother, realizing she is about to leave.*

135 **REBECCA**   I'll call you every day. We'll talk.

136 **KEVIN**   You don't have to call me every day.

137 **REBECCA**   All right. Every week. Hey, we're all the family we got, right?

138 *Kevin nods his head "yes."*

139	REBECCA	We've got to try and remember everything . . . the happy moments . . . .

140 *We see scenes of happier times. We see Rebecca and her father at Kevin's graduation, Thanksgiving dinner, Rebecca*
141 *and her new car.*

142 **REBECCA**   We have to remember the sad ones too . . . We have to remember it all . . .

143 *We see scenes of sad times. We see Mr. Casey at the hospital, Kevin walking alone, Kevin standing up to Jack, the*
144 *funeral.*

145 **REBECCA**   I guess it's time.

146 **KEVIN**   I guess so.

147 **REBECCA**   We never talk about Mom, do we? It's like she never existed. Why?

148 **KEVIN**   I don't know.

149 **REBECCA**   I remember everything . . . little things. I miss her combing my hair and the way she'd
150   tuck me in at night. The lullaby she wrote.

151 **KEVIN**   I don't remember any of it.

152 **REBECCA**   You were too young. I tried. I even sang it to you when you were little.

153 *Rebecca sings the first verse of a lullaby.*

154 **REBECCA**   (*singing*) Go to sleep,
155   The stars are shining brightly. Go to sleep,
156   The moon is on the rise . . .

157 **KEVIN**   Maybe I remember the lullaby.

158 *The two exchange warm smiles.*

159 **REBECCA**   Could I have a hug, please?

160 *They hug in the barn. It's the hug of two kids whose parent has died, leaving them alone. Somehow being together*
161 *makes it seem better.*

162 **KEVIN**   Have a terrific life in San Francisco.

163 **REBECCA**   Thanks. I'll give it a shot.

PART 3

164 FARM—DAY

165 *Rebecca gets into the truck with Brendan, and Anne and Kevin wave to her as the truck drives away.*

166 **ANNE**   Bye-bye. (*to Brendan*) You take care of her . . . Drive slowly.

167 *The truck drives off.*

168 **ANNE**   Take care!

169 INSIDE THE PICKUP TRUCK

170 *Brendan and Rebecca ride toward the airport.*

171 **BRENDAN**   So . . . are you excited about going back to San Francisco?

172 **REBECCA**   Yes.

173 *They ride for a moment in silence.*

174	REBECCA	Can I ask you something personal?
175	BRENDAN	Sure . . . go ahead.
176	REBECCA	Why didn't you and my father talk for so many years? What happened?
177	BRENDAN	Your father never told you?
178	*Rebecca shakes her head "no." Brendan stops the truck.*	
179	BRENDAN	(*looks at her closely*) Are you sure you want to know?
180	REBECCA	Yes.
181	BRENDAN	Well . . . When we were young and both living in Boston, your father and I had a lot of
182		friends in common . . . When the Korean War broke out, I got drafted. But before I left,
183		I asked Patrick to keep an eye on my new girlfriend. And your father said he would . . .
184		and he did. You know, absence doesn't make the heart grow fonder. I got a letter from
185		each of them, saying they had fallen in love.
186	REBECCA	It was my mother, wasn't it?
187	*Brendan nods "yes."*	
188	BRENDAN	Things never were the same between your father and me . . . They got married, and then
189		Lady Luck smiled and I met my Anne. You know the rest of story . . .
190	REBECCA	Thank God you got to the hospital in time.
191	BRENDAN	I'm sorry it took your father's illness to bring us together . . . Well, now you know.
192		(*He puts on his glasses.*) We'd better get you on that plane to San Francisco.
193	*We see the truck on the way to the airport.*	

EPISODE 38

Starting Over

PART 1

1 *We see a plane flying through the air.*

2 INSIDE THE PLANE—DAY

3 *Rebecca Casey sits in the plane, looking sadly and thoughtfully out the window.*

4 RAMÓN'S HOME—DAY

5 *Ramón puts the star atop his Christmas tree.*

6 ALBERTO'S OFFICE

7 *Alberto sits at the desk in his office, holding an envelope. A fellow architect looks over the partition. He holds a similar*
8 *envelope.*

9 **ALBERTO** Pete—Christmas bonus. Yes!

10 **COWORKER** (*reluctant to open it*) Yeah, what did we get this year?

11 **ALBERTO** Ahh—same as last year. Two seats to the opera.

12 **COWORKER** Boss sure likes his opera, huh? (*looking at Alberto's tickets*) Hey, you did well this year.
13 Grand Tier, Row A.

14 **ALBERTO** Just what I needed . . . uh-huh—for a special friend.

15 **COWORKER** The woman in the photo?

16 *A copy of the photo of Rebecca in the desert sits in his office.*

17 **ALBERTO** Yup, and right now she could use a little tender loving care . . .

18 **COWORKER** Better be careful, my friend. People are gonna start thinking you're in love.

19 **ALBERTO** Hey! Rumors like that can ruin a man's reputation!

20 **COWORKER** Couldn't happen to a nicer guy.

21 *ON NANCY'S FRONT PORCH*

22 *Rebecca opens the door with her key and enters.*

23 **NANCY** (*voice from above*) Rebecca, is that you?

24 *INSIDE NANCY'S HOUSE*

25 *Rebecca carries her suitcases into the living room and greets Nancy.*

26 **REBECCA** Yes, it's me.

27 *Nancy Shaw gives her a warm hug. She regards Rebecca with loving concern.*

28 **NANCY** Are you all right?

29 **REBECCA** I'm OK. I'm just exhausted, that's all.

30 **NANCY** You'll feel better after you get settled.

31 *NANCY'S FAMILY ROOM*

32 *Rebecca sits on the couch, looking around gratefully.*

33 **REBECCA** For a while, I didn't know if I'd ever be back.

34 **NANCY** I understand. You must miss your father terribly.

35 **REBECCA** Yes, I do. How's your uncle?

36 **NANCY** Truthfully, not so good.

37 **REBECCA** I'm sorry. What's wrong? He's not happy at the nursing home?

38 **NANCY** (*nods "yes"*) Edward keeps asking to come home. It breaks my heart. I can't take care of
39 him anymore. I did what I thought was best.

40 **REBECCA** You did the right thing. It's sad, though.

41 **NANCY** Well—glad to have you back. We've all missed you.

42 **REBECCA** I've missed my life here. And a lot of schoolwork. I hope I can make it up . . .

43 NANCY   Take it one step at a time . . .

44 REBECCA   Ooh—the first step is to call my advisor.

45 *She reaches for her address book.*

46 NANCY   Would you like some tea?

47 REBECCA   Yeah.

48 *We see Rebecca opening her address book. A picture of Rebecca, Kevin, and their dad on Kevin's graduation day is*
49 *inside. Rebecca dials.*

PART 2

50 SAN FRANCISCO COLLEGE OF MUSIC, FACULTY OFFICE

51 *Professor Thomas, a music professor and Rebecca's college advisor, is working on his computer. The phone rings and*
52 *Professor Thomas picks it up.*

53 PROFESSOR THOMAS Thomas here . . .

54 REBECCA   Hello, this is Rebecca Casey.

55 PROFESSOR THOMAS Oh, Rebecca, how are you?

56 REBECCA   Pretty well. I just got back.

57 PROFESSOR THOMAS Your father was sick, wasn't he? How's he doing?

58 REBECCA   (*quietly*) He passed away.

59 PROFESSOR THOMAS I'm very sorry to hear that.

60 REBECCA   Thank you . . . .Uh, the reason I'm calling is that I would like to get together and talk
61   about my courses. Is there any chance we could meet today or tomorrow?

62 PROFESSOR THOMAS I'm planning to be in my office late today. Why don't you come by—say,
63   around five o'clock?

64 REBECCA   I'll be there.

65 PROFESSOR THOMAS See you then.

66 *She hangs up the receiver. Nancy returns with the tea.*

67 NANCY   Here's your tea.

68 REBECCA   Oh, thanks.

69 NANCY   Did you reach the college?

70 REBECCA   Um-hmm. I'm gonna meet my advisor today at five o'clock. I'll see what he says. I've
71   missed so many classes.

72 NANCY   Well, don't worry about that right now. Things have a way of working out.

73 REBECCA   You're right. Did you hear anything from Emma Washington?

74 NANCY   No. I called her as you asked me to. She was very sorry to hear about your father.

75 REBECCA   I should probably give her a call, too . . . see if I still have a job.

76 *Nancy looks at the graduation picture.*

77	NANCY	Ahh—your father looks so happy here.
78	REBECCA	You know, Nancy, I found out what the problem was between my dad and Uncle
79		Brendan . . . why they didn't talk for so many years.
80	NANCY	Oh?
81	REBECCA	Uncle Brendan told me about my mom . . . that they were both in love with her.
82	NANCY	And that's why your father and I never got along. I always told your mother that
83		Brendan was the man for her. Your father got very angry at me when he found that out.
84		But your mother had a mind of her own. She went ahead and married Patrick anyway.
85		That's when they stopped talking . . .
86	REBECCA	They had a chance to talk before Dad . . .
87	NANCY	Good. They made peace?

88 *Rebecca nods "yes."*

PART 3

89 AFTER-SCHOOL PROGRAM

90 *We see Rebecca walking toward the school; the children approach her and welcome her back. Rebecca walks into the*
91 *empty cafeteria. Emma is getting snacks ready for the kids. Emma sees Rebecca and gives her a big hug.*

92	EMMA	Rebecca, how are you?
93	REBECCA	OK, I guess.
94	EMMA	I was so sorry to hear about your dad.
95	REBECCA	Thanks. How are things goin' here?
96	EMMA	Frantic as usual. Listen . . . um—I hope you understand . . . You know, I had to find
97		someone for your old job.
98	REBECCA	Oh . . .
99	EMMA	I didn't know whether you were coming back—and, uh, we're so shorthanded. I—I—I
100		had to replace you. I hope you will understand.
101	REBECCA	I understand.
102	EMMA	There might an opening next semester . . . right after the New Year.
103	REBECCA	Please, keep me in mind.
104	EMMA	You know I will. You're so great with children! Um—are you going back to college?
105	REBECCA	I hope to. I have a meeting with my advisor at five o'clock today. I have so much
106		catching up to do.
107	EMMA	You'll do just fine. Listen, are you still giving guitar lessons?
108	REBECCA	I sure am.
109	EMMA	Good. I'll put a notice on the bulletin board.
110	REBECCA	Thanks.

111 AFTER-SCHOOL PROGRAM, YARD

112 *Ramón, who has been coaching a group of boys in soccer, sees Rebecca watching the group from behind a fence. Ramón*
113 *walks over, and talks to her.*

114 **RAMÓN**   Rebecca? Are you really here? I don't believe it!

115 **REBECCA**   I'm here! Really here.

116 *Ramón heads for the gate so he can join Rebecca.*

The Pressure's On

PART 1

1 AFTER-SCHOOL PROGRAM, YARD—DAY

2 *A group of children practice their soccer skills.*

3 *Ramón greets Rebecca with a big hug. We see on his face that he's just as happy to see her as she is to see him.*

4 **RAMÓN**   Hah-hah—It's great to have you back.

5 **REBECCA**   It's good to be back.

6 *Alex, who's just spotted Rebecca, comes running up and gives her a big hug.*

7 **ALEX**   Rebecca! You're back!

8 *Rebecca gives Alex a big hug, too.*

9 **ALEX**   We beat the Hawks! And they were city champs!

10 **REBECCA**   See, I knew you could do it! Alex, I want to thank you for that nice letter and drawing
11   you sent to me. It meant a lot.

12 *Alex looks embarrassed by her attention.*

13 **ALEX**   That's OK. I like drawing, anyway.

14 **RAMÓN**   Hey . . . your team's waiting for you!

15 **ALEX**   See ya!

16 *Alex runs off to rejoin his friends.*

17 **RAMÓN**   So . . . . where are you off to?

18 **REBECCA**   I have an appointment at school.

19 **RAMÓN**   How are you doin'? Really.

20 **REBECCA**   Most of the time I'm fine.

21 **RAMÓN**   The other times?

22 **REBECCA**   The other times . . . well . . . I see something, and I think . . . 'I have to tell Dad about
23   that.' Then I remember . . .

24 *Rebecca is near tears again. Ramón gives her his handkerchief.*

25 **REBECCA**   Thanks.

26 **RAMÓN**   Give yourself time to grieve. The pain will go away. But it takes time.

27 **REBECCA**   The letter from you and Alex meant a lot to me. I was trying not to cry, you know . . .

28 **RAMÓN**   It happened to me when my abuela died. But there's nothing worse than seeing a grown
29   man cry . . . except maybe seeing two grown men crying.

30 **REBECCA**   (*smiling*) Right!

31 **RAMÓN**   See, a smile. Laughter is the best medicine. So, you're going back to school?

32 **REBECCA**   Oh, I'm going back, one way or another.

33 **RAMÓN**   Good for you. Are we gonna see you around here?

34 **REBECCA**   Emma had to hire someone to take my place.

35 **RAMÓN**   Sorry . . . I was afraid that . . . But you'll still be giving guitar lessons? I'm still a paying
36   customer.

37 **REBECCA**   Good. I can pick up Alex's lessons where we left off.

38 **RAMÓN**   We need you badly. Alex can't tune his guitar, and I'm totally tone deaf. Hah! The guitar
39   sounds like someone stepped on a cat.

40 **REBECCA**   Well, that should be easy to fix now that I'm back.

41 **RAMÓN**   Well—I should get back to the game . . .

42 **REBECCA**   Right . . . and I have to go see my advisor.

43 **RAMÓN**   Ah—yo—maybe—uh—Alex and I can buy you a—ice cream cone, one of these days,
44   you know, when you . . . when you have time.

45 **REBECCA**   I love ice cream. I'll find the time.

46 **RAMÓN**   OK.

47 **REBECCA**   Bye.

48 *She leaves, and Ramón watches her.*

PART 2

49 PROFESSOR THOMAS'S OFFICE—DAY

50 *Rebecca knocks. Her college advisor looks up from his desk.*

51 **PROFESSOR THOMAS**   Oh, come in, Rebecca. I've been expecting you.

52 *She sits down in a chair across from her professor.*

53 **REBECCA**   I wanted to talk to you about school . . . where things stand for me since I missed so
54   many classes. And, please, be honest.

55 **PROFESSOR THOMAS**   I've talked your situation over with my colleagues. I don't want to frighten you,
56   but I have to be frank. The finals are going to be tough. Real tough. If you don't pass,
57   you risk losing your partial scholarship.

58 *Rebecca looks disappointed.*

59 **PROFESSOR THOMAS** You can take incompletes and repeat your courses next semester . . . or you can
60 study like mad and go for it.

61 **REBECCA** I'd like to try to take the exams.

62 **PROFESSOR THOMAS** Well, I do admire your spirit. Maybe this'll help get you started.

63 *He hands her several sheets of paper.*

64 **PROFESSOR THOMAS** It's last year's exam. I gave it to the rest of the class to look at. It's a good
65 example of what to expect on this year's final.

66 **REBECCA** Thanks.

67 **PROFESSOR THOMAS** Get together with your classmates. Get their notes. Study with them. You're
68 probably not gonna get much sleep, but you just might pull it off.

69 **REBECCA** I'll give it my best shot.

70 **PROFESSOR THOMAS** Good luck.

71 **REBECCA** Thanks again.

72 HALLWAY OF THE SCHOOL

73 *Rebecca walks down the hallway, past students, music in the background. She moves through the school with*
74 *confidence.*

75 INSIDE NANCY'S HOUSE—EVENING

76 *Rebecca walks down the stairs, carrying one of her textbooks, and goes into the kitchen. Angela and Melaku are getting*
77 *dinner ready as Rebecca enters. They see her.*

78 **ANGELA** Rebecca, you're back! Oh!

79 *Angela gives her a big hug. They speak quietly.*

80 **ANGELA** I'm so sorry about your father.

81 **REBECCA** It was a total shock.

82 **MELAKU** It's nice to have you back here, Rebecca. My condolences on your father's death.

83 **REBECCA** Thank you, Melaku.

84 **MELAKU** In my country, we do not work for a time after the death of a loved one. We take time to
85 remember.

86 **REBECCA** Sounds like a good idea. In the United States, sometimes we move too fast.

87 **MELAKU** Is everything OK at school? Can you make up the work you missed?

88 **REBECCA** My advisor says I could start over next semester or cram for the finals this year.

89 **ANGELA** So?

90 **REBECCA** You won't be seeing much of me for a while. I'll be in my room studying!

91 *She takes a can of soda and heads back upstairs. Angela catches Rebecca near the stairs.*

92 NANCY'S HOUSE, STAIRS

93 *Angela stops Rebecca before she goes up the stairs.*

94 **ANGELA** Rebecca, we thought you might stay in Boston for Christmas.

95 **REBECCA** San Francisco is my home now. I'm going to finish school and write my songs. I'm gonna
96 make it happen. Here.

97 **ANGELA** Good for you. What are you doin' for the holidays?

98 **REBECCA** Hmm—not much. I'll be right here.

99 **ANGELA** Um—you're gonna be all alone. Melaku is going to visit some Ethiopian friends out
100 of town . . .

101 **REBECCA** (*interrupting*) Oh, it'll be good for him to be with friends—I'm sure he misses his family!

102 **ANGELA** (*continuing*) . . . and I'm going home to see my parents.

103 **REBECCA** Well, Nancy will be here. I'm sure we'll be fine.

104 *The doorbell rings.*

105 **ANGELA** I'll get that. You go study.

PART 3

106 NANCY'S HOUSE, STAIRS

107 *Angela goes to the door as Rebecca goes upstairs. Rebecca disappears around the corner. Angela calls up to Rebecca.*

108 **ANGELA** Rebecca, you have a visitor—a male visitor.

109 *Rebecca reappears on the stairs.*

110 **REBECCA** Who is it?

111 **ANGELA** (*whispers*) Alberto.

112 **REBECCA** (*frustrated*) Oh. Just ask him to wait in the living room. I—I'll be right there.

113 *Rebecca goes back upstairs. Angela whispers to Rebecca:*

114 **ANGELA** I forgot how handsome he is!

115 NANCY'S HOUSE, LIVING ROOM

116 *Alberto is checking his reflection as Rebecca enters the room. He gives her a big, warm hug.*

117 **ALBERTO** Rebecca, welcome back. I sure have missed you.

118 **REBECCA** This is such a surprise . . .

119 **ALBERTO** I just had to see you. I know things have been . . . been very tough for you. And I'm sorry
120 about your loss.

121 **REBECCA** Thank you. And I appreciated your beautiful flowers. Please, sit down.

122 *Rebecca motions to the couch as they both sit down.*

123 **ALBERTO** Well, it was the least I could do. Now, I wanna help you get back into the swing of
124 things. So . . . I have something here to cheer you up.

125 *He takes out the tickets to the opera and shows them to her.*

126 REBECCA Tickets to the San Francisco Opera.

127 ALBERTO Best seats in the house. They're doing *Amahl and the Night Visitors*. You know, the 'Night
128 Visitors' are the three kings, and they're following the star to Bethlehem . . .

129 REBECCA Huh—that's very nice of you . . .

130 ALBERTO (*interrupting*) I'm sure you'll enjoy it.

131 REBECCA I'm sure I would, too, but—I can't make any plans. I have to cram for my final exams.

132 ALBERTO A ton of schoolwork, huh?

133 REBECCA Yeah. I lost so much time because of . . . It's gonna take every waking hour just to
134 catch up.

135 ALBERTO Well, maybe a little diversion might help.

136 REBECCA Look, if I fail my exams, I lose my scholarship. Now, I would really love to . . .

137 ALBERTO (*interrupting*) I'll take that as a 'yes,' and you can see how your studying is going later on in
138 the week . . .

139 *Rebecca looks frustrated.*

140 REBECCA Thank you.

141 ALBERTO Well, I've gotta get going. Don't panic over your exams—I know you—I'm sure you'll do
142 just fine.

143 *She nods, but she's not so sure.*

144 NANCY'S HOUSE, FRONT HALLWAY

145 *Rebecca walks Alberto to the door.*

146 ALBERTO So . . . I'll call you later in the week.

147 REBECCA OK.

148 ALBERTO I'm really happy you're back.

149 REBECCA Me, too.

150 *He kisses her softly and gently on the lips.*

151 ALBERTO Bye.

152 REBECCA Bye.

153 *Rebecca closes the door. She leans against it, uncertain of her feelings. Angela comes down the stairs.*

154 ANGELA Lucky woman!

155 REBECCA He wants to take me out Saturday . . . to the opera.

156 ANGELA To the opera? Oh! Very nice. Maybe you two will spend the holidays together.

157 REBECCA I don't think so. I'm not even sure about the opera . . . I mean, I have so much studying
158 to do.

159 ANGELA What's that expression—all work and no play . . .

160	REBECCA	You know, if I don't study for my exams, I'm not gonna pass my finals. I don't know,
161		Angela, I'm just so exhausted.
162	ANGELA	It's probably just the trip and all. My advice—go out and have a grand time. You'll be
163		able to study better, believe me. And Alberto seems to really care for you.
164	REBECCA	I guess so. Well, it's time to get back to the books.
165	*Rebecca goes to the upstairs hallway.*	
166	ANGELA	Are you all right?
167	REBECCA	Just overwhelmed by everything.
168	*Rebecca continues walking up the stairs.*	

EPISODE 40

Sharing Feelings

PART 1

1 SAN FRANCISCO COLLEGE OF MUSIC, LIBRARY—DAY

2 *Rebecca is studying, surrounded by books. She looks totally worn out. Bill, Rebecca's friend at school, approaches and*
3 *sits down next to her.*

4	BILL	Don't you ever leave the library?
5	REBECCA	No. What day's today?
6	BILL	Friday.
7	REBECCA	Friday! Oh, no . . .
8	BILL	Well, you only have seventeen shopping days left till Christmas.
9	REBECCA	Shopping? You must be kidding!
10	BILL	You've gotta get out. You're not gonna take that musical dictation final, are you?
11	REBECCA	Yup.
12	BILL	Huh—no wonder you're goin' crazy. I'm going over to the music lab to study for it. Do
13		you wanna join me?
14	REBECCA	Yeah. Thanks. I need all the help I can get.
15	BILL	Hmm.

16 PRACTICE ROOM

17 *Bill helps Rebecca practice taking musical dictation. Bill plays a series of notes on his guitar, while Rebecca attempts to*
18 *write down the notes she hears on a piece of music paper.*

19	BILL	How you doin'?

20 *He leaves the piano bench, goes over to Rebecca, and looks over her shoulder at the notes Rebecca has penciled in.*

21	BILL	Terrific. You got all the right notes this time.
22	REBECCA	Really?
23	BILL	Except there should be a dot above these to indicate staccato.
24	REBECCA	I'll fix that.

25 *She uses her pencil to place dots on the chart.*

26	BILL	You're gonna ace this test. I know it.
27	REBECCA	I have a lot to learn real fast.
28	BILL	Don't we all! I hope all these exams are worth it.

29 *Bill starts playing one of his own pieces. It's rock 'n' roll.*

30	REBECCA	HEY! Hey! I—I can't keep up with you!
31	BILL	That's not for you—it's for me. All I wanna do is play my music, not go to school.
32	REBECCA	Why on earth are you here?
33	BILL	I'm just tryin' to get my parents off my back. 'Billy, you'll never make money playing in a
34		band. You have to go to college. Do something respectable.' Wrong. (*He begins to sing.*)
35		Don't you know, baby?
36		Hey, baby!
37		Wanna be a rock 'n' roll star! Whoo!

38 *The song makes Rebecca smile.*

39	REBECCA	I don't think my dad ever really approved of my plans to go to music school. It was so
40		hard to make him understand why music was so important to me.
41	BILL	Did he tell you you'd never make a living?
42	REBECCA	Constantly.
43	BILL	(*sigh*) Parents are all alike. Well, they don't know what they're talking about. I've got
44		plans. I'm gonna pitch my songs to The Moles.
45	REBECCA	You're kidding, right?
46	BILL	No. The word is, is that they're looking for new material. You should audition for
47		them, too . . .
48	REBECCA	Oh, I don't do their kind of music. Anyway, I don't think I'm ready for that.
49	BILL	Don't be so sure. You have big-time talent. Don't sell yourself short!
50	REBECCA	They're a hard-rock group, aren't they?
51	BILL	Rock is where the money is these days.
52	REBECCA	Money isn't all that important to me.
53	BILL	Come on!
54	REBECCA	No, really. Making music is all I care about. Making music is like breathing.
55	BILL	Uh-oh. She's getting sappy on me.
56	REBECCA	Bill, I'm serious. I have to make music. I can't imagine my life without it.

57	**BILL**	Listen . . . seriously . . . Think about the audition. You never know how school will work
58		out, so the more irons you have in the fire, the better off you are. Anyway, meeting them
59		will be a real education!

60 *Rebecca doesn't look persuaded.*

61	**BILL**	Hey, it might even be fun.
62	**REBECCA**	I don't know.
63	**BILL**	Listen, I help you study. You come with me, you know, to the audition, as my backup
64		singer.

65 *She thinks for a second and then nods.*

66	**REBECCA**	All right. It's a deal.

PART 2

67 SAN FRANCISCO COLLEGE OF MUSIC, LIBRARY—DAY

68 *Rebecca pulls a book off the shelf and returns to her carrel. She opens her calendar to Saturday. She sighs. Printed in*
69 *pencil is "opera w/Alberto?"*

70 ALBERTO'S OFFICE

71 *A phone is ringing in Alberto's office. Alberto answers it.*

72	**ALBERTO**	Hello? Rebecca, how are you? . . . You can't go? Oh. Well, I'm disappointed. No, I . . .
73		I . . . I get it. Maybe we can go out after your exams. OK. Happy homework! Bye.

74 *He hangs up and sits at his desk for a moment. We see the disappointment on his face.*

75 MENDOZA RESTAURANT—LATE NIGHT

76 *Ramón is closing up the restaurant, which is decorated for Christmas. Alberto arrives. He is in his dress clothes and*
77 *carries a copy of the opera program.*

78	**ALBERTO**	Hello? Ramón. Hey, man.
79	**RAMÓN**	What are you doing here at this hour? It's almost midnight!
80	**ALBERTO**	I went to the opera.
81	**RAMÓN**	Ah. *Amahl and the Night Visitors*? Ha. Who didja go with?
82	**ALBERTO**	No one. Thought I'd just drop by.
83	**RAMÓN**	You want a drink?
84	**ALBERTO**	No, not really. You probably wanna get home . . .
85	**RAMÓN**	No need to rush. Alex is home with the baby-sitter.
86	**ALBERTO**	Your ex-wife gets him for Christmas?
87	**RAMÓN**	Yeah. He's gotta fly to L.A. alone. Feel sorry for him. It's not easy being shipped back and
88		forth.
89	**ALBERTO**	You must really be angry at Chris.
90	**RAMÓN**	Nah. She's his mother. I understand . . . She loves Alex as much as I do. It's just this
91		divorce has screwed everything up.

92	ALBERTO	I don't know. Sometimes falling in love can be the worst thing.
93	RAMÓN	Yeah. Or it can be the best thing.
94	ALBERTO	I suppose. Just don't get married. That's when all the problems start.
95	RAMÓN	What's with you? You're usually so positive. Are you sick or somethin'?
96	ALBERTO	Listen, I'm considering a vacation in Aspen. Spend the holidays skiing. Maybe you can
97		come with me. You know, spend some time in the great outdoors, take a break from the
98		restaurant.

99 *Ramón reaches to touch his brother's forehead.*

100	RAMÓN	Let me feel your forehead. You must have a fever.
101	ALBERTO	Cut it out! I'm fine. I thought we might enjoy the time together. You know, especially
102		now, since Mama and Papa are in Mexico visiting the relatives for the holidays.
103	RAMÓN	Ah, it's a great idea, really. But I can't—not with the restaurant. And Alex will want to
104		be home for New Year's . . . Sorry, it's impossible.

105 *Alberto sighs.*

PART 3

106 MENDOZA RESTAURANT, BAR

107 *Alberto sits at the bar.*

108	ALBERTO	I guess this is what it means to be getting old. All my friends are either married or moved
109		out of town, my brother's all tied up with work and his kid, my retired parents are now
110		traveling around the world, and the woman I'm interested in is busy with school . . .
111	RAMÓN	Oh, now I get it. Woman trouble.
112	ALBERTO	No, not really. Rebecca was supposed to go out with me tonight, but her schoolwork got
113		in the way. I guess I'm losing my fatal charm.
114	RAMÓN	So, Rebecca's resisting? Amazing . . . !
115	ALBERTO	Thanks for the sympathy, brother.
116	RAMÓN	Let me get you a drink. Here, these will cheer you up . . . .

117 *Ramón walks behind the bar, grabs an envelope, and tosses it to Alberto.*

118	RAMÓN	Pictures from the retirement party. They just came back.

119 *Ramón pours Alberto a drink. Alberto picks up the pictures. We see the pictures—one of his parents dancing, one of*
120 *Rebecca at the party, another of her with Ramón and Alex, and one of Ramón and Rebecca dancing at the party.*

121	RAMÓN	You know, Rebecca is a very dedicated student.
122	ALBERTO	That she is. Maybe too dedicated.

123 *Ramón is curious and asks another question.*

124	RAMÓN	What does that mean?
125	ALBERTO	I'm surrounded by dedicated career women all day. It'd be nice to be the center of
126		attention once in a while.
127	RAMÓN	Oh, come on! Remember Elena? You were the center of attention with her.

128 **ALBERTO** That was different. Maybe she wasn't the right one for me.

129 **RAMÓN** Well, what about Rebecca?

130 **ALBERTO** Maybe, maybe not. She's all tied up with her music. It doesn't have much to do with my
131 life.

132 **RAMÓN** You sound just like a spoiled brat. She's been through a lot. Her father just died. She has
133 a lot of pressure at school. She probably needs some understanding right now.

134 **ALBERTO** As usual, my older brother provides insight into the workings of the opposite sex.

135 **RAMÓN** With age comes wisdom.

136 **ALBERTO** Ah, well . . . You're tired, I have to get up early in the morning. It's time to go home.

137 *The two brothers get ready to leave. Ramón decides to ask another question.*

138 **RAMÓN** So, what is it you want in a woman?

139 **ALBERTO** (*with a smile*) Everything.

140 **RAMÓN** (*smiling back*) Good luck!

141 *We see the Christmas tree.*

142 **ALBERTO** Nice tree. Maybe I should put one up this year.

143 **RAMÓN** Absolutely. This was good . . . talking, I mean. We haven't done that for a long time.

144 **ALBERTO** So, do you miss having someone in your life?

145 **RAMÓN** I liked being married. But the next time, she's gonna have to be the right woman—for
146 me, and for Alex. It's not so simple. You and Rebecca—now that's simple.

147 **ALBERTO** Things are never as simple as they might appear. Let's just say at the moment, Rebecca
148 doesn't seem to be very interested.

149 **RAMÓN** What—if it's what you want, you have to be patient.

150 **ALBERTO** Me . . . patient? You kidding me? I've never been patient in my entire life.

151 **RAMÓN** Yeah, don't I know. Hey, remember when we were waiting for Abuela at the train
152 station . . .

153 **ALBERTO** Yeah, yeah, yeah. Stop! Don't remind me . . .

154 *The brothers leave the restaurant.*

Unexpected Offers

PART 1

1 SAN FRANCISCO AIRPORT—DAY

2 *Ramón looks at his son on board the plane.*

3 **RAMÓN** Fasten your seat belt.

4 **ALEX** (*grumpily*) Yeah.

5 **RAMÓN** Are you gonna be all right? . . . Don't act like that.

6 **ALEX** Don't act like what?

7 **RAMÓN** Like this is a big ordeal. It's not . . . You'll have a great time. You'll be back for New
8 Year's, and we'll celebrate Christmas then, OK? (*The boy nods.*) And you'll get together
9 with Vincent.

10 **ALEX** Promise?

11 **RAMÓN** Yeah, I promise.

12 **ALEX** And you promise to call me on Christmas day?

13 **RAMÓN** Of course I will. And so will Grandma and Grandpa from Mexico.

14 **ALEX** And you have to promise to give Vincent, Rebecca, and Uncle Alberto their presents
15 from me . . . .

16 **RAMÓN** Certainly . . .

17 **ALEX** You have to, Dad, right away, so they get them before Christmas. Don't forget.

18 **RAMÓN** Don't worry. I'll do it right away.

19 **ALEX** Today.

20 **RAMÓN** I promise. I'll do it today. Vincent, Rebecca, and Uncle Alberto will have their presents
21 today. It's time to go . . . How about a smile?

22 *Alex gives his father a wide fake grin.*

23 **RAMÓN** And smile when you see your mother.

24 **ALEX** Yeah.

25 **RAMÓN** All right. I love you. I'll call you Christmas day! Que Diós te bendiga.

26 THE WANGS' LIVING ROOM—DAY

27 *Vincent is putting a Christmas present under the Wangs' Christmas tree. Mrs. Wang enters.*

28 **MRS. WANG** Vincent, Alex's father came here with this today.

29 **VINCENT** A gift from Alex! I didn't give him one before he left.

30 **MRS. WANG** Alex will be in Los Angeles for Christmas.

31 **VINCENT** I know. I feel bad for Alex, Mom.

32 **MRS. WANG** Why?

33 **VINCENT** He didn't want to go to L.A. No way.

34 **MRS. WANG** Well, many times we must do things we do not want. (*in Mandarin*) Nǐ bàba huílai le.
35 ("*Your father is home.*") We will have our dinner soon. And so go up and wash your hands,
36 please, OK?

37 *Vincent heads upstairs to the bathroom. Mrs. Wang goes to the front door, where she greets Mr. Wang.*

38 **MR. WANG** We have to talk.

39 *They move upstairs.*

40 BATHROOM

41 *Vincent is wiping his hands on a towel. He sees his parents walk past the bathroom and enter their bedroom. Curious,*
42 *he walks into his bedroom and enters a connecting closet.*

43 *He listens at the connecting closet door. Here, he can hear their voices more clearly.*

44 THE WANGS' BEDROOM

45 *Mr. Wang is handing Mrs. Wang a letter.*

46 **MR. WANG** This is the letter we've been waiting for.

47 **MRS. WANG** (*concerned*) The letter . . . ?

48 **MR. WANG** Yes. From the company in Taiwan . . . It's a definite offer.

49 **MRS. WANG** They want you?

50 **MR. WANG** They want me to work for them . . .

51 **MRS. WANG** In Taiwan?

52 **MR. WANG** Yes.

53 CLOSET

54 *Vincent peeks through the halfway open door. His parents do not realize he is there.*

55 **MR. WANG** Mei-Lin, this may be our golden opportunity.

56 *Mrs. Wang turns around to face her husband. She is upset but trying not to show it.*

57 **MRS. WANG** We have done well in United States. We have good life. We have good business . . .

58 **MR. WANG** We knew this difficult decision would come.

59 **MRS. WANG** Vincent, too, he has good life here. He is in good school. He has friends.

60 **MR. WANG** Vincent's friends were not always his friends here.

61 **MRS. WANG** (*in Mandarin*) Nǐ cóng lái méi yǒu kuānshù guò nàxiē háizi, duì bù duì? ("*You have never*
62 *forgiven those children, have you?*")

63 **MR. WANG** They hurt our child . . . by calling him names. And those words hurt us, too.

64 *Mr. Wang is silent for a minute.*

65 **MR. WANG** Vincent was born here. But to some people in the United States, Vincent will always be
66 a foreigner.

67 **MRS. WANG** This is our home now.

68 **MR. WANG** We will adjust.

69 **MRS. WANG** Well, when do we have to go?

70 **MR. WANG** Soon. Very soon.

71 *We see Vincent's frightened face in the crack of the door.*

PART 2

72 NANCY'S HOUSE—DAY

73 *The doorbell rings. Rebecca goes to answer it.*

74 **REBECCA** Ramón! What a nice surprise.

75 **RAMÓN** I just dropped by to give you this. It's a Christmas present from Alex.

76 **REBECCA** Alex is so sweet. He's a great kid!

77 **RAMÓN** I just put him on a plane to L.A. . . . (*Rebecca looks confused.*) He's visiting his mother.

78 **REBECCA** It must be difficult not having Alex around for Christmas.

79 *Ramón looks very lost and upset. He stands there for a few seconds.*

80 **REBECCA** Are you all right?

81 **RAMÓN** I don't know. It just hit me, I guess.

82 **REBECCA** Do you want to come in . . .

83 **RAMÓN** Yeah . . . yeah.

84 *Ramón enters. She closes the door behind him. She holds the present from Alex.*

85 **REBECCA** Would you care for anything to drink?

86 **RAMÓN** No, no. I really don't have much time. I have to open the restaurant soon. You probably
87 have a lot of studying to do.

88 *He starts to leave.*

89 **REBECCA** No, it's fine. I have a minute . . .

90 *It is an awkward moment for them, the first time they have been alone together in this house.*

91 LIVING ROOM

92 *We see Rebecca and Ramón sitting near the Christmas tree.*

93 **REBECCA** It's heavy. Wonder what it is?

94 **RAMÓN** I had to stop by. Alex insisted that I bring you that gift today.

95 **REBECCA** Kids that age . . . . they get an idea into their heads, and they just don't let it go.

96 **RAMÓN** Yeah, you can say that again . . . I guess sending Alex off to Los Angeles is hitting me
97 harder than I thought.

98 **REBECCA** I can imagine.

99	RAMÓN	I've never been alone at Christmas.
100	REBECCA	What about your Mom and Dad?
101	RAMÓN	They're in Mexico, visiting relatives . . . and I'm all alone in the house.
102	REBECCA	Well, at least you'll have your brother.
103	RAMÓN	Alberto said he's going skiing for the holidays. Aren't you going with him?
104-105	REBECCA	No. We never talked about it. Anyway, skiing's not my thing. I'm sure he'll have a great time.
106	RAMÓN	He makes friends, wherever he goes . . . Are you doing anything special for Christmas?
107-108	REBECCA	No. I'll be here. It'll be pretty quiet. Melaku and Angela will be gone. It'll be just Nancy and me.
109	RAMÓN	What about your brother?
110-112	REBECCA	No, I'm not going to see him. He's at my uncle's farm. I'll call him, for sure. This will be our first Christmas without my dad. I guess we'll both be without families for the holidays.
113-114	RAMÓN	We have a family tradition. On Christmas day, I'll bring food over to the community center in our neighborhood. It's like a posada.
115	REBECCA	A posada?
116-117	RAMÓN	The posada is a Mexican tradition. During Christmas, we go from house to house and we ask for shelter. We sing Christmas carols, eat, and share the Christmas story.
118	REBECCA	It's a beautiful tradition.
119-120	RAMÓN	Well, my family has been doing it for years. This year, I'll have to do it by myself, but it wouldn't be Christmas without it.
121	REBECCA	I should have known that you'd have the true Christmas spirit.
122	*The hall clock chimes.*	
123	RAMÓN	Well, I'd better go.
124	REBECCA	Yeah, I should get to my studying.
125	*Ramón heads toward door.*	

126 HALLWAY

127 *Rebecca walks him to the door. He turns and talks.*

128	RAMÓN	I don't want to make a fool of myself, but I . . . I have to ask you something.
129	REBECCA	Sure.
130-131	RAMÓN	If things were different . . . I mean if . . . would you consider . . . spending Christmas with me?
132	REBECCA	(*surprised*) Christmas with you? Wow, Ramón . . . I don't know what to say I . . .
133	RAMÓN	I . . . I figured cause . . . since we're both alone . . .
134-135	REBECCA	(*struggling for words*) Ramón . . . You are one of the sweetest men I know . . . and . . . and a wonderful father . . . and I love spending time with you.

136	RAMÓN	That's what I thought. No, no, I'm sorry I bothered you.
137	REBECCA	You didn't bother me. Because I'd like to . . .
138	RAMÓN	Have a great holiday.

139 *He starts to open the front door. Rebecca stops him short.*

140	REBECCA	Wait. Please don't misunderstand me. I didn't mean that . . .
141	RAMÓN	No, I understand. Really . . . really I . . . I don't know why I asked . . . I just, you
142		know . . . No, really, I have to go.
143	REBECCA	Goodbye . . . Oh, man . . .

144 *This time he leaves for good. Rebecca is left standing in the doorway, confused and upset.*

PART 3

145 ALBERTO'S OFFICE

146 *Alberto is working on a blueprint, talking with a fellow architect. Ramón appears in the doorway, carrying Alex's*
147 *present. He enters.*

148	ALBERTO	Ramón. What're you doing here?
149	RAMÓN	Alex made me promise to drop this off—pronto. So, here I am.

150 *Alberto looks at the present.*

151	ALBERTO	What a thoughtful nephew I have. Well, I have a present for him, too.
152	RAMÓN	He won't be home until after Christmas.
153	ALBERTO	You drove him to the airport already?
154	RAMÓN	Yeah. Hey, I gotta go, get back to the restaurant.
155	ALBERTO	Hey, I need a break. I'll walk you to the door . . .

156 *The brothers head out.*

157	ALBERTO	So . . . I've made a reservation at a ski lodge in Aspen.
158	RAMÓN	(*without much enthusiasm*) Sounds great.
159	ALBERTO	What's with you?
160	RAMÓN	I think I'm starting to hate the holidays.
161	ALBERTO	There's only one answer . . . escape. I told you. Come with me.
162	RAMÓN	And I told you . . . it's impossible.
163	ALBERTO	You've got to do something, brother, before you turn into the Grinch.
164	RAMÓN	I tried.
165	ALBERTO	What do you mean, you tried?

166 *Ramon looks uneasy.*

167	RAMÓN	I think I did something out of line.
168	ALBERTO	What was that?
169	RAMÓN	I had to deliver Alex's present to Rebecca . . .

170	**ALBERTO**	Rebecca . . .
171	**RAMÓN**	And we got to talking. And I told her that I'd be all alone on Christmas . . . and you'd be
172		gone . . . and so would Alex, and Mama and Papa . . . And she said she was going to be
173		alone . . . so before I knew it . . . I asked her to join me for Christmas.
174	**ALBERTO**	So . . . what did she say?
175	**RAMÓN**	That I was a nice man, and a good father . . .
176	**ALBERTO**	It's all true.
177	**RAMÓN**	It was so dumb to ask her. I realize I was out of line. I meant it in more than a friendly
178		way. And she picked up on that.
179	**ALBERTO**	Hey, you were just lonely. It happens.

180 *Alberto looks at his brother; he is realizing that Ramón's feelings for Rebecca go deep.*

181	**RAMÓN**	This Rebecca thing might be something we should talk about . . .
182	**ALBERTO**	Definitely, but not now. We've both got work to do . . . and these chats are great, but
183		not on company time.
184	**RAMÓN**	All right.
185	**ALBERTO**	See ya.
186	**RAMÓN**	All right. See ya.

187 *Ramón leaves, encouraged by Alberto's gentle persuasion. After Ramón has left, Alberto's happy exterior changes into a*
188 *more serious mood. How does he feel about this incident?*

The Audition

PART 1

1 *NANCY'S HOUSE—NIGHT*

2 *Rebecca is sitting at the table, alone, looking miserable. She is stirring sugar into a large mug of coffee, a schoolbook*
3 *open in front of her. Nancy appears in her robe.*

4	**NANCY**	May I join you?

5 *Rebecca looks up and nods. Nancy sits down opposite her.*

6	**NANCY**	I thought you drank your coffee black . . . no sugar.
7	**REBECCA**	Tonight, I need sugar.
8	**NANCY**	Studying for exams can certainly burn up energy.
9	**REBECCA**	You can say that again.
10	**NANCY**	I saw Alex's father leaving.
11	**REBECCA**	He dropped off a present from Alex . . . Ramón is such a great dad.

12 NANCY   Just a great dad?

13 REBECCA   OK, he's a good dancer, too.

14 NANCY   There's something in the way he looks at you.

15 REBECCA   I think we understand each other . . .

16 NANCY   What ever happened to Alberto? Wouldn't it be a little awkward, dating two brothers?

17 REBECCA   What makes you think I would date both of them?

18 NANCY   Stranger things have happened.

19 REBECCA   I came here to get a college education.

20 NANCY   So?

21 REBECCA   I can't be involved with either Ramón or Alberto. I've got to focus on school.

22 NANCY   You mean, you can't do both?

23 REBECCA   No, I can't. Right now, it's got to be my music—and my music alone. It hasn't been easy
24   to get this far.

25 NANCY   You've been through a lot . . . But don't worry. You'll pass your exams. I know you will.

26 REBECCA   I've got to. I've just got to!

27 COLLEGE CLASSROOM—DAY

28 *Rebecca is now in a final exam at school.*

29 PROFESSOR Time. That's it for Beethoven.

30 *Bill hands Rebecca a note. It says: "Audition, Friday night, 8:00 p.m. Be there!" Rebecca shakes her head "no." He*
31 *nods "yes." She nods "OK."*

32 PROFESSOR Can I have your attention, please? We will now proceed to the second part of the exam,
33   which will be an analysis of this cord progression. I'll play it for you once.

PART 2

34 SOUND RECORDING STUDIO—EVENING

35 *Rebecca and Bill are standing in the lobby of a sound studio. They are excited and nervous at the same time. The lobby*
36 *is filled with records and pictures of stars all over the walls. They stand for a few seconds.*

37 BILL   Well, here goes nothing . . .

38 REBECCA   I still have another exam. I mean, I'd be happy to leave . . . .

39 BILL   C'mon. Give it a go.

40 REBECCA   All right, but just a minute, though, OK?

41 *Finally, someone comes down the hallway. It's the group's manager.*

42 MANAGER   Who are you?

43 BILL   I'm Bill Ellis and this is Rebecca Casey. We're here for The Moles' audition.

44 MANAGER   Follow me.

45 SOUND RECORDING STUDIO, CONTROL ROOM

46 *The door opens, and the manager enters, followed by Bill and Rebecca. Longhaired band members turn to look at*
47 *them. One of them waves his hand to signal that he's busy.*

48 **MANAGER**   He's tied up right now. Wait outside.

49 *The manager holds the door open, and they leave the control room. The band members continue to work.*

50 SOUND RECORDING STUDIO, WAITING ROOM

51 *Rebecca and Bill walk out into the waiting room. Through the wall they can hear the music from the control room.*
52 *Finally, they sit down on a couch.*

53 **MANAGER**   You can wait out here.

54 **REBECCA**   Do you really still want to wait?

55 **BILL**   Of course we're gonna wait.

56 **REBECCA**   All right, we'll wait.

57 **BILL**   Hey, did you see that studio in there? All that equipment?

58 *We see a sound technician and the band members at work in the studio.*

59 SOUND RECORDING STUDIO, WAITING ROOM—NIGHT

60 *Rebecca and Bill continue to wait. They are really tired of waiting. Rebecca studies and Bill stretches out on the couch.*

61 **BILL**   What time is it?

62 **REBECCA**   Ten minutes later than the last time you asked me. How much longer do you want to
63   wait?

64 **BILL**   Let me go find out what's happening.

65 *Bill gets up and goes to the studio door. Rebecca watches. Bill talks to the manager for a second. Then he returns.*

66 **BILL**   He doesn't know how much longer.

67 **REBECCA**   Oh, let's go!

68 **BILL**   No way, wait, man. This is gonna be worth it.

69 *He sits and they wait.*

70 MENDOZA RESTAURANT—NIGHT

71 *Ramón is sitting at the bar where he often does his work, going over the bills. He finds the envelope with the pictures*
72 *from the retirement party. He takes out the pictures. He stops to look carefully at one picture. We see a closeup of the*
73 *photo: Rebecca with him and Alex. We also see a photo of Rebecca and Ramón dancing . . . Ramón looks at the photo*
74 *for a long minute. He then puts it back in the envelope and puts the envelope down on the table. It's clear that he has*
75 *decided to put Rebecca out of his thoughts.*

PART 3

76 SOUND RECORDING STUDIO, WAITING ROOM—NIGHT

77 *Rebecca and Bill are sleeping on the couch. The music has stopped. The manager comes out and talks to Bill.*

78 **MANAGER**   I've got some bad news. The band had to leave.

79	BILL	What do you mean, had to leave?
80	MANAGER	Sorry. The band had to go. But if you two want to leave your tapes....
81	BILL	Tapes? I don't have a tape with me.

82 *The manager starts to leave.*

83	BILL	Hey, wait, I was told we could play for them . . . and we've been here for hours . . .

84 *The manager takes pity on them.*

85	MANAGER	(*after a sigh*) All right. I'm full of Christmas spirit today. Come into the studio, and I'll do
86		a quick scratch track for you both. But hurry up. I want to get out of here.

87 *Bill and Rebecca follow him.*

88 SOUND RECORDING STUDIO, CONTROL ROOM

89 *Bill's voice is heard with Rebecca doing backup. We see them in the studio, recording.*

90	MANAGER	Cut the monitor for a second. I've got to make a phone call. (*on phone*) Hi, baby. It's me.
91		Yeah, another few minutes and I'm on my way. Milk and diapers. I'll pick them up on my
92		way home. Bye.

93 *During the conversation, Bill and Rebecca have finished singing. They stand there waiting.*

94	MANAGER	You done?
95	BILL	Yes.
96	MANAGER	What about you?
97	REBECCA	Me?
98	MANAGER	Yeah, you. Are you auditioning too?

99 *Rebecca doesn't know what to say. Bill motions for her to go ahead.*

100	BILL	Sure she is! . . . I'll play piano. What key are you in?
101	REBECCA	G.
102	MANAGER'S VOICE	Tape's rolling. Any time you're ready. Start with your name and phone number.
103	REBECCA	My name is Rebecca Casey. My phone number is 555-1998. And this is a song I wrote.
104		It's called 'Dream Catcher.'

105 *She sings the song. Bill plays the piano.*

106	REBECCA	(*singing*) All the lights are shinin' bright down in the city,
107		Shinin' like a million dreams . . .
108		Sometimes I feel like I'm upside down,
109		And all those dreams are fallin' right past me . . .
110		Everybody needs a dream catcher,
111		Someone to be there when your dreams start to fall . . .
112		Everybody needs a dream catcher,
113		Someone to be there when the bad dreams are all you can see . . .
114		Dream catcher . . . catch me.

115 *We see a dream catcher as the song ends.*

Dream Catcher

PART 1

1 *Rebecca auditions, singing her song, "Dream Catcher." We see scenes of:*

2 *Meeting Alberto in the desert*

3 *Ramón leaving*

4 *Kissing Alberto*

5 *The dream catcher*

6 *Dancing with Ramón*

7 REBECCA (*singing*) All the lights are shinin' bright down in the city,
8   Shinin' like a million dreams . . .
9   Sometimes I feel like I'm upside down,
10   And all those dreams are fallin' right past me . . .
11   Everybody needs a dream catcher,
12   Someone to be there when your dreams start to fall . . .
13   Everybody needs a dream catcher,
14   Someone to be there when the bad dreams are all you can see . . .
15   Dream catcher . . . catch me.

16 NANCY'S KITCHEN—NIGHT

17 *Nancy's on the the phone. As she is speaking, a voiceover of Rebecca continuing to sing can be heard.*

18 NANCY   Hello . . . oh, yes, Alberto. And a Merry Christmas to you. No, Rebecca's isn't here. Yes.
19   She has your phone number? Yes. I'll be certain to give her your message. Bye.

20 *Nancy writes on a piece of paper. "Rebecca—call Alberto. Important."*

21 SOUND RECORDING STUDIO, CONTROL ROOM—NIGHT

22 *Rebecca is finishing her song.*

23 REBECCA   . . . catch me . . . catch me . . . catch me.

24 *The manager enters the studio door.*

25 MANAGER   Thanks for coming in. I have to get going—so if you don't mind. Here's a copy of your
26   performance. Listen, if they like the songs, we'll call you. Remember, don't call us; we'll
27   call you.

28 *Rebecca and Bill nod and take their copy of the performance.*

29 MANAGER   C'mon, you guys. Let's get going.

30 *The two exchange amused glances and turn to leave.*

31 SOUND RECORDING STUDIO, LOBBY

32 *Rebecca and Bill are exhausted from their night's adventure.*

33 **BILL**   (*cynical*) Some audition, huh?

34 **REBECCA**   They probably won't even listen to the tapes.

35 **BILL**   Who cares! That was a beautiful song you wrote. I'd love to orchestrate it for you.

36 **REBECCA**   Really?

37 **BILL**   Yeah. We need some strings . . . and maybe some brass . . .

38 *They walk out of the lobby and into the hallway.*

39 **REBECCA**   Don't overdo it . . . I mean, it's a simple song . . .

40 **BILL**   Relax! . . . Just leave everything to me!

PART 2

41 NANCY'S HOUSE—NIGHT

42 *Nancy is sitting in the living room, lit by the Christmas tree. She has opened a box of chocolates. She has eaten one*
43 *from the assortment. Rebecca enters.*

44 **REBECCA**   Nancy, you're up late.

45 **NANCY**   I couldn't sleep. Come over here and tell me how your exams went.

46 *Rebecca enters and sits down on the sofa.*

47 **REBECCA**   (*sigh*) I think I did all right, but I have one more.

48 **NANCY**   When will you get your grades?

49 **REBECCA**   They'll mail them to me in January. I could go over to school this week and find out
50   sooner. I hope I have the strength for one more.

51 **NANCY**   You deserve a special treat.

52 *Nancy reveals the box of chocolates and offers them to Rebecca.*

53 **REBECCA**   Ooh, chocolates!

54 *Rebecca takes one, as does Nancy. They get chewy ones.*

55 **NANCY**   Caramel.

56 **REBECCA**   Mine, too.

57 *They speak to each other even though they are chewing.*

58 **NANCY**   You had a phone call.

59 **REBECCA**   Who was it?

60 **NANCY**   Alberto. He wants you to call him. It's important.

61 *Rebecca makes no move to go to the phone.*

62 **NANCY**   Are you going to call?

63 **REBECCA**   Maybe it's too late to call him back.

64 *Nancy looks at Rebecca intently.*

65 **REBECCA** Maybe not. I guess I'll call him.

66 *Rebecca still doesn't move.*

67 **NANCY** I'm sorry to put my nose into your business, but that's the way I am. I think you're going
68 to have to make up your mind about these brothers. We don't want history to repeat
69 itself, do we?

70 **REBECCA** I know what I have to do.

71 **NANCY** I know you do.

PART 3

72 SAN FRANCISCO COLLEGE OF MUSIC, LIBRARY—DAY

73 *We see Bill in the library.*

74 **NARRATOR** Rebecca's friend Bill reflects on the story.

75 **BILL** I definitely do not belong in a library. Too quiet. Too serious. Like Rebecca. She is a
76 serious person.

77 FLASHBACK—REBECCA TALKING TO HER PROFESSOR

78 **PROFESSOR THOMAS** You can take incompletes and repeat your courses next semester. Or you can
79 study like mad and go for it.

80 **REBECCA** I'd like to try and take the exams.

81 **PROFESSOR THOMAS** Well, I do admire your spirit.

82 END OF FLASHBACK

83 **BILL** I wanna get her to lighten up a little, so I asked her to come with me to The Moles'
84 audition. You know, get her nose out of the books. Getting out there is part of learning.

85 FLASHBACK—AUDITION AT THE STUDIO

86 **MANAGER** He's tied up right now. Wait outside.

87 END OF FLASHBACK

88 **BILL** But Rebecca only has one thing on her mind. Her exams. I have a feeling she's given up
89 a lot to be in school. There's a lot at stake for her . . .

90 FLASHBACK—REBECCA AND KEVIN SAYING GOODBYE

91 **KEVIN** Have a terrific life in San Francisco.

92 **REBECCA** Thanks. I'll give it a shot.

93 END OF FLASHBACK

94 **BILL** Don't get me wrong. I think Rebecca's very cool. She knows who she is, and she knows
95 what she wants.

96 FLASHBACK—ALBERTO ASKING REBECCA TO THE OPERA

97 **ALBERTO** I have something here to cheer you up.

98 *He takes out the tickets to the opera and shows them to her.*

99 **REBECCA** Tickets to the San Francisco Opera?

100 **ALBERTO** Best seats in the house. They're doing *Amahl and the Night Visitors.* You know, the 'Night
101 Visitors' are the three kings, and they're following the star to Bethlehem . . .

102 **REBECCA** That's very nice of . . .

103 **ALBERTO** I'm sure you'll enjoy it.

104 **REBECCA** I'm sure I would too, but . . . I can't make any plans. I have to cram for my final exams.

105 **ALBERTO** A ton of schoolwork, huh?

106 **REBECCA** Yeah. I lost so much time because of . . . It's going to take every waking hour just to
107 catch up.

108 **ALBERTO** Well, maybe a little diversion might help.

109 **REBECCA** Look, if I fail my exams, I lose my scholarship. Now, I would really love to, but . . .

110 **ALBERTO** I'll take that as a 'yes,' and you can see how your studying is going later on in the week . . .

111 *She thinks for a moment, and then nods "yes."*

112 **REBECCA** Thank you.

113 END OF FLASHBACK

114 **BILL** She's got a great voice. There's real talent there . . .

115 FLASHBACK—REBECCA AUDITIONING

116 **REBECCA** (*singing*) All the lights are shinin' bright down in the city . . .

117 END OF FLASHBACK

118 **BILL** But you need more than talent to make it in this business. 'Cause this is a business, you
119 know. I mean, being a success in the music business means more than just making music.
120 It means making money—lots of money—selling product, doing big tours on the road,
121 and making money.

122 FLASHBACK—REBECCA TALKING TO BILL ABOUT MUSIC

123 **REBECCA** Making music is all I care about. Making music is like breathing.

124 **BILL** Uh-oh, she's getting sappy on me.

125 **REBECCA** Bill, I'm serious. I have to make music. I can't imagine my life without it.

126 *Cut to Rebecca singing*

127 **REBECCA** (*singing*) Everybody needs a dream catcher . . .

128 END OF FLASHBACK

129 **BILL** But that's what I want. Everyone's different, I guess. Rebecca's kind of success isn't mine.
130 Still, we make a great team—when we're making music . . . I bet we both make it—each
131 in our own way.

132 *He turns and looks at Rebecca.*

133 **REBECCA** Shh . . . !

134 **BILL** (*whispering*) Sorry!

Gifts

PART 1

1 SAN FRANCISCO—DAY

2 **REBECCA** (*voice on phone*) Hi, Alberto. This is Rebecca. I got your phone message. What's up?

3 SAN FRANCISCO COLLEGE OF MUSIC, SOUND ROOMS

4 **REBECCA** (*voice continues on phone*) I'm at school. I'll be in the sound studio for the next two days. I
5 need to talk to you, too. Bye.

6 *Bill and two other musicians tune their instruments.*

7 SAN FRANCISCO COLLEGE OF MUSIC, STAIRWELL—DAY

8 *Alberto walks through the school, dressed in a ski parka and pants and carrying a very large manila envelope. He asks*
9 *for directions to the studio.*

10 **ALBERTO** Uh, could you tell me where the studio is?

11 **STUDENT** (*pointing the way*) Upstairs . . .

12 **ALBERTO** Thank you.

13 *Alberto goes up the stairs and enters the studio.*

14 STUDIO

15 *Bill is discussing sheet music with Rebecca. Alberto enters the control room.*

16 *Rebecca sees Alberto through the control room window. He waves.*

17 **REBECCA** (*waving*) Hey! (*to Bill*) Hold on.

18 *She leaves the studio and enters the control room, where Alberto waits.*

19 **REBECCA** Hi. Is everything OK?

20 **ALBERTO** Yes. Is there someplace quiet where we can talk?

21 **REBECCA** Yeah, sure. C'mon.

22 *They leave the control room.*

23 STUDIO LOBBY

24 *Rebecca finds an unoccupied practice room and enters with Alberto.*

25 **REBECCA** Let's go in here.

26 STUDIO PRACTICE ROOM

27 *The two enter. Rebecca motions for Alberto to sit.*

28 **REBECCA** You can sit right there.
29 **ALBERTO** So, have you finished your exams?
30 **REBECCA** Yeah, thank goodness. So what's up?
31 **ALBERTO** Well, I'm leaving town for a while. I'm hitting the slopes . . . skiing for the holidays.
32 **REBECCA** Oh, yeah, Ramón mentioned it to me. I'm sure you'll have a great time.
33 **ALBERTO** Yeah . . .

34 *He pauses.*

35 **ALBERTO** Have you ever tried it?
36 **REBECCA** No . . . it's not my thing.
37 **ALBERTO** Yeah, that's what my brother says. Ramón thinks tying boards to your feet and going
38 down a hill is crazy. But one of these days, I'll get him to try it.

39 *They both smile. He looks at her. We see in his face that he has come to a final decision, and that it has been a hard*
40 *one for him.*

41 **ALBERTO** It's been one heck of a relationship, hasn't it? I mean, you and me . . . .
42 **REBECCA** Yeah. You're the best stranger I ever met in the desert.
43 **ALBERTO** You're the prettiest!
44 **REBECCA** Compliments and everything. Thank you.
45 **ALBERTO** You're welcome. My friends at the gallery said that you were stunning.
46 **REBECCA** Well, it was your photography, I'm sure.
47 **ALBERTO** No, it's you . . . Those were good times.
48 **REBECCA** Yeah, they were.

49 *Rebecca and Alberto both start to speak at the same time, but catch themselves.*

50 **REBECCA** Alberto . . .
51 **ALBERTO** Rebecca . . . I . .

52 *They laugh.*

53 **REBECCA** Go ahead. You go first . . .
54 **ALBERTO** OK. I just wanna say how much I enjoy having you as a friend . . .
55 **REBECCA** That goes for me too . . .

56 **ALBERTO** And this friendship is going to last a long time, I know it. And I guess, somehow, a few
57 things got misunderstood, but it's probably my fault. Our relationship is a friendship,
58 right?

59 *Rebecca takes all of this in, realizing that what she was going to do (break off the relationship), Alberto is doing for her.*

60 **REBECCA** The very best friendship.

61 *They smile. He reaches his hand across the table.*

62 **ALBERTO** Friends.

63 **REBECCA** Friends.

64 *They shake hands.*

65 **ALBERTO** I wanted you to have this. I remember how much you admired it . . . at the opening . . .

66 *He gives Rebecca a large envelope. She pulls out a copy of the large studio print of the photograph of Ramón and Alex*
67 *that was part of his photo exhibit at the gallery.*

68 **REBECCA** Oh, thank you. It's a beautiful photo.

69 **ALBERTO** Yeah. I guess it catches Alex's innocence . . .

70 **REBECCA** . . . and his spirit.

71 **ALBERTO** . . . and you can see in Ramón's eyes how much he loves his son . . .

72 **REBECCA** Yeah. He's a very loving person . . .

73 **ALBERTO** And a great brother. And I hope this new year brings him all the love and care he
74 deserves.

75 *There is a quiet moment between them. Then Alberto smiles.*

76 **ALBERTO** Well, I've gotta get going. Ramón's giving me a ride to the airport.

77 **REBECCA** I should probably get back to rehearsal, too.

78 *The two exit the room and walk out into the hallway.*

79 STUDIO CONTROL ROOM

80 **REBECCA** Lemme walk you out.

81 **ALBERTO** No, that's OK. Get back to your music. Sounds like a great song.

82 **REBECCA** It's called "Dream Catcher." Your gift inspired me to write it.

83 **ALBERTO** Well, I'm glad. Gotta get goin' . . . um . . . See ya.

84 **REBECCA** Take care.

85 **ALBERTO** OK. Bye.

86 **REBECCA** Bye.

87 *Alberto quickly walks down the hallway. Rebecca watches him walk down the corridor.*

PART 2

88 SAN FRANCISCO COLLEGE OF MUSIC, STAIRWELL

89 *We see Alberto walking, trying to forget Rebecca and missing her already. Rebecca begins to sing. Alberto listens on the*
90 *stairwell, remembering the times he and Rebecca have shared.*

91 *We see scenes of:*

92 *The kiss*

93 *Alberto, Ramón, and Rebecca at the party*

94 *Alberto buying the dream catcher*

95 **REBECCA**   (*singing*) All the lights are shinin' bright down in the city,
96   Shinin' like a million dreams . . .
97   Sometimes I feel like I'm upside down,
98   And all those dreams are fallin' right past me . . .
99   Everybody needs a dream catcher,
100   Someone to be there when your dreams start to fall . . .
101   Everybody needs a dream catcher,
102   Someone to be there when the bad dreams are all you can see . . .
103   Dream catcher . . . catch me.

104 *Alberto continues down the stairway, a bit sad.*

105 ALBERTO'S OFFICE—DAY

106 *Ramón and Alberto enter.*

107 **ALBERTO**   Hope you don't mind stoppin' on the way to the airport to pick up my skis. I really hate
108   leavin' them in the car.

109 **RAMÓN**   No problem. By the way, I picked up something you might be able to use.

110 *He gives Alberto a very expensive pair of ski goggles.*

111 **ALBERTO**   Hey, top of the line. Thanks. I can really use these goggles.

112 **RAMÓN**   Now you can see the tree before you hit it on the way down.

113 **ALBERTO**   One of these days, I'm gonna get you out on the slopes.

114 **RAMÓN**   Huh, right.

115 **ALBERTO**   Both you and Rebecca.

116 **RAMÓN**   She didn't wanna go with you?

117 **ALBERTO**   I had a hunch she might want to spend the holidays . . . with someone else. Besides, you
118   know me—always on the move. Let's go.

119 NANCY'S KITCHEN—EVENING

120 *Rebecca is wrapping gifts. Nancy comes in.*

121 **NANCY**   I found some more tape, Rebecca.

122 **REBECCA**   Oh thanks. I just finished my last roll.

123 *Nancy looks at the picture.*

124	NANCY	What's this?
125	REBECCA	Oh, it's a picture I just finished framing.
126	NANCY	What a charming photograph. Did Alberto take that?
127	REBECCA	Yeah, he gave it to me. This is Ramón and his son, Alex. It is special, isn't it?
128	NANCY	Alberto gave you a picture of his brother and then went off skiing?
129	REBECCA	That's right.
130	NANCY	I think that young man may have been trying to tell you something.
131	REBECCA	You may be right.

132 *Rebecca thinks for a minute.*

PART 3

133 MENDOZA RESTAURANT, KITCHEN—DAY

134 *Ramón is handing out Christmas bonus checks to his kitchen staff.*

135	RAMÓN	Luis . . . Michael . . . Suzy. Happy Holidays. Just a little Christmas bonus. Of course, the restaurant will be closed on Christmas Day, but, you know, every year we take Christmas dinners over to the community center. I'll come in and take the food over, but I'm gonna to ask you to help out, too. Here's the menu . . . We'll prepare the food the day before Christmas . . .

140 MENDOZA RESTAURANT, INTERIOR

141 *Rebecca has come to the restaurant with a box of food for the community center. She enters, but there is no one*
142 *around. She sees the restaurant's Christmas tree and she goes to put the box under the tree. Suddenly, Ramón's voice*
143 *startles her.*

144	RAMÓN	I always wanted to know what Santa Claus looked like.

145 *Rebecca stands.*

146	REBECCA	Oh, you startled me! Well, I can't lie. Santa Claus is a woman.
147	RAMÓN	I always suspected something like that . . .
148	REBECCA	I wanna help you with the dinner at the community center. I brought some canned food and . . . an extra hand.
150	RAMÓN	You can be here on Christmas?
151	REBECCA	I can't think of any other place I'd rather be. Have you talked to Alex?
152	RAMÓN	Oh, yeah . . . couple times. He's havin' a good time, but he can't wait to get back.
153	REBECCA	Yeah.
154	RAMÓN	How 'bout your brother?
155	REBECCA	I got a long letter from him. I'm gonna talk to him on Christmas Day.
156	RAMÓN	This Christmas is shaping up better than I thought!

157 COMMUNITY CENTER—CHRISTMAS DAY

158 *Ramón is handing out food at a long table. People are seated at tables eating. Rebecca comes out of the kitchen with*
159 *another tray of food. She helps pour coffee. Rebecca leads the singing of a Christmas song, "Silent Night." During the*
160 *song everyone joins in. We see Ramón's love for this woman.*

161 **ALL:** (*singing*) Silent night, holy night,
162 All is calm, all is bright,
163 Round yon virgin, mother and child,
164 Holy infant, so tender and mild,
165 Sleep in heavenly peace,
166 Sleep in heavenly peace.

167 MENDOZA RESTAURANT—NIGHT

168 *Rebecca and Ramón enter the restaurant. They are both carrying dirty, empty trays from the community center.*

169 **RAMÓN** Put the trays in here.

170 **REBECCA** It was a lotta work, but, boy, what an experience.

171 **RAMÓN** Amazing group of people, huh?

172 **REBECCA** In these hard times, it could be any one of us.

173 **RAMÓN** I haven't felt this much Christmas spirit since I was a kid. Would you like something to
174 drink?

175 **REBECCA** Sure.

176 **RAMÓN** How 'bout some champagne?

177 **REBECCA** Champagne?

178 **RAMÓN** Yeah, well, Christmas comes only once a year.

179 **REBECCA** All right.

180 **RAMÓN** OK.

181 *They walk off to the bar area.*

182 MENDOZA RESTAURANT, BAR

183 *Two glasses sit on the bar. Ramón pops the cork.*

184 **RAMÓN** Get your glass ready . . . here—here goes! Any minute now . . .

185 **REBECCA** Careful . . .

186 **RAMÓN** Aah, there . . .

187 *The cork pops and Ramón pours them each a glass of champagne.*

188 **REBECCA** Whoa—

189 **RAMÓN** Whoa— . . . You know, I almost had tears in my eyes when you were singing and
190 everyone joined in. Here's to a very special Christmas.

191 **REBECCA** To a very special person . . .

192 **RAMÓN** To a great singer . . . (*They sip their champagne.*)

193 **RAMÓN** Now, to make my day complete . . . I'm gonna call Alex.

194 REBECCA Lemme wish him a Merry Christmas, too.

195 *Ramón picks up the phone and begins to dial.*

196 RAMÓN Hi, Champ. It's me. Merry Christmas. You got what? Great . . . what else? Yeah, you
197   have some presents here, too. You even got one from somebody who'd like to say
198   hello . . .

199 *He hands the phone to Rebecca.*

200 REBECCA Merry Christmas, Alex. Yes, it's me. Your dad and I had a terrific day. I'll let him tell you
201   about it. I just wanted to wish you a Merry Christmas. And I can't wait until you get
202   back so we can continue our guitar lessons . . . Right? I will. Here's your dad . . .

203 *She hands the phone back to Ramón.*

204 RAMÓN Yeah, you'll be back in a few days. I can't wait to see ya. What? You're glad Rebecca's
205   here?

206 *Rebecca and Ramón smile at each other.*

207 RAMÓN Yeah, I'm glad she's here too!

True Love

PART 1

1 SAN FRANCISCO—CHRISTMAS NIGHT

2 *The brightly lit streets are jammed with people as Rebecca and Ramón head home from the restaurant.*

3 NANCY'S HOUSE—CHRISTMAS NIGHT

4 *Rebecca is being dropped off by Ramón. Ramón is carrying a small wrapped present. They enter Nancy's house.*

5 *Rebecca calls out in the empty house.*

6 REBECCA Hello? Nancy?

7 *No answer.*

8 REBECCA Oh. She must be at the retirement home with her uncle.

9 RAMÓN Retirement home?

10 REBECCA Yeah. He just went to live there.

11 RAMÓN That must be rough, especially at Christmas.

12 REBECCA Yeah.

13 RAMÓN Would you like to open your present?

14 REBECCA I'd love to. I have a present for you, too . . . under the Christmas tree.

15 *She heads for the living room. Ramón and Rebecca sit in front of the Christmas tree and a warm fire.*

16 **RAMÓN** Well, you open your gifts first.

17 **REBECCA** (*reading from card*) 'Merry Christmas and a Happy New Year. Your friend, Alex.'

18 *She opens the package. It is a clay figure of a woman baseball hitter. It is engraved on the bottom: "Mighty Casey at*
19 *the bat."*

20 **RAMÓN** He made the statue at school.

21 **REBECCA** 'Mighty Casey at the Bat' . . . What a riot! I'll keep it forever. It's so cute. All right, now
22   you open your present.

23 **RAMÓN** OK. . . .

24 *Ramón opens the package and pulls out the audiotape.*

25 **RAMÓN** A tape . . . what could this be?

26 **REBECCA** Here. Let me play it for you.

27 *Rebecca takes the tape and inserts it in a cassette recorder. Her lovely voice fills the room. This is a moment of peace*
28 *and quiet.*

29 **REBECCA** (*singing*) All the lights are shinin' bright down in the city,
30   Shinin' like a million dreams . . .
31   Sometimes I feel like I'm upside down
32   And all those dreams are fallin' right past me . . .
33   Everybody needs a dream catcher,
34   Someone to be there when your dreams start to fall . . .
35   Everybody needs a dream catcher,
36   Someone to be there . . . catch me.

37 FLASHBACK *of the dance between Rebecca and Ramón*

38 *We see the dream catcher twirling in the air.*

39 NANCY'S HOUSE

40 *The song ends.*

41 **RAMÓN** That was really beautiful.

42 **REBECCA** Thank you.

43 **RAMÓN** Well—wait till you see what Santa left for you.

44 *She opens another gift. It is a little statue of a Peruvian man. On him are strung several items—a gold record, a*
45 *diploma, a guitar, the name Kevin, money.*

46 **REBECCA** Oh. What is it?

47 **RAMÓN** It's from Peru. It's called an ekeko.

48 **REBECCA** I love it.

49 **RAMÓN** Legend has it that he can bring you good luck and fulfill your dreams. You hang all your
50   dreams on ekeko, and they'll come true.

51 **REBECCA** A diploma . . .

52	**RAMÓN**	That you get your degree and graduate . . .
53	**REBECCA**	And Kevin . . .
54	**RAMÓN**	That you and your brother will be together again . . .
55	**REBECCA**	So the gold record . . . .
56	**RAMÓN**	. . . your first recording will be a big hit.
57	**REBECCA**	I love it!
58	**RAMÓN**	There's only one problem. For your dreams to come true, he has to smoke once a day.
59	**REBECCA**	What?
60	**RAMÓN**	You have to give him a cigarette once a day . . . to smoke.
61	**REBECCA**	You're joking?
62	**RAMÓN**	No, I'm not.
63	**REBECCA**	Well, Nancy doesn't allow smoking in the house, so I guess he'll have to smoke outside,
64		like every other smoker in America! . . . Uh, the fire looks like it needs some work.

65 *In the firelight, Ramón sees the photo of himself and Alex under the tree.*

66	**RAMÓN**	Alberto's picture. How did that get here?
67	**REBECCA**	Oh. Alberto gave it to me. He knew I really liked it.
68	**RAMÓN**	It's my favorite picture of Alex.
69	**REBECCA**	It's a great picture of the both of you.

70 *There is an awkward silence as they look at each other. Rebecca quickly goes to fix the fire.*

71	**RAMÓN**	Let me help here . . . Watch this.

72 *Both start working on the fire, touching and being close to each other. Finally the fireplace bursts into flames. Ramón's*
73 *gotten a smudge on his hand.*

74	**RAMÓN**	Ow!
75	**REBECCA**	Ooh, are you OK? Did you burn yourself?
76	**RAMÓN**	No, just a—

77 *She touches Ramón gently on the hand. The touch is electricity between them.*

78	**REBECCA**	You should put it under cold water. My mom always said put a burn under cold water . . .

79 *They lean toward each other, their first kiss . . . and then . . . Nancy walks in. They draw back.*

PART 2

80 *NANCY'S HOUSE—NIGHT*

81	**NANCY**	Oh, hello. I was wondering whose car that was.
82	**REBECCA**	Nancy, hello. You remember Ramón, Alex's father. Ramón, this is Nancy, my godmother.
83	**RAMÓN**	It's nice to see you again.

84	NANCY	Oh, yes, I remember. We met at your parents' retirement party. It's so nice to see you at
85		Christmas time.
86	REBECCA	Ramón and I were just exchanging presents.
87	NANCY	And you've got the fire going. A glass of warm cider would make everything perfect!

88 LIVING ROOM

89 *Nancy, Rebecca, and Ramón are sipping cups of cider. Nancy is looking at the ekeko.*

90	NANCY	Well, isn't that something . . . An ekeko, is that how you say it? I hope the legend is real
91		and your dreams do come true.
92	REBECCA	Thanks. How's Edward?
93	NANCY	Not too bad. The retirement home was decorated very nicely, and we had a delicious
94		Christmas dinner. How did your dinner go?
95	REBECCA	The people at the shelter seemed pleased with the meal.
96	RAMÓN	I think we got as much pleasure out of serving them as they got out of eating it. Listen,
97		I—I should be going. Merry Christmas again, Nancy. Happy New Year if I don't see you
98		before then.
99	NANCY	Happy New Year to you, too.

100 *Rebecca stands.*

101	REBECCA	Thanks again for the presents.
102	RAMÓN	You're welcome. I'll play your tape on my way home.
103	REBECCA	Well, I'll have a whole new version of it this week, with backup singers and full
104		orchestration and the works.
105	RAMÓN	It sounds like your dreams are coming true even before ekeko has his first cigarette.

106 *Rebecca smiles.*

107	REBECCA	I'll walk you out.

108 *The two enter the front room on their way to the door.*

109	RAMÓN	I was wondering . . . what are you doin' for New Year's Eve?
110	REBECCA	I don't have any plans yet.
111	RAMÓN	Well, it's a big night at the restaurant. I have to be there, but it'll be a fun place to be on
112		New Year's Eve . . . So, if you don't have anything else to do, why don't you come and be
113		my guest? Alex will be there. Whaddya you say?
114	REBECCA	Thanks. I'd love to.
115	RAMÓN	Great. We'll ring in the new year together.

116 *They kiss once more.*

117	RAMÓN	Oh—ah—and let me know how the recording session goes!
118	REBECCA	I will.
119	RAMÓN	All right.

120 *Ramón leaves. Rebecca lingers at the door for a moment, smiling excitedly.*

PART 3

121 NANCY'S FRONT ROOM—NIGHT

122 *Nancy Shaw has gotten her present for Rebecca. Rebecca returns from the front door.*

123	**NANCY**	Well?
124	**REBECCA**	What does that mean?
125	**NANCY**	Oh, don't be coy with your godmother. Are you two an item yet?
126	**REBECCA**	Well, he asked me to spend New Year's Eve with him. And I'm going.
127	**NANCY**	Good. So it looks like it's going to be an interesting new year. Merry Christmas, Rebecca.

128 *Nancy hands her a present. Rebecca gets hers from under the tree.*

129 **REBECCA**   Oh. Merry Christmas to you, too, Nancy.

130 FARMHOUSE—NIGHT

131 *The house sits quietly in the snow piled high on the driveway.*

132 *Inside, Kevin, Uncle Brendan, and Aunt Anne are playing Scrabble.*

133	**KEVIN**	Oh, I have a word. U-P-L-I-N-K. Uplink. That's a word.
134	**ANNE**	Is it? What does it mean?
135	**BRENDAN**	It's computer talk, Hon.
136	**ANNE**	(*sigh*) I can't keep up with all this new jargon.
137	**KEVIN**	This has been a great Christmas. I just wish Rebecca were here.
138	**ANNE**	Ah, you miss her, don't you?
139	**KEVIN**	Yeah . . . I sure do.
140	**BRENDAN**	Why don't you go out and visit her?
141	**ANNE**	Yeah.
142	**KEVIN**	It's a long way.
143	**ANNE**	That's what airplanes were made for, Kev.

144 *Kevin sits, thinking about the idea.*

145 NANCY'S HOUSE, KITCHEN—NIGHT

146 *Rebecca is on the phone.*

147 **REBECCA**   Yeah . . . and thanks for the CD, Kevin. Did you like your gift? Good. OK, I'm ready for
148   the news. Uncle Brendan and Aunt Anne did what? They gave you what? A round-trip
149   ticket to San Francisco? When are you coming? The day after tomorrow? God, I can't
150   believe it! Well, well, I'll show you the town. We'll have a great time.

Episode 46

Friendship

PART 1

1 SAN FRANCISCO COLLEGE OF MUSIC, RECORDING STUDIO—DAY

2 *The band is practicing and talking. The engineer is setting up the equipment. Bill is tuning his guitar.*

3 *Rebecca enters, followed by her brother, Kevin. They stand and look around, finally smiling at each other.*

4 KEVIN So this is what you've been up to all this time . . . Man, look at all this equipment! You
5   know how to use all this stuff?

6 REBECCA I don't know how it all works technically. But I know how to make it work for my music.

7 KEVIN I just didn't know my sister was so cool.

8 REBECCA Oh, I want you to meet my friend Bill. He's the one that's cool. He's putting it all
9   together.

10 *Bill pulls away from the other musicians to meet Rebecca and her brother. Rebecca introduces her brother to Bill.*

11 REBECCA Kevin, this is Bill. Bill, meet my brother, Kevin.

12 BILL Nice to meet you. How do you like San Francisco?

13 KEVIN It's great. Not too big, not too small.

14 BILL Rebecca, we only have the studio for an hour, so we better get crackin'.

15 REBECCA Oh, yeah, you bet. Kevin, you can sit in the control room. Let me know what you think
16   of the song. Come this way.

17 *Kevin is led into the control room by Rebecca.*

18 CONTROL ROOM

19 *Rebecca introduces Kevin to the engineer.*

20 REBECCA Hey, Jay. This is my brother, Kevin.

21 JAY Hey.

22 KEVIN Hello.

23 REBECCA Jay's the best engineer at the school. Is it OK if Kevin sits in here to watch?

24 JAY No problem. Grab a seat. We 'bout ready for a rehearsal?

25 REBECCA Yeah, all set.

26 KEVIN This is so exciting.

27 REBECCA I've been dreaming about this for years.

28 KEVIN Knock 'em dead!

29 REBECCA I'll do my best.

30 OUTSIDE THE MENDOZAS' HOUSE—DAY

31 *Ramón and Alex open the trunk of the car to get his luggage and his presents.*

32 **RAMÓN** It's a good thing we have a big car. Look at all these gifts.

33 **ALEX** (*picking up something*) This one is the best.

34 **RAMÓN** How does it feel to be home?

35 **ALEX** Great! Are my other presents under the tree?

36 **RAMÓN** Right where Santa left them.

37 *Alex hurries up the stairs.*

38 **ALEX** All right!

39 *Ramón just shakes his head as he brings the stuff up the stairs.*

40 THE MENDOZAS' HOUSE, LIVING ROOM

41 *Presents and wrapping paper are everywhere. Alex is opening a small package.*

42 **RAMÓN** This one's from Rebecca.

43 *Alex opens it.*

44 **ALEX** Look! It's a baseball with autographs all over it!

45 **RAMÓN** Oh, yeah? Who are all these people?

46 **ALEX** They're the Oakland Athletics. This is the first baseman, and this is a pitcher.

47 **RAMÓN** I'm so out of touch, I don't even know who they are. Once upon a time I used to know
48 the names of the players.

49 **ALEX** Well, Rebecca knows 'em.

50 **RAMÓN** I got a present from Rebecca, too. It's a song she wrote. Wanna hear it?

51 **ALEX** Sure.

52 **RAMÓN** All right.

53 *Ramón puts on the tape. He sits with his arms around Alex. They're quiet for a moment.*

54 **RAMÓN** (*quietly*) It's nice to have you home, Alex.

55 *Alex just smiles as they listen to the music.*

56 COLLEGE RECORDING STUDIO AND CONTROL ROOM

57 *We see Rebecca singing her song. She is singing very well, and she sounds very professional. At the end of the song,*
58 *everybody claps. Rebecca is very happy.*

59 **KEVIN** Oh, Rebecca. That was totally cool.

60 **REBECCA** Thanks. You really liked it?

61 **KEVIN** It was better than good—it was the best. I didn't know you could write songs like that!

62 **REBECCA** It was there. It just never had the chance to come out before.

63 **KEVIN** I'm glad I was here to see this.

64 REBECCA I'm glad you were, too.

65 KEVIN I wish Dad could have been here just now . . .

66 REBECCA Yeah, me too.

67 BILL We're going to mix this right now.

68 REBECCA (*reaching for the phone*) Oh—

69 KEVIN What are ya doin'?

70 REBECCA I have to make a phone call.

71 *Rebecca picks up the phone in the control room and dials. We hear a recorded message on the other end of the line.*

72 ANSWERING MACHINE This is the Casa Mendoza restaurant. For reservations, please leave your
73 name and number.

74 REBECCA Hi, Ramón. It's me. I did it! We just finished recording my song. The toughest critic I
75 have . . . my brother, Kevin . . . thinks it's really cool. I'm so excited . . . I can't wait till
76 you can hear it. Bye.

PART 2

77 THE WANGS' APARTMENT—DAY

78 *Ramón is dropping off Alex at the Wangs' house. He is met by Mrs. Wang.*

79 RAMÓN That's right, Rebecca's brother is in town. That's why she can't give the boys a lesson
80 today. But the kids haven't seen each other for a while, so I thought they might like to
81 practice together.

82 MRS. WANG Yes, a very good idea. Thank you.

83 RAMÓN (*to Alex*) I'll pick you up in an hour, Alex. See ya later.

84 MRS. WANG Bye.

85 VINCENT Come on, let's go practice in my room.

86 *The two boys leave the living room. Mrs. Wang goes about her housework.*

87 VINCENT'S BEDROOM

88 *The boys sit on Vincent's bed and practice their guitars.*

89 ALEX Are you sure you heard your parents right?

90 VINCENT Yeah. They wanna go back to Taiwan.

91 ALEX What a drag.

92 VINCENT I don't wanna go to Taiwan. Maybe I'll hate it there.

93 ALEX Is it very far?

94 VINCENT It's a different place. I won't know anybody.

95 ALEX Do they speak English there?

96 VINCENT I dunno. I think they speak Mandarin.

97 ALEX I can speak Spanish . . . a little. But I don't think I'd like to move to Mexico.

98 VINCENT Yeah, we belong here.

99	ALEX	Well, do you really have to go to Taiwan?
100	VINCENT	If my parents go, I guess I have to go, too. Do you have to move to L.A.?
101	ALEX	I don't know. My parents may have to go to court to figure out what to do with me.
102	VINCENT	This is really bad, Alex.
103	ALEX	So we have to do something.
104	VINCENT	Yeah.
105	ALEX	Hey, I have an idea. Maybe we can live together.
106	VINCENT	My parents wouldn't let me do that.
107	ALEX	How come parents always make the decisions?
108	VINCENT	Yeah, kids have rights, too.
109	*They are silent for a moment.*	
110	VINCENT	Why can't things just stay the way they are?
111	ALEX	And we could be friends and not have to move any place.
112	*Mrs. Wang appears in the doorway.*	
113	MRS. WANG	(*in Mandarin*) Vincent, Alex de bàba dǎ diànhuà lái shuō tā wǎn diǎnr lái. Wǔ fēn zhōng
114		nèi, tā jiù dào zhè lǐ le.
115	VINCENT	(*translating for Alex*) Your father called. He's running a little late. He'll pick ya up in
116		five minutes.
117	ALEX	Thank you, Mrs. Wang.
118	MRS. WANG	You are welcome.
119	*She leaves the boys alone.*	
120	ALEX	What are you doing Saturday?
121	VINCENT	You mean, New Year's? Nothing, I guess. Why?
122	ALEX	Well, this could be our last New Year's together, right?
123	VINCENT	Yeah. Next year, I'll be in Taiwan, and you'll be in L.A.
124	ALEX	So let's make it the best New Year's we've ever had!
125	VINCENT	Yeah!
126	ALEX	I've got an idea.
127	VINCENT	Is this idea gonna get us in trouble?
128	ALEX	Trouble? No way! Do you have any money?
129	VINCENT	Yeah. In my bank.
130	*The boys go to Vincent's dresser. He picks up his bank and shakes it. It clanks with lots of coins.*	
131	ALEX	Wow! Sounds like a lot of money.
132	VINCENT	Thirty-five dollars and fifty-two cents.
133	ALEX	And with my Christmas money, we could have a blast!

PART 3

134 SAN FRANCISCO COLLEGE OF MUSIC, CONTROL ROOM—EVENING

135 *Bill and Jay do the last mix of the music. The last chords end.*

136 **BILL** Whaddya think?

137 **REBECCA** It's perfect. Thanks, Jay, for all your help.

138 **JAY** I gotta run. This took longer than I thought.

139 **BILL** Thanks, man. Maybe we'll work together again someday.

140 **JAY** Sounds good. I'll see you, Becky.

141 **REBECCA** Take care.

142 **JAY** It was nice meeting you, Kevin.

143 **KEVIN** See you later.

144 *He shakes hands all around and then leaves. Bill has taken off the tape and presents it to Rebecca.*

145 **BILL** Here it is . . . 'Dream Catcher' by Rebecca Casey.

146 **REBECCA** It's hard to believe. (*She gives Bill a kiss on the cheek.*) Thanks.

147 **KEVIN** I'm gonna wait outside. Get some fresh air.

148 **REBECCA** We just have to close up the studio, and then I'll be right out.

149 **BILL** It was nice meeting you.

150 **KEVIN** Nice meeting you, too.

151 *He leaves. Rebecca and Bill stay in the studio.*

152 **BILL** Listen, I have to tell you something. I'm not coming back to school next term.

153 **REBECCA** You're kidding me . . .

154 *He shakes his head "no."*

155 **BILL** I'm just wasting time here. I'm heading to L.A. I've some friends in the record industry
156 there, and they say if I'm there, they'll get me a job.

157 **REBECCA** I guess it wouldn't make any difference if I told you you were nuts.

158 **BILL** No. You have your dream and I have mine. Let's just hope my dream catcher lets in only
159 the good dreams.

160 **REBECCA** I'm sure it will. I'm gonna miss you.

161 **BILL** Me, too. You have a great voice, girl.

162 **REBECCA** Take care of yourself.

163 **BILL** I will. You, too.

164 *They hug.*

The Lost Boys

PART 1

1 THE WANGS' APARTMENT, VINCENT'S BEDROOM—DAY

2 Vincent sneaks into his bedroom. He takes the money out of his bank.

3 THE WANGS' FRONT ROOM

4 Vincent walks past his mother, who is vacuuming the rug. Mrs. Wang sees him.

5 **MRS. WANG** Vincent, where are you going?

6 **VINCENT** Out. I'll be back . . . soon . . . Bye.

7 He leaves the house quickly. His mother looks concerned.

8 STREET, CHINATOWN

9 **VINCENT** This is gonna to be an awesome New Year!

10 **ALEX** The best! How much does it cost?

11 **VINCENT** Five dollars and fifty cents to get in, plus three dollars to rent the skates. Ya have some
12 money?

13 **ALEX** (holding up piece of ripped newsprint) Yeah, tons. And this is where we go.

14 **VINCENT** Let's go!

15 The boys run off down the street.

16 VINCENT'S BEDROOM—LATE AFTERNOON

17 Mrs. Wang enters Vincent's room. She finds the empty bank on the bed.

18 **MRS. WANG** Oh, no. Where did the money go?

19 THE WANGS' STORE

20 The phone rings as Mr. Wang waits on a customer. He picks up the phone.

21 **MR. WANG** Hello. Ah, hello. Mei-Lin . . . No, no Vincent's not here . . . Perhaps he's with his
22 cousins . . . He's not? . . . His bank? . . . It's empty? . . . He took his money? . . .

23 CHINATOWN—EARLY EVENING

24 Mrs. Wang walks the streets looking for Vincent.

25 THE WANGS' STORE

26 Mrs. Wang enters the store.

27 **MR. WANG** Did you find him?

28 MRS. WANG   No.

29 MR. WANG   Where do you think he is?

30 MRS. WANG   (*in Mandarin*) Wǒ bù qīng chu . . . ("*I'm not sure.*") But I know who he is with. Alex
31   Mendoza.

32 MR. WANG   Well, then don't worry. They probably went to the . . . library.

33 MRS. WANG   On New Year's Eve?

34 MR. WANG   Where else could they be?

35 CHINATOWN LIBRARY

36 *Mrs. Wang walks into the library and looks around. There is no sign of either Vincent or Alex.*

37 MENDOZA RESTAURANT—EARLY EVENING

38 *The place is very busy. Balloons and other New Year's decorations are being put up by the kitchen staff and waiters.*
39 *Ramón is supervising the whole thing. Rebecca arrives with Kevin.*

40 RAMÓN   Great . . . ah . . . Put those over there . . . yeah . . . in the corner.

41 REBECCA   Ramón . . . Hi. Is this a bad time?

42 RAMÓN   Rebecca, no. Come in. This must be your brother, Kevin.

43 KEVIN   Hi.

44 REBECCA   Kevin and I are sightseeing—just checking out the city.

45 RAMÓN   This is a great time to be in San Francisco. New Year's is one long party from morning
46   till night.

47 KEVIN   It sounds like my kinda town.

48 REBECCA   I hope you don't mind if Kevin comes tonight.

49 RAMÓN   Not at all . . . I'd be honored to have Kevin here for our New Year's party. Put on your
50   dancing shoes—the band is very good.

51 *A worker comes up to Ramón and asks him something in Spanish. Rebecca and Kevin talk.*

52 REBECCA   I think we should go. He's really busy right now.

53 KEVIN   I thought you wanted to play him your tape . . .

54 *Ramón turns his attention back to them.*

55 REBECCA   Ramón, you're busy. We'll see you tonight.

56 RAMÓN   Forgive me, there is so much to do . . .

57 REBECCA   Don't worry. We'll see ya later . . .

58 KEVIN   Bye.

59 *They turn to leave as Mr. Wang enters the restaurant. Ramón has already moved off to the back part of the restaurant.*

60 REBECCA   Mr. Wang . . . This is my brother, Kevin. This is the father of one of the boys I give
61   guitar lessons to.

62 KEVIN   Nice to meet you.

63	MR. WANG	Nice to meet you, too. Have you seen Vincent today?
64	REBECCA	No.
65	MR. WANG	Excuse me.
66	*He heads off to the back part of the restaurant.*	
67	KEVIN	Should we go?
68	REBECCA	Wait. Something's wrong . . .

PART 2

69 MENDOZA RESTAURANT

70 *Mr. Wang and Ramón are talking as Rebecca and Kevin approach them.*

71	MR. WANG	Ramón, have you seen Vincent?
72	RAMÓN	No, Vincent hasn't been here all day.
73	MR. WANG	We don't know where he is. He didn't come home for lunch, and my wife is getting
74		worried. Somebody saw him with Alex.
75	RAMÓN	That can't be. Alex is home. Let's call and see if he's heard from Vincent.
76	*Ramón notices Rebecca and Kevin.*	
77	RAMÓN	Vincent's missing.
78	REBECCA	I heard. Is there anything I can do, Mr. Wang?
79	MR. WANG	I don't know, but thank you for offering.
80	*Ramón has been dialing on the phone.*	
81	RAMÓN	It's ringing.

82 THE MENDOZAS' HOUSE

83 *We see the empty house as the phone rings.*

84	RAMÓN	No one's answering.

85 MENDOZA RESTAURANT

86	RAMÓN	I'm going to have to go to the house to see if anything's wrong.
87	MR. WANG	Maybe your phone is out of order . . .
88	RAMÓN	No. The answering machine picked up.
89	MR. WANG	Sooner or later, we'll get a call from one of them. My wife is at home in case Vincent
90		calls there. Is there anyone that can stay at your house to answer the phone?
91	REBECCA	Kevin and I would be glad to answer the phone.
92	RAMÓN	I don't want to spoil your day.
93	REBECCA	No. Those two boys are very important to me. I insist. Kevin and I will answer the phone
94		at your house.
95	MR. WANG	I'm going out to drive around to see if I can find them. Please call my wife as soon as you
96		have any information.

97 **RAMÓN**   I will. José . . .

98 *Ramón goes to talk with his head waiter as Mr. Wang leaves. Rebecca and Kevin are left alone in the*
99 *restaurant entrance.*

100 **REBECCA**   Kevin, I didn't think our New Year's Eve would turn out like this.

101 **KEVIN**   Well, things happen.

102 **REBECCA**   I just can't imagine what those boys are doing right now.

103 **KEVIN**   Hey . . . It's New Year's. They're probably out celebrating.

104 **REBECCA**   They're only ten . . . They wouldn't do that.

105 **KEVIN**   (*interrupting*) You'd be surprised what kids will do. Do you remember when I ran away from
106   home? I was only seven . . .

107 **REBECCA**   Right. You went down two blocks and then chickened out.

108 **KEVIN**   That's right. Kids'll do crazy things. Hey, tomorrow, this'll be funny.

109 *Ramón returns.*

110 **RAMÓN**   OK, we can go now!

111 *They leave.*

112 THE MENDOZAS' HOUSE—EARLY EVENING

113 *Ramón enters, followed by Rebecca and Kevin.*

114 **RAMÓN**   Alex! Alex!

115 **REBECCA**   I don't think he's here.

116 **RAMÓN**   I'm going next door to check with Mrs. Lynch. She keeps an eye on Alex when my
117   parents are out of town. Um, make yourselves at home, or . . .

118 *Rebecca looks worried.*

119 EMBARCADERO—EVENING

120 *The square is filled with people. We see a crowded skating rink. Vincent and Alex are having a good time skating.*
121 *Suddenly, a big kid crashes into Alex and he falls on the ice. He lies very still. Vincent looks on in horror.*

122 **VINCENT**   Are you all right . . . ? Come on, Alex.

123 **ALEX**   I can't skate!

124 THE MENDOZAS' HOUSE—EVENING

125 *Ramón is calling Mrs. Wang on the phone.*

126 **RAMÓN**   Wait till I get my hands on that kid. Of all the days to pull a crazy stunt . . . Mrs. Lynch
127   hasn't seen him since early this afternoon. (*pause*) Hello, Mrs. Wang? Alex and Vincent
128   are not here. They're not in the house. You haven't heard? . . . Yes, I'll call you soon as I
129   hear something . . .

130 *He hangs up the phone.*

131 **RAMÓN**   Now what do I do?

132 **REBECCA**   Call the police?

133	**RAMÓN**	No, please. They're not in trouble . . . They're probably fooling around or something . . .
134	**REBECCA**	Kevin, tell Ramón your idea . . .
135	**KEVIN**	Well, ah . . . maybe they went somewhere to celebrate New Year's—you know, wherever
136		kids go in this town . . .
137	**RAMÓN**	Alex left his bag in the hall . . . (*Ramón goes immediately to Alex's bag. Inside is the San Francisco*
138		*newspaper with an ad cut out.*) He usually puts it away. He ripped an ad out of the paper.
139	**REBECCA**	What?
140	**RAMÓN**	It's an ad for the Embarcadero . . .

141 *Rebecca and Ramón are about to leave. Kevin talks to them on the porch.*

142	**RAMÓN**	Thanks for volunteering to answer the phone, Kevin. We'll check in every half hour or
143		so to find out if you've heard anything. Here's my work number, just in case.

144 *Ramón hands Kevin a business card.*

145	**KEVIN**	Hey, good luck. I hope you find them.
146	**REBECCA**	Thanks, Kev, for being such a good sport. I owe you one.
147	**KEVIN**	Get going—so we can find them before midnight. Then we party!
148	**RAMÓN**	I almost forgot. The baby-sitter. She's coming at seven. There's an envelope on the
149		counter. Please give it to her and apologize for me . . .
150	**KEVIN**	No problem.

151 EMBARCADERO—NIGHT

152 *Ramón and Rebecca walk through the crowd looking for the boys. They are nowhere to be seen.*

153	**RAMÓN**	They would have rented skates . . .

154 *He and Rebecca go to the skate stand. Ramón shows a picture of Alex.*

155	**SKATE ATTENDANT**	Yeah, I think they were here earlier. This one was limping around.
156	**RAMÓN**	He was hurt?
157	**SKATE ATTENDANT**	I asked if he wanted to see our first aid person. But he and his friend just left.
158	**RAMÓN**	How long ago?
159	**SKATE ATTENDANT**	Maybe an hour . . .

160 *Ramón and Rebecca look worried.*

161	**RAMÓN**	Uh, thanks.

PART 3

162 RAMÓN'S CAR—NIGHT

163 *Ramón and Rebecca hunt for the boys.*

164	**RAMÓN**	This is ridiculous, driving around on New Year's Eve! Wait till I get my hands on
165		that kid . . .
166	**REBECCA**	He's been through a lot . . . the trip to Los Angeles, being away from you at
167		Christmas . . . Maybe this is his way of reacting to what he's been going through.

168 RAMÓN   It's this custody thing. If only I . . . (*He gets quiet.*) I guess he's more upset than I
169   realized . . . But still, that's no reason to scare us to death . . .

170 THE MENDOZAS' HOUSE—NIGHT

171 *Kevin answers the ringing phone.*

172 KEVIN   Hello, Mendoza residence. Oh, hi . . . No, I haven't heard anything. Mr. Wang went
173   down to the police and filed a missing person's report . . .

174 *The doorbell rings.*

175 KEVIN   There's someone at the door . . . OK, hang on, I'll be right back . . .

176 *Kevin rushes to the door and opens it. It's the baby-sitter, a very pretty girl.*

177 MONICA   Hi! I'm the baby-sitter. Who are you?

178 KEVIN   Oh. Just a minute. Mr. Mendoza is on the phone. There's an emergency.

179 *Kevin rushes back to the phone.*

180 KEVIN   No, it was the baby-sitter . . . OK. All right. I'll call Mrs. Wang and let her know.
181   Thanks.

182 *Kevin hangs up the phone. The baby-sitter still stands in the doorway.*

183 KEVIN   Oh, you must be the baby-sitter. You were going to baby-sit Alex and his friend?

184 MONICA   Yeah.

185 KEVIN   Well, they seem to be missing.

186 MONICA   Missing?

187 KEVIN   Yeah. Mr. Mendoza wanted me to give you this money and to apologize for him . . . He's
188   out looking for them now.

189 MONICA   Who are you, anyway?

190 KEVIN   My name's Kevin . . . I'm a friend of the family's . . . Just helping out.

191 MONICA   I'm Monica. I usually baby-sit for Alex. I live across the street.

192 *They stand there for a few moments.*

193 KEVIN   Kids do crazy things . . .

194 MONICA   Yeah.

195 KEVIN   I have to to call Mrs. Wang . . . She's the mother of the other kid . . . And I have to give
196   her a message.

197 MONICA   Do you mind if I stick around a bit and see if they turn up?

198 *Kevin picks up the phone and starts dialing.*

199 KEVIN   No, that'd be fine. Some crazy New Year's—missing kids, police, you name it . . .

200 MONICA   It's scary what's going on today . . .

201 KEVIN   Hello, Mrs. Wang . . . What? You heard from them? They were what? OK, OK, I'll tell
202   Mr. Mendoza when I see him. Thank you.

203 *He hangs up the phone.*

204	MONICA	They found them? (*He nods his head "yes."*) Are they all right?
205	KEVIN	They're at the hospital.
206	MONICA	Oh, my God . . .

EPISODE 48

A Very Good Year

PART 1

1 RAMÓN'S CAR—NIGHT

2 *Ramón and Rebecca wait for the light to change.*

3	RAMÓN	I hope Alex is safe.
4	REBECCA	I'm sure he's fine . . . Maybe he got involved in . . . I don't know, lost track of time, or
5		something . . .
6	RAMÓN	This isn't how I had planned this New Year's Eve . . .
7	REBECCA	I'm sure we'll find him.
8	RAMÓN	Maybe he took a shortcut through the park . . . Let's check it out.
9	REBECCA	Yeah . . .

10 PARK—NIGHT

11 *The park is lit by a few lights.*

13	RAMÓN/REBECCA	(*shouting into darkness*) Alex . . . ! Vincent . . . ! Vincent . . . ! Alex . . . !

14 *They walk in the park.*

15	RAMÓN	I don't think they're here.
16	REBECCA	No. Should we go back?
17	RAMÓN	Yeah, and I should call in . . . Maybe someone's heard from the kids. This is my worst
18		nightmare . . . Not knowing where your child is . . . . is just . . .

19 *The two walk off looking for the missing boys.*

20 SAN FRANCISCO HOSPITAL—NIGHT

21 *Mr. and Mrs. Wang, Vincent, and Alex are in the hospital lobby.*

22	MRS. WANG	Are you all right?

23 *Alex nods "yes."*

24	VINCENT	What's your dad going to do?
25	ALEX	Probably have a fit.

26 *Mr. Wang talks to the boys.*

27 **MR. WANG** Well, what do the two of you have to say for yourselves?

28 **ALEX/VINCENT** Sorry . . . I'm sorry, Dad.

29 **MRS. WANG** Later, we will talk.

30 **MR. WANG** No. I want to know what's going on . . . Alex, I'm sorry about your ankle, but tonight has
31 been very . . . very disturbing. I even went to the police, and now the hospital . . . I don't
32 think I can trust you two ever again.

33 **MRS. WANG** (*stopping him*) Not right now. (*in Mandarin*) Xiànzài . . . bù shì shíhou . . . ("*Not now . . .*
34 *This is not the time . . .*")

35 **MR. WANG** No, I want to get to the bottom of this. Why did you two run away?

36 *Neither boy speaks.*

37 **MR. WANG** Vincent?

38 *Vincent mutters.*

39 **MR. WANG** What did you say?

40 **VINCENT** Alex is my best friend, and we just wanted to do something special before I have to go to
41 Taiwan.

42 *Mr. Wang and Mrs. Wang exchange looks.*

43 **MR. WANG** Vincent, how did you know about Taiwan?

44 **VINCENT** I heard you and Mom talking . . . the other day . . . in your bedroom.

45 *Mrs. Wang and Mr. Wang look at each other.*

46 **MRS. WANG** I will tell him . . .

47 *Mr. Wang nods "yes."*

48 **MRS. WANG** Vincent, your father and I have talked. And we think to stay in San Francisco is best
49 for you.

50 *Vincent looks surprised.*

51 **MRS. WANG** You and I . . . will stay here. And your father will go and work in Taiwan.

52 **VINCENT** Really?

53 **MRS. WANG** Your father will go for one year. And that is a very long time. I . . . I will need your
54 help to (*She asks Mr. Wang in Mandarin for the right word.*) . . . Liàolǐ shāng diàn . . .

55 **MR. WANG** . . . manage . . .

56 **MRS. WANG** . . . manage the store.

57 **VINCENT** I'll help . . . I promise . . .

58 **MR. WANG** We expect you to keep up your grades and to be an obedient son to your mother . . .

59 **VINCENT** I will . . .

60 **MR. WANG** After tonight, I'm not so sure . . .

61 **VINCENT** Honest, Dad. We just thought this would be our last New Year's together . . .

62 **MRS. WANG** You see. You will have another.

63 *Alex doesn't look happy. Vincent responds for him.*

64 **VINCENT** Naw, it's still the last time. Alex has to move to Los Angeles to live with his mom.

65 **MR. WANG** Is that right, Alex?

66 *He nods "yes."*

PART 2

67 PARK—NIGHT

68 *Rebecca and Ramón are still walking in the park.*

69 **REBECCA** Kevin disappeared once, when he was a little kid . . . I thought I was going to die until I
70 found him. He had decided to go visit our father at the fire station . . . When I found
71 him, he was crying . . . and lost—totally lost, just a couple of blocks from our apartment.

72 **RAMÓN** Maybe this whole episode is to remind me to pay attention to what's important . . .
73 Enough of this 'poor Ramón' . . . I've got to do what's right for Alex . . .

74 **REBECCA** You are doing what's right . . .

75 **RAMÓN** No, I've put him in a terrible situation. I'm asking him to choose between his mother
76 and me. I'm ashamed to admit it.

77 **REBECCA** Ramón . . . you love your son . . .

78 **RAMÓN** But I made him feel like a piece of baggage being shipped back and forth between his
79 mother and me . . . Who knows? I was probably trying to get back at my ex-wife.

80 **REBECCA** Oh, come on . . .

81 **RAMÓN** . . . How about that for . . . for being a total jerk.

82 **REBECCA** Come on . . . You wouldn't do that . . .

83 **RAMÓN** No, no, no, I'm serious. Enough is enough. Everybody says that a child should be with his
84 mother . . . everybody, the courts, the newspapers, everybody . . . Anyway, I cause him
85 nothing but heartache . . .

86 **REBECCA** Stop this, right now.

87 **RAMÓN** No, no, no. It's the truth. I can't do it—manage a restaurant, Alex . . . a personal life . . .

88 **REBECCA** I can't believe that I'm hearing this nonsense.

89 **RAMÓN** It's true . . .

90 **REBECCA** No, it isn't. Come on Ramón . . . I've seen you with your son . . . You are a caring and
91 giving father who wants what's best for his son. I've seen the sacrifices you make for Alex
92 and for your work . . . Look, I don't know what your ex-wife is like, but I can't imagine
93 that anyone could love him as much as you do.

94 **RAMÓN** I don't know if I can do it anymore, Rebecca . . . Sometimes I get so tired . . .

95 *She stops him. They look at each other.*

96 **REBECCA** When I was a little kid, my dad gave me something that always worked.

97 *She hugs him, and he hugs her back.*

98	**RAMÓN**	I'm sorry. I must sound like a big crybaby.
99	**REBECCA**	No, you sound like a man who is suffering because his son is missing. Ramón, you are
100		such a good man . . . capable of great love . . .

101 *They look at each other with a look that stops both of them.*

102	**REBECCA**	Why don't we go back and make a phone call and see if anyone's heard from them . . .
103		OK?

104 **STREET CORNER—NIGHT**

105 *Ramón is on the phone with Kevin. Rebecca reacts to the phone call.*

106	**RAMÓN**	. . . They what? The hospital? Kevin, is he all right? Where are they? Vincent's dad is
107		bringing him to the house. OK. We'll be right there . . .

108 **THE MENDOZAS' HOUSE—NIGHT**

109 *Ramón and Rebecca enter. Kevin comes out from the kitchen.*

110	**RAMÓN**	Are they here?
111	**KEVIN**	No, not yet.

112 *The baby-sitter comes out from the kitchen. Rebecca gives a strange look as Ramón goes to the window.*

113	**MONICA**	Is it Alex?

114 *Kevin quickly introduces the girl to his sister.*

115	**KEVIN**	This is my sister, Rebecca. This is Monica, the baby-sitter . . .
116	**MONICA**	Hi . . .
117	**KEVIN**	She's waiting around to see if the kids are OK.
118	**REBECCA**	Oh . . .

119 *We hear the sound of a car in the driveway. Rebecca and the other two join Ramón at the door.*

PART 3

120 **THE MENDOZAS' HOUSE**

121 *Ramón and Rebecca open the door as Mr. Wang carries Alex up the stairs.*

122	**RAMÓN**	Are you all right?

123 *Alex nods "yes."*

124	**RAMÓN**	Let me see your ankle.

125 *The boy puts his leg out.*

126	**ALEX**	Ow!
127	**RAMÓN**	Well, you won't be playing much baseball for a while.
128	**ALEX**	I'm sorry, Dad . . .

129 *Ramón lifts the boy up in his arms and holds him close.*

130	**RAMÓN**	(*to Mr. Wang and his wife*) Thanks, thanks to both of you.

131 **RAMÓN** You know you're grounded, right?

132 *Alex nods "yes."*

133 **RAMÓN** Grounded for a very, very long time . . . Come on . . . Can you walk?

134 **ALEX** Yeah . . .

135 **RAMÓN** All right . . .

136 *Kevin and Monica hold the door open.*

137 **MONICA** Hi, Alex. Happy New Year!

138 THE MENDOZAS' HOUSE

139 *Alex and Vincent sit on the sofa, being quiet and still. Rebecca has given each of the boys a glass of juice.*

140 **REBECCA** Here you go. At least you're home now.

141 **ALEX** What do you think my dad's going to do?

142 **REBECCA** I'm not sure . . .

143 **ALEX** Maybe he'll just forget about all this?

144 **REBECCA** I doubt it.

145 *Ramón and the Wangs join them.*

146 **RAMÓN** Mr. and Mrs. Wang have told me why you boys did what you did. I can understand your
147 feelings, but you must promise never to do a foolish thing like this again. OK?

148 **ALEX** Yes.

149 *Vincent nods "yes."*

150 **MR. WANG** It's time to go, Vincent.

151 *He gets up and goes to the door with his parents. Ramón walks them to the door.*

152 **VINCENT** (*to Alex*) See ya!

153 **ALEX** Yeah.

154 **MONICA** Well, I guess I should go home. Goodnight. It was nice meeting you.

155 **KEVIN** I'll walk you home.

156 **MONICA** That's not necessary. I live right across the street.

157 **KEVIN** No, I insist. Really. (*She smiles and agrees.*)

158 **REBECCA** Nice meeting you, Monica. Have a Happy New Year.

159 **MONICA** You, too.

160 **KEVIN** I'll be right back.

161 *They head to the door. Rebecca and Alex reflect on the situation.*

162 **REBECCA** How's your ankle?

163 **ALEX** It's better, I think.

164 *He tries to stand, but it hurts. Ramón joins them and lifts his son up into his arms.*

165 **ALEX** Ouch . . .

166 **REBECCA** Careful...

167 **RAMÓN** I don't think you should try to walk on that foot. Listen carefully to what I'm going to
168 say. You don't have to worry about who you're going to live with. I promise, your mother
169 and I are going to work things out... somehow. And I promise that your happiness will
170 be our first priority. Understood?

171 *Alex nods "yes."*

172 **RAMÓN** Listen, I want us to spend New Year's Eve together. You can come with us to the
173 restaurant and celebrate, but don't get me wrong, you're still grounded... starting
174 tomorrow.

175 MENDOZA RESTAURANT—NIGHT

176 *The crowd has gathered to count down the last few seconds before midnight. Kevin and Alex, with his foot up on a*
177 *pillow, watch the others. Rebecca stands next to Ramón.*

178 **CROWD** ...ten...nine...eight...seven...six...five...four...three...two...one...
179 (cheer)

180 *People in the crowd wave noisemakers, throw confetti into the air, and kiss. Alex and Kevin also wave their*
181 *noisemakers.*

182 *Ramón and Rebecca kiss. Ramón quietly talks to Rebecca.*

183 **RAMÓN** Well... Happy New Year.

184 **REBECCA** Happy New Year.

185 **RAMÓN** You know, I think this is going to be a very good year.

186 **REBECCA** I think so, too. Happy New Year!

187 *They look very happy to be together and in love.*

全新版新世纪走遍美国
会话练习 4

Pam Tiberia   Janet Battiste
Michael Berman   Linda Butler

北京市版权局著作权合同登记号　图字01-2008-1460

图书在版编目（CIP）数据

全新版新世纪走遍美国.会话练习4/Pam Tiberia 等编著.—北京：北京大学出版社，2008.11
ISBN 978-7-301-14380-3

Ⅰ.全… Ⅱ.P… Ⅲ.英语－听说教学－教材 Ⅳ.H319.9

中国版本图书馆CIP数据核字（2008）第164900号

Pam Tiberia　Janet Battiste　Michael Berman　Linda Butler
Connect with English, Conversation Book 4
ISBN: 0-07-292767-4

Copyright © 1998 by the WGBH Educational Foundation and the Corporation for Public Broadcasting. All rights reserved. Printed in the United States of America. Except as permitted under the United States Copyright Act of 1976, no part of this publication may be reproduced or distributed in any form or by any means, or stored in a data base or retrieval system, without the prior written permission of the publisher.

All rights reserved. This edition is authorized for sale in the People's Republic of China only, excluding Hong Kong, Macao SARs and Taiwan.

此书只限在中华人民共和国境内（不包括中国香港、澳门特别行政区及台湾地区）销售。未经出版者预先书面许可，不得以任何方式复制或抄袭本书的任何部分。

本书封面贴有McGraw-Hill公司防伪标签，无标签者不得销售。

书　　　名：全新版新世纪走遍美国·会话练习4
著作责任者：Pam Tiberia　等编著
责 任 编 辑：张建民
标 准 书 号：ISBN 978-7-301-14380-3/H·2089
出 版 发 行：北京大学出版社
地　　　址：北京市海淀区成府路205号　100871
网　　　址：http://www.pup.cn
电 子 信 箱：zbing@pup.pku.edu.cn
电　　　话：邮购部62752015　发行部62750672　编辑部62755217　出版部62754962
印　刷　者：世界知识印刷厂
经　销　者：新华书店
　　　　　　889毫米×1194毫米　16开本　6印张　150千字
　　　　　　2008年11月第1版　2008年11月第1次印刷
定　　　价：98.00元（包括视频理解、会话练习、学习指导及光盘）

未经许可，不得以任何方式复制或抄袭本书之部分或全部内容。
版权所有，侵权必究
举报电话：(010)62752024　电子信箱：fd@pup.pku.edu.cn

Table of Contents

TO THE TEACHER v

A VISUAL TOUR OF THIS TEXT vii

	THEMES	TWO-PAGE ACTIVITY	OPTIONAL PROJECT
EPISODE 37 **THANKSGIVING**	• Family Holidays • Family Secrets • Thanksgiving Day	GAME: THANKSGIVING FOOTBALL	Computer Classes (Appendix 1)
EPISODE 38 **STARTING OVER**	• Christmas Bonuses • Giving Advice • Losing a Job	INFORMATION GAP: DECORATING A CHRISTMAS TREE	Sports for Children (Appendix 2)
EPISODE 39 **THE PRESSURE'S ON**	• Managing Priorities • Stress • Being Direct	GAME: STUDYING FOR EXAMS	Opera (Appendix 3)
EPISODE 40 **SHARING FEELINGS**	• Things That Are Important to You • Being Patient or Impatient • Making Money	INFORMATION GAP: ROCK AND ROLL MUSIC	Using the Library (Appendix 4)
EPISODE 41 **UNEXPECTED OFFERS**	• Moving to a Different Place • Invitations • Christmas Spirit	GAME: GIVING CHRISTMAS PRESENTS	Vacations (Appendix 5)
EPISODE 42 **THE AUDITION**	• Waiting • The Importance of Education • An Audition	SONG: DREAM CATCHER	Dedication (Appendix 6)

	THEMES	TWO-PAGE ACTIVITY	OPTIONAL PROJECT
EPISODE 43 *DREAM CATCHER*	• Success • Talent • Having Confidence	INFORMATION GAP: TAKING A MESSAGE	Chocolates (Appendix 7)
EPISODE 44 *GIFTS*	• The Community Center • Breaking Up • Inspirations	GAME: SKIING	Helping People in the Community (Appendix 8)
EPISODE 45 *TRUE LOVE*	• An Ekeko • Exchanging Christmas Presents • Falling in Love	INFORMATION GAP: PLANNING A TRIP	Legends (Appendix 9)
EPISODE 46 *FRIENDSHIP*	• Being Impressed • Collecting Autographs • Sharing Good News	GAME: THE MUSIC BUSINESS	Languages (Appendix 10)
EPISODE 47 *THE LOST BOYS*	• Changing Plans • Baby-sitting • Children and Money	INFORMATION GAP: A MISSING PERSON'S REPORT	Ice Skating (Appendix 11)
EPISODE 48 *A VERY GOOD YEAR*	• New Year's Resolutions • Trust • Parenting	GAME: GROUNDING	New Year's Eve (Appendix 12)

APPENDICES 1–12   OPTIONAL PROJECT PAGES, EPISODES 37-48

APPENDIX 13   MANIPULATIVES

To the Teacher

The primary goal of each *Conversation Book* is to help students develop oral communication skills using the themes found in **Connect with English** as a springboard for classroom discussion. This introduction and the following Visual Tour provide important information on how each *Conversation Book* and the corresponding video episodes can be successfully combined to teach English as a second or foreign language.

LANGUAGE SKILLS:

Each *Conversation Book* has 12 chapters which contain a variety of pair, group, team, and whole-class activities that are based on important issues and ideas from the corresponding video episodes.

The activity types vary with each chapter but generally include an assortment of role-plays, discussions, opinion surveys, games, interviews, and questionnaires. In each chapter, a special two-page section is devoted to longer games, information gaps, and songs from the **Connect with English** soundtrack. Students also have the opportunity to work on special project pages found in appendices in the back of the book. These projects provide students with the opportunity to explore key themes outside of the classroom.

THEMATIC ORGANIZATION:

Events and issues that are familiar and important to all ESL/EFL learners have been purposely included in the **Connect with English** story. These topics were carefully chosen for their relevant cultural content, and they provide a rich context for the communicative activities found in the *Conversation Books*. As students watch the video story and become familiar with the events and characters, the *Conversation Books* provide a framework within which students can freely discuss the ideas presented in each episode. Throughout *Conversation Books 1-4,* students are given the opportunity to explore such varied themes as the following:

- Pursuing Your Dream
- Making Future Plans
- Looking for a Job
- Making New Friends
- Money vs. Love
- Having Fun
- Apologizing
- Making a Difficult Decision
- Gossip
- Divorce and Remarriage
- Regrets
- Anger
- Making Compromises
- Spending Money
- Adulthood
- Best Friends
- Managing Priorities
- Parenting
- Helping Others
- The Death of a Loved One
- Dedication
- Moving
- Holidays
- Life Lessons

PROFICIENCY LEVEL:

The activities found in each *Conversation Book* are designed for use with high-beginning to intermediate students. Special icons are used to identify the difficulty level of each activity in the book. These icons help teachers tailor the activities for the needs of students at different levels of language proficiency.

 Arrows pointing up indicate that the difficulty of an activity can be increased.

 Arrows pointing down indicate that an activity can be simplified.

 Arrows pointing in both directions indicate that the difficulty level of the activity can be either increased or simplified.

Detailed teaching suggestions on modifying each activity are found in the accompanying Instructor's Manual.

OPTIONS FOR USE:

The *Conversation Books* are specifically designed for classroom use. While it is assumed that students have watched the corresponding video episode at least once before attempting the activities in the book, it is not necessary to have classroom access to a TV or VCR. Teachers may choose to show the video during class time, or they can assign students to watch the video episodes prior to class, either in a library, language lab, or at home. Class time can then be used for completion of the activities found in the *Conversation Book*.

Each *Conversation Book* can be used as the sole text in any course that emphasizes oral communication skills. Teachers also have the option of combining the *Conversation Books* with other corresponding texts in the **Connect with English** print package:

- *Video Comprehension Books 1-4* contain a variety of comprehension activities that enhance and solidify students' understanding of main events in the video story.

- *Grammar Guides 1-4* provide multilevel practice in grammar structures and vocabulary items derived from the **Connect with English** video episodes.

- *Connections Reader Series* (16 titles) offer students graded reading practice based on the **Connect with English** story.

- *Video Scripts 1-4* include the exact dialogue from each of the video episodes and can be used in a variety of ways in conjunction with any of the other texts in the **Connect with English** program.

For additional information on these and other materials in the **Connect with English** program, please refer to the inside back cover of this book.

A VISUAL TOUR OF THIS TEXT

This visual tour is designed to introduce the key features of *Conversation Book 4*. The primary focus of each *Conversation Book* is to help students develop oral communication skills within the context of the *Connect with English* story. *Conversation Book 4* corresponds to episodes 37-48 of *Connect with English*, and it presents an assortment of activities dealing with various aspects of communication, including explaining, questioning, interviewing, reporting, paraphrasing, describing, stating feelings/opinions, and more.

Themes drawn directly from the video episodes are listed at the start of each chapter. In Episode 42, activities are based on the themes of Waiting, The Importance of Education, and An Audition. A two-page activity is devoted to the song "Dream Catcher," and an optional project focuses on the theme of Dedication.

Variety of Activity Types

Each chapter contains a variety of activity types that feature different student combinations and communicative objectives. For example, Activity 1 features a brainstorming activity to be done as a class, while Activity 2 contains a group survey in which students collect and synthesize information.

Conversation Book 4 often features a logical progression of activities. For example, a partner interview about waiting in Activity 3 is followed by an analysis of interview responses in Activity 4. This organization reinforces important concepts and vocabulary and provides an additional opportunity to discuss various issues evolving from each theme.

Activities such as discussions and opinion surveys invite students to share personal experiences and opinions as they relate to the themes from the video story. In Activity 5, students discuss their ideas about the importance of education.

EPISODE 42

THEMES
- Waiting
- The Importance of Education
- An Audition

SONG
- Dream Catcher

OPTIONAL PROJECT
- Dedication (Appendix 6)

The Audition

THEME Waiting

1 CLASS — BRAINSTORM

In this episode, Rebecca and Bill have to wait a long time for an audition. As a class, think of a list of eight common situations in which people wait. Use the pictures to get some ideas. Write your list below the pictures. (You will use the boxes in Activity 2.)

1. _____ 5. _____
2. _____ 6. _____
3. _____ 7. _____
4. _____ 8. _____

2 GROUP — SURVEY   group number ___

Find out when the members of your group hate to wait the most.
A. Divide into groups. Look at the list of situations from Activity 1.
B. Ask this question: *When do you really hate to wait?* Each person can vote for only three situations. Count the votes for each situation and write the number in the boxes in Activity 1.
C. Compare your group's answers with those of other groups. Are the answers alike? When do your classmates really hate to wait?

EPISODE 42 PAGE 1

---

3 PARTNER — INTERVIEW   partner's name ___

How long would you wait for certain things? Write the times in the chart. Then, ask your partner the questions and write his/her times.

How long would you wait...	TIME You	Your partner
to get a table in a restaurant?		
to buy a ticket for a concert?		
to buy something on sale?		
for a job interview?		
for an appointment with a friend?		
for an appointment with a doctor?		

4 CLASS — DATA ANALYSIS

As a class, tell the teacher your times from Activity 3. The teacher will write the numbers on the board. Find the average waiting time for the class for each item. Then, answer these questions:
- For how many items are you above the class average?
- For how many items are you below the class average?

As a class, discuss this question: *Are you surprised by how long people wait for things?*

THEME The Importance of Education

5 CLASS — DISCUSSION

School is very important to Rebecca. How important do you think school is? Read the following sentences. Check (✓) *I agree* or *I disagree*. Discuss your answers with the class.

	I agree	I disagree
1. Education is necessary to be successful.		
2. Education is helpful to be successful.		
3. Education doesn't help people be successful.		
4. You have to go to an expensive school to get a good education.		
5. You have to go to school to get an education.		
6. It's possible to have too much education.		

EPISODE 42 PAGE 2

Activity bars identify the start of each numbered activity and indicate whether the activity is designed for pairs, groups, teams, or whole-class participation. Descriptors such as **Discussion**, **Interview**, or **Role-Play** alert teachers to the type of activity that follows.

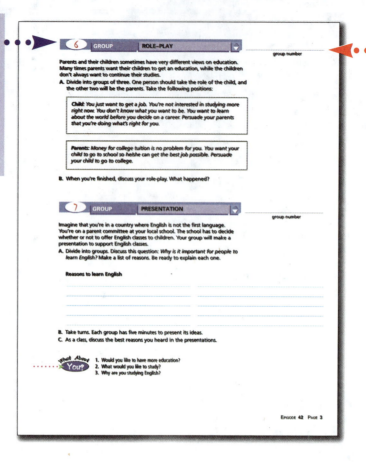

Spaces that allow students to indicate partner name, group number, and team number make it easier for students and teachers to keep track of student collaborations. Group and team numbers also are useful when different student groups are asked to compare and contrast survey or discussion results with one another.

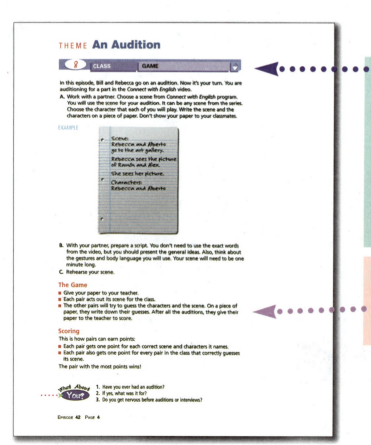

Multilevel Activities

Special icons are used to show the difficulty level of each activity in the book. These icons are designed to help teachers tailor the activities to the needs of a multilevel group of students. An arrow pointing up △ indicates that the difficulty of an activity can be increased, while an arrow pointing down ▽ indicates that an activity can be simplified for lower-level students. Arrows pointing in both directions ◇ indicate that the activity can be adjusted in either direction. Detailed teaching suggestions for how to change the level of each activity in *Conversation Book 4* are included in the accompanying Instructor's Manual.

This interactive game based on the concept of auditions simultaneously encourages communication among pairs of students and the larger class, and also serves to be a timely review of previous events from the *Connect with English* story.

A VISUAL TOUR viii

Two-Page Activity

Each episode contains an extended theme which is covered in a longer, two-page activity. These themes are developed into games, information gaps, or activities based on songs from the *Connect with English* soundtrack.

Rebecca's song "Dream Catcher" provides the basis for this two-page activity. In all activities involving songs from the *Connect with English* soundtrack, the lyrics are presented to the students for purposes of review and discussion.

Comprehension and interpretation questions bring students close to the content of the song lyrics, and prepare them for subsequent activities.

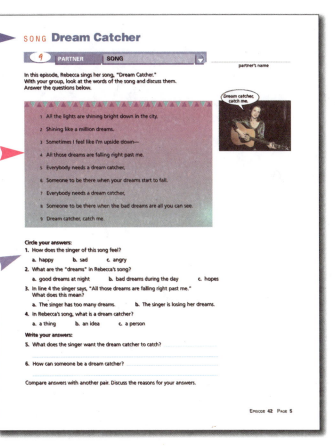

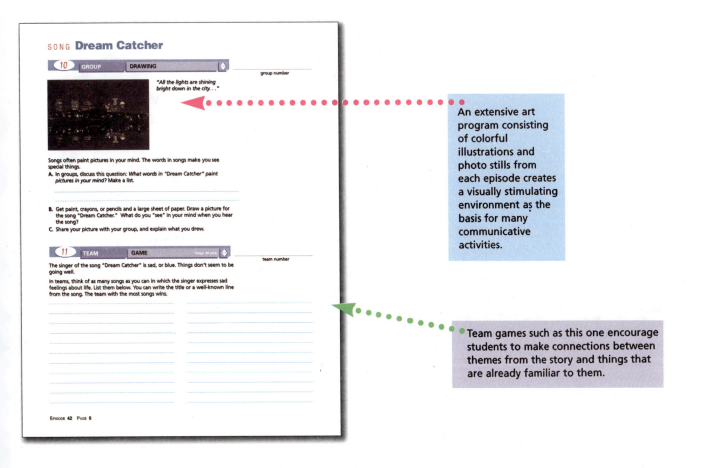

An extensive art program consisting of colorful illustrations and photo stills from each episode creates a visually stimulating environment as the basis for many communicative activities.

Team games such as this one encourage students to make connections between themes from the story and things that are already familiar to them.

A VISUAL TOUR ix

Project Page

Optional project pages correspond to each episode and are found in appendices located at the back of the book. Project pages contain research-oriented activities or community surveys and polls based on important themes from each episode. These projects reinforce the communicative nature of the *Conversation Books* and invite students to expand their learning and conversation to areas beyond the classroom environment.

Project pages throughout the *Conversation Books* encourage students to use a variety of research tools, including books, encyclopedias, newspapers, magazines, almanacs, and the Internet.

On this project page, students are invited to research the lives of well-known people who were dedicated to a certain cause or field of study. Many times, students will be asked to make a class presentation, which serves the dual purpose of solidifying their own knowledge of the material and successfully communicating it to their classmates.

What About You? activities provide open-ended questions that encourage students to express their personal feelings and opinions as they relate to the themes from the story. These activities create a springboard for more sophisticated discussions among students who are at higher levels of oral proficiency. **What About You?** activities can also be used as optional writing assignments.

EPISODE **42**

PROJECT **Dedication**

1 | PARTNER | RESEARCH

partner's name

"Right now, it's got to be my music... and my music alone."

Rebecca is dedicated to her music. She will do anything necessary to be a songwriter and performer.

A. Work with a partner. Choose any dedicated person in the history of the world. This person can be alive or dead, famous or not famous. Here are some examples:

Nelson Mandela   Louis Pasteur
Dian Fossey   Maria Taglioni
Leo Tolstoy   Mahatma Gandhi
Katharine Hepburn   Elizabeth Cady Stanton
Simón Bolívar

B. Complete the information below. You can use your school library, a biographical dictionary, an encyclopedia, the Internet, and so on.

Name of the dedicated person _____

Where the person was/is from _____

What the person was dedicated to _____

What the person accomplished _____

C. Present the information to the class. Show a picture of the person if possible.

What About you?
1. If you could meet one of the people from Activity 1, who would it be?
2. Why would you want to meet this person?
3. What are you dedicated to?
4. What have you accomplished?

APPENDIX 6 EPISODE 42 PROJECT

Thanksgiving

EPISODE 37

THEMES
- Family Holidays
- Family Secrets
- Thanksgiving Day

GAME
- Thanksgiving Football

OPTIONAL PROJECT
- Computer Classes (Appendix 1)

THEME Family Holidays

 CLASS BRAINSTORM

cook

play games

sing

Look at the photos above. They show things the Casey family did on Thanksgiving. As a class, make a list of things families do on holidays. Think about the Casey family. Think about your family. For example, do you tell family stories? Do you talk about the past? Your teacher will write your list on the board.

 PARTNER INTERVIEW

_____
partner's name

A. Write five things your family does on holidays. Use the list from Activity 1 for ideas.

B. Interview your partner. Ask your partner this question: *What does your family do for family holidays?*

C. Write your partner's answers. How many of your answers are the same?

Your answers

1. _____
2. _____
3. _____
4. _____
5. _____

Your partner's answers

1. _____
2. _____
3. _____
4. _____
5. _____

3 GROUP DISCUSSION

group number

Uncle Tim

The family members below are coming to your house for a holiday dinner.

A. Read the descriptions of each person.

B. With your group, discuss where each person should sit at the table above. Write each person's name next to a chair at the table. One name is done for you. *Note: There is more than one way to seat people around the table.*

Dad:	He smokes.
Uncle Tim:	He wants to sit at one end of the table.
Aunt Betty:	She wants to sit across from Jane.
Grandpa Joe:	He doesn't like little children.
Cousin Jane:	She doesn't like smoke.
Cousin Peter:	He is seven years old.
Mom:	She doesn't like Aunt Betty.
You:	You want to sit next to Peter.

C. When you've finished, compare your answers with those of other groups. Do your tables look the same? Talk about which table is the best.

1. What holidays do you and your family celebrate together?
2. Do you usually cook something for family holidays?
3. How are family holidays like other parties? How are they different?
4. Do you ever travel far for family holidays?

THEME Family Secrets

4 PARTNER — ROLE-PLAY

partner's name

In this episode, Rebecca learns a family secret.

With a partner, write a dialogue for one of the following situations. Practice the dialogue. Then, present it to the class.

Situations

- At your family house, you find an old picture of your mother. In the picture, your mother is kissing a man. The man is not your father. You ask about it.
- Your father has lived in the same house for 20 years. You have never seen him go down to the basement. You think this is very strange. One day, you ask him about it.
- Your sister buys an expensive new car. The next week, she rents a nice apartment. You don't understand where the money is coming from. You ask her about it.
- Your mother never talks about her parents. One day, you ask her about them.

Why didn't you and my father talk for so many years? What happened?

THEME Thanksgiving Day

5 PARTNER — MAKING GUESSES

partner's name

Thanksgiving Day celebrates an important event in the history of the United States. Make guesses about the dates and times of the historical events below. Use the clues in the box. You will read a story in Activity 6 and see how close your guesses are.

	Your guess	Actual date	Difference
1. When was the first Thanksgiving?			
2. When was the first national day of thanksgiving in the United States?			
3. When did Thanksgiving become an official holiday?			
4. When did the day of Thanksgiving become the fourth Thursday in November?			
		Total difference:	

CLUES

▶ George Washington, the first president of the United States, called for the first national day of prayer and thanksgiving.

▶ Because of Franklin Roosevelt, Thanksgiving is always on a Thursday. He was president during the bad economic times of the 1930s.

▶ The Pilgrims celebrated the first Thanksgiving. They came to the new land in 1620.

▶ President Abraham Lincoln made Thanksgiving an official holiday. He lived during the 1800s.

6 PARTNER STORYTELLING

partner's name

A. Read the following story.

The Story of Thanksgiving

In 1620, a group of people from Europe arrived in what is now Massachusetts. They wanted to make a home in this new land. These people were called Pilgrims. They were the first people who spoke English to come and stay in what is now the United States.

The Pilgrims had a long, hard journey across the Atlantic Ocean. There were 102 people on a small ship. It took 65 days for the ship to cross the sea.

When they arrived, they had an even worse time. It was winter. Many of the Pilgrims died before the spring.

The Pilgrims had to learn how to live in the new land. They got help from a group of Native Americans called the Wampanoags. These Native Americans taught the Pilgrims how to hunt, fish, and grow food. A Native American named Squanto was very helpful to the Pilgrims. He spoke some English!

That first year, the Pilgrims grew a lot of food, and they were thankful. So, in 1621, the Pilgrims celebrated the first Thanksgiving with the Wampanoags. It was a celebration of the food and of their success. They had a feast with turkey, corn, beans, and other foods.

Over 150 years later, George Washington, the first president of the United States, decided to made November 26, 1789, a day of thanksgiving and prayer. It was first national day of thanksgiving. In 1863, President Abraham Lincoln made Thanksgiving an official national holiday. It was to be celebrated every year in November. Finally, in 1939, President Franklin Roosevelt changed Thanksgiving Day to the fourth Thursday of November.

B. Retell the story to your partner from Activity 5. Do not look back at the story. Try to tell the important events. Also tell the most interesting fact you learned.

C. Your partner will retell the story to you. Check (✔) the information that he/she says.
- ❏ who the Pilgrims were
- ❏ what the Pilgrims learned from the Native Americans
- ❏ why the Pilgrims wanted to celebrate
- ❏ what they did to celebrate
- ❏ when Thanksgiving became an official holiday

D. Go back to Activity 5. Fill in the correct dates. Find the difference between your guesses and the real dates. Then, find the total difference.
Finally, compare your answers with those of other pairs. Which pair has the smallest total difference?

1. Is there a holiday of thanksgiving in your country?
2. If there is, what do people do on the thanksgiving day?
3. What is an important event in the history of your country? Tell the story.
4. What are you most thankful for?

EPISODE 37 PAGE 4

GAME Thanksgiving Football

   | TEAM | GAME |

team letter

The American version of football is one of the most popular sports in the United States. On Thanksgiving Day, there are many football games on television. In football, two teams move up and down a field. One team moves toward one side of the field, the other team moves to the other side. When a team comes to the end of the field (crosses the goal), it scores (makes a touchdown). The field is divided into yards. (A yard is about 1 meter.)

In this game, your team moves up and down the field when it answers questions correctly.

Get Ready to Play

Step One

Divide into two teams. One is team A and the other is team B. Each team will write 20 questions about the *Connect with English* story. Write each question on a separate piece of paper. After each question, write 10, 20, or 30 in parentheses ( ). These are the number of yards a team will move when it answers the question.

About this episode:

- What is one food the Casey family eats on Thanksgiving? (20)
- What is the game Kevin and the girls play outside on Thanksgiving? (10)

About the story:

- What is the name of Rebecca's school? (20)
- What is Alberto's job? (30)

Step Two

Give your questions to your teacher. He/she will read the questions and check them over. Your teacher will also write some questions about the story.

Play the Game

- Each team uses a different coin as a marker. Place them at the 50-yard line. Flip a coin to see which team starts.
- The teacher picks a question at random and reads it to the team. If a team answers correctly, it moves its coin toward its goal line. The coin should be moved forward the number of yards written on the card.
- If a team answers incorrectly, it moves its coin *away* from its goal line. The coin should be moved backward the number of yards written on the card. *Note: Team A moves toward Team A's goal line. Team B moves toward Team B's goal line.*

EXAMPLE

What is the name of Rebecca's school? (20)

If a team answers this question correctly, it moves its coin 20 yards toward its goal line. If a team doesn't answer this question correctly, it moves its coin 20 yards away from its goal line.

- Each team has a chance to answer three questions on every turn.
- Every time a team gets to the goal line, it scores a touchdown. Then the team starts over again at the 50-yard line. If a team doesn't score a touchdown on its turn, it starts over again at the 50-yard line on its next turn.
- The first team to score three touchdowns wins!

GAME **Thanksgiving Football**

Starting Over

EPISODE 38

THEMES
- Christmas Bonuses
- Giving Advice
- Losing a Job

INFORMATION GAP
- Decorating a Christmas Tree

OPTIONAL PROJECT
- Sports for Children (Appendix 2)

THEME Christmas Bonuses

1 GROUP SURVEY

group number _____

In this episode, Alberto receives a Christmas bonus. His boss gives him two opera tickets.

A. Write your name in the first line of the chart. Next to your name, write the Christmas bonus that you would like to get. You can use the ideas below, or some of your own.

Kinds of Christmas Bonuses
- tickets to a sports game or a concert
- a basket of food
- a gift certificate for a store or a restaurant
- a day off
- money

B. Divide into groups. Ask your group members this question:
What Christmas bonus would you like to get? Write their answers in the chart.

Name	What Christmas bonus would you like to get?
You:	
1.	
2.	
3.	
4.	
5.	
6.	

EPISODE 38 PAGE 1

2 GROUP COMPARISON

_____
group number

Join another group. Compare your answers from Activity 1.

A. Count the total number of people who chose each of these Christmas bonuses. Write the number in the spaces below.

_____ tickets to a sports game or a concert

_____ a basket of food

_____ a gift certificate for a store or a restaurant

_____ a day off

_____ money

Which is the most popular answer? _____

B. List three other ideas for Christmas bonuses.

1. _____
2. _____
3. _____

C. How many people in your group have ever gotten a Christmas bonus? _____

3 GROUP DISCUSSION

_____
group number

Divide into groups. Your group is the board of directors for a company. Your company has had a good year. You are having a meeting about Christmas bonuses for the employees of your company. Discuss and answer the questions below. When your group finishes, present your answers to the class. Explain your decisions.

1. Which employees will get Christmas bonuses? Check (✔) your answer.

   _____ only full-time employees who did great work this year

   _____ all full-time employees

   _____ all full-time and part-time employees

   _____ only full-time and part-time employees who did great work this year

   _____ Nobody will get bonuses.

2. What kind of bonus will you give your employees? Check (✔) your answer.

   _____ money

   _____ a gift (tickets to the opera, for example)

   _____ money and a gift

3. If you give money, how much will you give to each person? _____
4. If you give a gift, what will it be? _____

THEME Giving Advice

 4 PARTNER — WAYS TO SAY IT

partner's name

In this episode, Rebecca needs to start over in San Francisco. She needs to go back to school and work. Nancy gives Rebecca advice.
Here are some ways that people give advice:

> **You should** get more rest.
>
> **If I were you, I'd** go to bed.
>
> **You ought to** get a job.
>
> **Why don't you** apply for a scholarship?

Work with a partner. Look at the situations below. Take turns. One person chooses a situation. The other person gives some advice. Then, make up your own situation.

EXAMPLE Student A: I have a headache.   Student B: You should take some aspirin.

Situations   **Expressions**

1. I need money for a college course.   _____
2. I have a bad cold.   _____
3. My wallet was stolen.   _____
4. I feel very stressed and anxious.   _____
5. Your situation: _____

 5 GROUP — DISCUSSION

group number

A. Divide into groups. Read the following information about Harry. Talk about his problems. Decide what advice to give him. Write your ideas on a separate piece of paper.

This is Harry. He's a very nice guy, but his life is a mess. Here are some of Harry's problems:
- He hates his job, but he needs money.
- His roommate got married and moved out. Now Harry is paying all the rent for a two-bedroom apartment.
- He thinks his girlfriend is in love with another man.
- His brother borrowed his car last week. He hasn't brought it back.

B. Join another group. Compare your advice for Harry. Discuss what is best for Harry to do.

1. When was the last time you asked someone for advice? What was it about?
2. Who do you usually ask for advice? Why do you ask that person?
3. Do you like to give advice?

THEME Losing a Job

6 GROUP DEBATE

group number

In this episode, Rebecca learns she has lost her job. Rebecca was away from work because of her father's death, so her boss hired a new person. Did Rebecca's boss do the right thing?

A. Your teacher will divide the class into three groups. Groups 1 and 2 will debate. Group 3 decides the winner of the debate.

B. Read the directions for each group.

> **Group 1**
> **Your position:** *People can't expect their employers to give them time off for family problems.* Talk about the reasons for this position. Write them down. Prepare to present your reasons.

> **Group 2**
> **Your position:** *Employees shouldn't lose their jobs because they need time off for family problems. Laws should protect them.* Talk about the reasons for your position. Write them down. Prepare to present your reasons.

> **Group 3**
> During the debate, take notes on good ideas. After the debate, choose the winner. Decide: *Which team presented the best ideas?*

C. Groups 1 and 2 take turns presenting their positions. Then Group 3 meets to decide which group gave the best presentation. Group 3 announces its decision.

D. The whole class votes on this question: *Do you agree with Position 1 or Position 2?*

7 PARTNER DISCUSSION

partner's name

Rebecca has lost her job. She needs to find a new one. Which of the jobs above do you think would be best for her?

A. Work with a partner. Discuss the three jobs. Look at all of the information in each advertisement. Decide which job would be best for Rebecca. Be ready to give your reasons to the class.

B. Write the number of the best job. _____

C. As a class, discuss the good and bad points of each job. Take a class vote: *Which job would be best for Rebecca: 1, 2, or 3?*

INFORMATION GAP Decorating a Christmas Tree

8 PARTNER — **INFORMATION GAP**

STUDENT A — Work with a partner. One of you works on this page. The other works on page 6. Don't look at your partner's page.

partner's name

Nancy Shaw decorates her Christmas tree in the same way every year. First, she puts on lights. Then, she hangs ornaments. These ornaments have been in her family for a long time.

You can see some of the ornaments on the tree in the picture below. Your partner has more ornaments in his/her picture of the tree. Make your trees match. *Note: You can see all the kinds of ornaments in the small pictures below. Some ornaments are on the tree in two places.*

A. Tell your partner what you can see hanging on the tree. For example, say: *In the first row of ornaments, there is a candy cane on the right.*

B. Find out what's missing. For example, ask, *What's next to the candy cane?* Write the names of the missing ornaments in the right places.

C. When you're finished, compare trees with your partner. Are they the same?

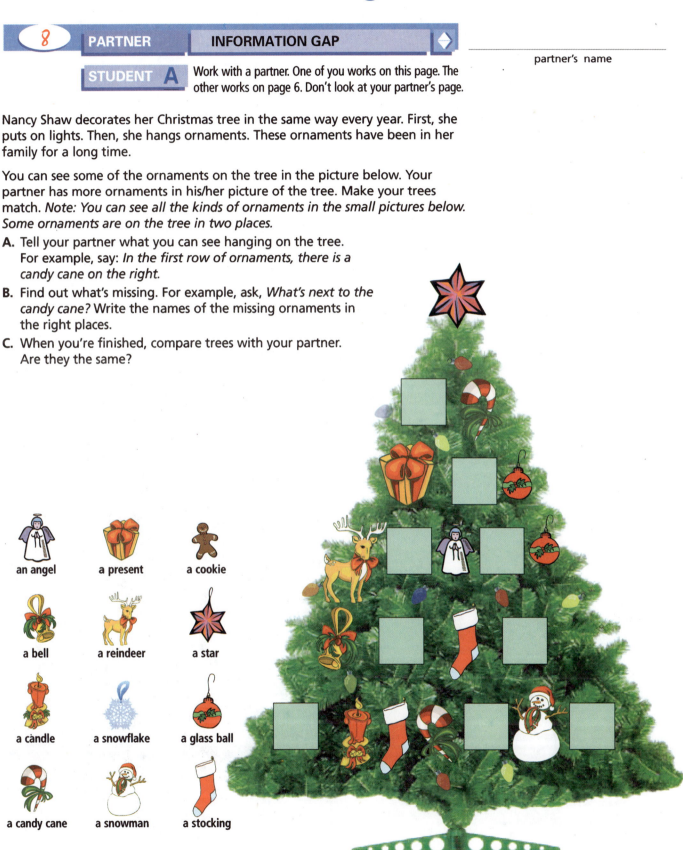

an angel · a present · a cookie
a bell · a reindeer · a star
a candle · a snowflake · a glass ball
a candy cane · a snowman · a stocking

EPISODE **38** PAGE **5**

INFORMATION GAP Decorating a Christmas Tree

8 PARTNER INFORMATION GAP

STUDENT B Work with a partner. One of you works on this page. The other works on page 5. Don't look at your partner's page.

partner's name

Nancy Shaw decorates her Christmas tree in the same way every year. First, she puts on lights. Then, she hangs ornaments. These ornaments have been in her family for a long time.

You can see some of the ornaments on the tree in the picture below. Your partner has more ornaments in his/her picture of the tree. Make your trees match. *Note: You can see all the kinds of ornaments in the small pictures below. Some ornaments are on the tree in two places.*

A. Tell your partner what you can see hanging on the tree. For example, say: *On the bottom row of ornaments, there is a reindeer on the right.*

B. Find out what's missing. For example, ask, *What's next to the reindeer?* Write the names of the missing ornaments in the right places.

C. When you're finished, compare trees with your partner. Are they the same?

an angel — a present — a cookie
a bell — a reindeer — a star
a candle — a snowflake — a glass ball
a candy cane — a snowman — a stocking

EPISODE 38 PAGE 6

The Pressure's On

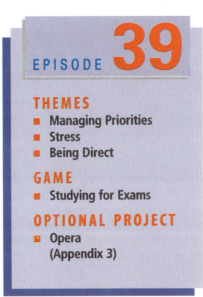

EPISODE 39

THEMES
- Managing Priorities
- Stress
- Being Direct

GAME
- Studying for Exams

OPTIONAL PROJECT
- Opera (Appendix 3)

THEME Managing Priorities

1 GROUP DISCUSSION

_____
group number

In this episode, Rebecca has too much to do. She must *manage her priorities*, and decide what things she must do first. Help Rebecca manage her priorities for one evening.

A. Divide into groups. Read the situation.

Situation

It's Tuesday night. Rebecca has a big final exam tomorrow. She knows that she needs to study three hours for it. She has to look over her notes from class. Also, she wants to get to bed by 11 o'clock. She doesn't want to feel tired during the exam tomorrow morning.
Things Rebecca has to do on Tuesday nights: ■ do the laundry ■ write her brother a letter ■ help Nancy clean the kitchen ■ practice the guitar ■ pay bills
When Rebecca arrives home from school at 4 o'clock, she finds these things: ■ a note from Nancy: It says that the rent is due today.　■ a message from an old friend: She's visiting San Francisco for only one night. She's at a hotel waiting for Rebecca's call. ■ a message from Alberto: He wants Rebecca to go to a party tonight.

B. Discuss the situation. What things should Rebecca do on Tuesday night? Decide on her *priorities*. Make a list, with number 1 as the most important thing.

1. _____   4. _____
2. _____   5. _____
3. _____   6. _____

C. What should Rebecca do about the things that aren't on the list in Part B? For example, if she isn't able to go to the party, should she call Alberto and tell him? Discuss your ideas with the group.

1. Are you good at managing priorities? Why or why not?
2. What are your three most important priorities in life?
3. What were your three most important priorities five years ago?

EPISODE 39　PAGE 1

THEME Stress

2 PARTNER INTERVIEW

_____
partner's name

| school | politics | work | your health | your family |
| your car | money | your apartment/house | your social life | your future |

In this episode, Rebecca has a lot of stress. She has to pass her exams! Look at the list above. Circle the three things that give you the most stress and write them below. Ask your partner the question: *What three things give you the most stress?* Write your partner's answers. Are your answers alike?

Your answers
1. _____
2. _____
3. _____

Your partner's answers
1. _____
2. _____
3. _____

3 PARTNER STRESS TEST

_____
partner's name

Take the "Stress Test" below. Check (✔) *Often, Sometimes,* or *Never*. Then ask your partner the questions below, and check (✔) your partner's answers. Discuss the results.

	YOU			YOUR PARTNER		
	Often	Sometimes	Never	Often	Sometimes	Never
1. Do you feel you have too much to do?						
2. Do you worry about school or work?						
3. Do you get angry with people easily?						
4. Do you feel tired and nervous?						
5. Do you think that people expect too much of you?						

Scoring: *Often* answers are worth 2 points.
Sometimes answers are worth 1 point.
Never answers are worth 0 points.

If your score is between 0–4 points: Don't worry. You're calm.

If your score is between 5–7 points: You're in the middle. But try to take more time to relax!

If your score is 8 points or more: You're stressed. Look at Activity 4 for ways to relieve stress!

4 GROUP SURVEY

group number

A. Ask the members of your group this question: *What do you do to relieve stress?* Write their answers. Here are some ideas for ways to relieve stress: exercise, talk with friends/relatives, listen to music, watch TV, meditate, and take breaks from work.

Name	What do you do to relieve stress?

B. Share results as a class. Then, in your group, discuss these questions:
- What is the most popular way to relieve stress?
- What is the most unusual way?
- Which new way would you try?

THEME Being Direct

5 PARTNER WAYS TO SAY IT

partner's name

In this episode, Professor Thomas is *direct* with Rebecca. He tells her clearly that her exams will be difficult. Here are some ways that people are direct in English. These are ways to begin a sentence:

| To be frank,... | To be perfectly honest,... | I don't want to lie to you, but... |
| To tell you the truth,... | Truthfully,... | If you want the truth,... |

To be frank, your exams are going to be tough. Real tough.

Work with a partner. Look at the situations below. One person chooses a situation. The other person chooses an expression from the box above. Take turns. Then, make up your own situation.

EXAMPLE   Student A: Do you like my new jacket?   Student B: To be honest, I don't like it.

Situations   **Expressions**

1. Does my music bother you?   _____
2. I'm sorry I didn't meet you yesterday. Are you angry?   _____
3. I was wondering. How much money do you make?   _____
4. Do you like my new outfit?   _____
5. Your situation: _____

PARTNER DISCUSSION

partner's name

In some situations, people prefer to be direct. For example, you would be direct if you want to be very clear about how you feel. In other situations, people prefer to be indirect. You might be indirect if you want to be more careful about what you're saying. Discuss the following situations with your partner. For each case, decide if it's best to be *direct* or *indirect*. Check (✔) your answers.

DIRECT   **INDIRECT**

   1. Two friends who share an apartment

   2. A husband and a wife

   3. Hosts and their guests at a party

   4. A proud mother and her friend

1. Are you usually direct or indirect with people?
2. Is it better to be direct or indirect with people?
3. In what situations is it better to be direct?

GAME Studying for Exams

 GROUP   GAME

group number

You're studying for an exam. If you study the right way, you'll pass the exam!

Get Ready to Play

Step One
Divide into groups of two to four players. Each group needs a coin.

Step Two
Each player will make at least six game cards. Game cards look like these:

 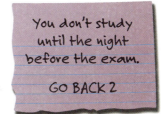 

Each game card should have either a good or a bad way to study. Good ways to study should say GO AHEAD. Bad ways to study should say GO BACK. Make each card for one or two spaces. You can work alone or with others to make the game cards. Here are some ideas:

Good Ways to Study
- You study a few hours every day before the test.
- You work with a classmate, and ask each other questions.
- You make a list of important words and their meanings.

Bad Ways to Study
- You stay up all night before the test.
- You lose your notes.
- You drink four cups of coffee the night before the exam and can't sleep.

Step Three
Make sure no two game cards are exactly the same. Shuffle the game cards and put them in a pile face down on the table. Turn to the game board on page 6. Cut out the markers on Appendix 13. Put your marker on START.

Play the Game
- Decide who will go first. That player tosses the coin. If it lands heads up, the player moves ahead one space. If it lands tails up, the player moves ahead two spaces.
- If there's something written on the space where you land, read the words aloud. Follow the directions. You may have to move ahead, move back, or draw a card.
- If you draw a card, read it aloud. Follow the directions on the card. You can draw only one card on each turn.
- If the card tells you to move AHEAD or BACK to a space, move your marker and stay there. Don't follow the directions on that space. Wait for your next turn.
- If you land on a FREE space, stay there, and wait for your next turn.
- The next player tosses the coin, and play continues. The first person to reach YOU PASSED! passes the exam and wins the game.

GAME Studying for Exams

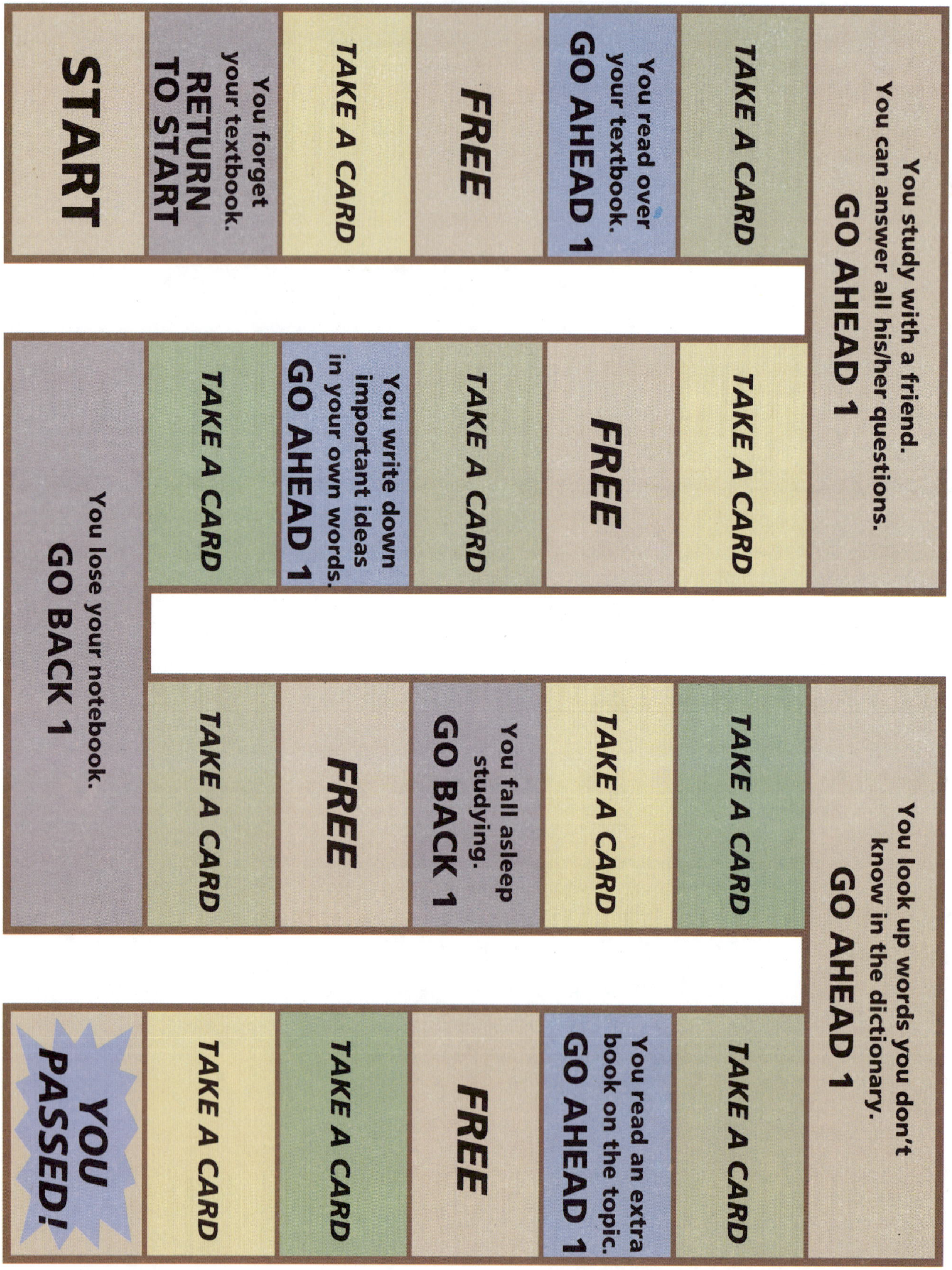

START

You forget your textbook. **RETURN TO START**

TAKE A CARD

FREE

You read over your textbook. **GO AHEAD 1**

TAKE A CARD

You study with a friend. You can answer all his/her questions. **GO AHEAD 1**

TAKE A CARD

FREE

You write down important ideas in your own words. **GO AHEAD 1**

TAKE A CARD

You lose your notebook. **GO BACK 1**

TAKE A CARD

FREE

You fall asleep studying. **GO BACK 1**

TAKE A CARD

TAKE A CARD

You look up words you don't know in the dictionary. **GO AHEAD 1**

TAKE A CARD

You read an extra book on the topic. **GO AHEAD 1**

FREE

TAKE A CARD

TAKE A CARD

YOU PASSED!

EPISODE 39 PAGE 6

Sharing Feelings

THEMES
- Things That Are Important to You
- Being Patient or Impatient
- Making Money

INFORMATION GAP
- Rock and Roll Music

OPTIONAL PROJECT
- Using the Library (Appendix 4)

THEME Things That Are Important to You

1 GROUP RANKING

People have different ideas about what's important in life.

A. First, work on your own. What's important to you? Rank the items on the list below. Write 1 for most important and 10 for least important.

____ having a nice house

____ getting a college education or a graduate school education

____ having a family

____ being rich

____ having lots of friends

____ traveling to many different countries

____ having an important job

____ doing good things for the community

____ being famous

____ doing lots of interesting things (crafts, music, sports, and so on) in your free time

B. Share your lists in groups. Answer these questions:

■ *Are there any items in the top three on everyone's list?* List them.

_____

_____

■ *Are there any items in the bottom three on everyone's list?* List them.

_____

_____

_____

group number

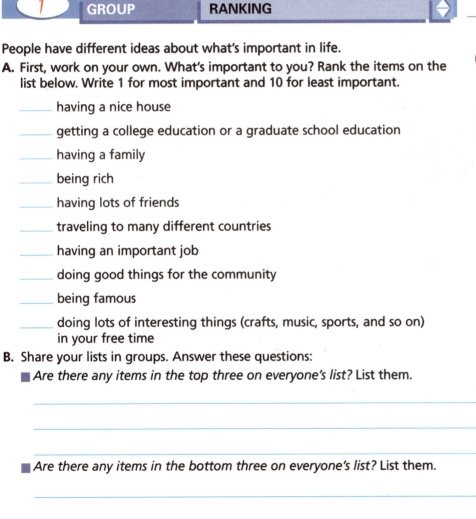

2 PARTNER INTERVIEW

partner's name

A. Are there any items you'd like to add to the list in Activity 1? Write three ideas on the lines below.
B. Interview your partner. Ask this question: *What other things are important to you in life?*
C. Write your partner's ideas. Did any of your partner's answers surprise you?

Your ideas	Your partner's ideas
1.	1.
2.	2.
3.	3.

THEME Being Patient or Impatient

3 CLASS BRAINSTORM

In what situations are you impatient? Are you impatient when you wait in line? Are you impatient in traffic? Are you impatient when you try to learn new things?

As a class, make a list of some situations when people are impatient. Write your answers on a separate piece of paper. Your teacher will write a "master list" on the board.

4 GROUP SURVEY

group number

A. Divide into groups.
B. Ask the people in your group this question: *In what situation are you the most impatient?* Write their answers. Use the list from Activity 3 or your own ideas.

Name	In what situation are you the most impatient?
1.	
2.	
3.	
4.	

5 GROUP DISCUSSION

group number

In many cultures, it's a good thing to be patient. Do you think it's ever good to be impatient? For example, is it good to be impatient in a store? Is it good to be impatient with family or friends? Is it good to be impatient in an emergency?

A. Divide into groups. Make a list of three times when it's good to be patient, and three times when it's good to be impatient.

B. Share your lists with another group.

Times to be patient
1. _____
2. _____
3. _____

Times to be impatient
1. _____
2. _____
3. _____

1. Are you a patient or impatient person?
2. What's better in your country, being patient or impatient?
3. Can you learn to be more patient? If so, how?

THEME Making Money

6 PARTNER BRAINSTORM

partner's name

Most people would like to make money, but they don't always know how to do it. Work with your partner to think of at least three ways for people to make money. Write your ideas below. Give details! Don't just say, "Open a business." Tell the kind of business. Don't just say, "Invent something." Tell the kind of invention.

_____
_____
_____
_____
_____
_____
_____
_____
_____

A Business

An Investment

An Invention

| 7 | TEAM | GAME | Time: 15 min. |

_____
team number

How much money is a good idea worth? This auction game will help you find out.

A. Work with your partner from Activity 6. Form teams with one or two other pairs. Decide on the five best ideas that your team had in Activity 6.

B. Write your team number and your ideas on a large piece of paper. Post your paper on a wall in your classroom.

C. In this game, your team and other teams will offer money for the ideas on the walls. These offers of money are called "bids."

The Game

Your team will win if it is the team with the most money at the end of the game. This is how your team will earn money:

> ■ Your team gets all the money that the other teams bid on your ideas.
> ■ Your team gets all the money it offers for an idea, but only if your team's bid was the *highest*.

Your team has $600 to spend on three good ideas from other teams. You can't bid on any ideas from your own team's paper. Remember: Your team needs to spend more than other teams in order to get the best ideas.

■ Read each paper on the wall. With your team, decide which three ideas to bid on. Do *not* let other teams know your choices.

■ Write down the three ideas your team wants to bid on. Also write the amount of money you want to spend on each idea. Remember you can't spend more than $600 in total.

Ideas to bid on   **How much money you'll spend**

1. _____   1. _____
2. _____   2. _____
3. _____   3. _____

■ Copy your bids onto a separate piece of paper. Your teacher will collect them when the time is up. Your teacher will also figure out your team's score. Remember—your score is a combination of the following:
  ▶ the amount of money other teams paid for your ideas
  ▶ the amount of money your team spent if it was the highest bidder on an idea

The team with the most amount of money wins!

1. What's the quickest way to make money?
2. Do you need to go to college to make a lot of money?
3. Do you want to make a lot of money? Why or why not?

EPISODE 40 PAGE 4

INFORMATION GAP **Rock and Roll Music**

8	PARTNER	INFORMATION GAP	
	STUDENT A	Work with a partner. One of you works on this page. The other works on page 6. Don't look at your partner's page.	_____ partner's name

With your partner, match each CD with a music review (description).

Part One
Below you'll find the covers for three CDs. Your partner has reviews of each of these CDs. Listen to your partner read the reviews. Decide which musicians and CD titles go with which CD covers. Ask your partner to repeat information if necessary. Write your answers below.

Name of Musician/Band   **Name of Musician/Band**   **Name of Musician/Band**
_____   _____   _____

Title of CD   **Title of CD**   **Title of CD**
_____   _____   _____

Part Two
Below you'll find the reviews of the CDs on page 6. Read them to your partner. Repeat any information if necessary. Help him/her match the reviews to the CD covers and write the names.

1. Mary Douglas's new CD, *Guitar Songs*, is fantastic! The variety of songs on this CD shows her great singing and song-writing talent. The song "New York Blues" is sure to be a hit!
2. Thomas Long plays rock saxophone at its best on his new CD, *All Night Long*. Most of the songs were written by Thomas, but there also are two jazz classics.
3. In her new CD, *Close Up*, Jane Collins sings about the sad side of life. By the end of the CD, I was tired of hearing about her bad relationships and disappointments. I don't recommend this one.

INFORMATION GAP **Rock and Roll Music**

 PARTNER | **INFORMATION GAP**

STUDENT B — Work with a partner. One of you works on this page. The other works on page 5. Don't look at your partner's page.

partner's name

With your partner, match each music review (description) with a CD.

Part One

Below you'll find the reviews of the CDs on page 5. Read them to your partner. Repeat any information if necessary. Help him/her match the reviews to the CDs and write the names.

1. The Good Notes, an all-female group, has a new CD called *Where Are We Now?* These women know rock and roll! I danced to all of the songs! I especially liked "Don't Listen." It has a fantastic piano solo by María Ricardo.
2. *Drum Head* is the first CD by the Boston hard rock group the Monsters. Their music is loud and angry. If that's what you like, you'll love this one!
3. The Blue Boys have a new CD, *Back to the Past*, and that's exactly where it takes you. They play rock versions of well-known songs, using traditional instruments like the fiddle, bass, banjo, and guitar.

Part Two

Below you'll find the covers for three CDs. Your partner has reviews of each of the CDs. Listen to your partner read the reviews. Decide which musicians and CD titles go with which CD covers. Ask your partner to repeat information if necessary. Write your answers below.

Name of Musician/Band | **Name of Musician/Band** | **Name of Musician/Band**

Title of CD | **Title of CD** | **Title of CD**

EPISODE 40   PAGE 6

Unexpected Offers

EPISODE 41

THEMES
- Moving to a Different Place
- Invitations
- The Christmas Spirit

GAME
- Giving Christmas Presents

OPTIONAL PROJECT
- Vacations (Appendix 5)

THEME Moving to a Different Place

1 GROUP BRAINSTORM

group number _____

In this episode, Mr. and Mrs. Wang talk about moving to Taiwan.

When people move to a different place, what do they have to adjust to? With your group, make a list. The first two are done for you.

When you move to a different place,…

1. sometimes you have to learn a new language.
2. the food is usually different.
3. _____
4. _____
5. _____
6. _____
7. _____
8. _____

2 PARTNER INTERVIEW

partner's name _____

A. Work with a partner from your group in Activity 1. Which three items in Activity 1 do you think are most difficult to adjust to? Circle your answers in the box below.

B. Find out what your partner thinks. Say: *You move to a different place. What three things are most difficult to adjust to?* Circle your partner's answers. Are your answers similar?

You

1	2	3	4
5	6	7	8

Your partner

1	2	3	4
5	6	7	8

THEME Invitations

3 PARTNER — WAYS TO SAY IT

Ramón invites Rebecca to go with him to the community center on Christmas. Here are some ways that people extend invitations:

Would you care to dance?	How about getting a cup of coffee?
Would you like to go out for dinner?	Would you consider going to the party with me?

Here are some ways to accept or refuse invitations:

Ways to accept an invitation:	Ways to refuse an invitation:
I'd like that.	Thank you, but no.
That would be very nice.	I'm afraid I can't. Maybe another time.
Sure, sounds great.	Thank you, but I have to _____.

partner's name

"Would you consider spending Christmas with me?"

Work with a partner. Look at the situations below. Take turns. One person chooses a situation and extends an invitation. The other person accepts or refuses the invitation. Then, make up your own situation.

EXAMPLE Student A: Would you like to come to the cafeteria with us? Student B: Thank you, but I have to study.

Invite your partner to do the following:

1. study together
   Student A _____
   Student B _____
2. practice speaking English
   Student A _____
   Student B _____
3. go to a movie
   Student A _____
   Student B _____
4. get something to drink in a café
   Student A _____
   Student B _____
5. Your situation:
   Student A _____
   Student B _____

1. What was the last thing you invited somebody to do?
2. When was the last time you received an invitation?
3. Do you ever get invitations to events that you don't want to go to? If so, do you usually accept or refuse the invitation?

4 PARTNER MATCHING

partner's name

a.
Dr. and Mrs. John Baker
request the pleasure of your
company
at the marriage of their
daughter
Kathleen Louise
to Mr. Alfred Jackson
on June 20
at four o'clock
at St. John's Episcopal
Church
Springfield, Connecticut

Reception at Young Manor.
RSVP on enclosed card.

b.
Hey grads—
WE DID IT!
LET'S PARTY!
Campus Center Ballroom
Friday, May 25
from 9:00 to whenever
Music by DJ Stan the Man
Campus Center snack bar
open till midnight

c.
It's a baby shower for
Jessica
Given by
Ann and Deborah
To be held at
Ann's—98 Bridge Rd., Apt. 224
on _Sunday the 12th_ at _7:00_
RSVP _Deb 555-8741_ (home)
or _555-4200_ (work)

d.
You're invited to a birthday party!
For: DANNY
On: Saturday, Oct. 15
From: 2:00 To: 4:00
At: 24 East Park Street
RSVP by: Monday, October 10
Phone: 555-8933

e.
Luis—
There's a cookout at Jones's beach on Friday after school. Please come. Call me if you need directions.
Rosa

f.
Come to a goodbye party!
For: Marilyn and Richard Sims
On: Friday, April 25
From: 7:00 To: 10:00
At: The Clarks' House
4515 North Ashland

A. With your partner, match the invitations and the events. Write the letter of the invitation next to the event below.

B. Check (✔) the invitations to which you should R.S.V.P. (R.S.V.P. means to answer the invitation—to write or call to say whether or not you can go.)

		RSVP?			RSVP?
____	1. a birthday party	____	____	4. a wedding	____
____	2. a graduation party	____	____	5. a beach party	____
____	3. a party for a woman who is having a baby	____	____	6. a party for someone who is moving	____

1. Which of the parties above would you like to go to?
2. When do people in your country send written invitations?
3. When was the last time you sent a written invitation? What was the invitation?

EPISODE 41 PAGE 3

THEME **The Christmas Spirit**

5 CLASS DISCUSSION

In this episode, Ramón talks about bringing food to the community center for Christmas. Rebecca tells him that he has the true Christmas spirit. The expression "having the Christmas spirit" means honoring Christmas traditions. It means giving to others, both the ones you love and strangers in need.

On what other holidays do people show a spirit of giving? Discuss this as a class. Your teacher will complete a chart like the following on the board.

What is the holiday?	Who celebrates it?	How do people show the spirit of giving?
1. Christmas	Christians	In the U.S. and Canada, families and friends give gifts. People give money to the poor. People serve Christmas dinners in community centers.
2.		
3.		

6 GROUP PRESENTATION

_____
group number

At Christmas time, people give money to charities. Charities help people in different ways. But all charities need money to give help. You're going to try to help a charity raise some money.

Preparation
A. Divide into groups. Each group chooses a different kind of charity. Groups can choose from the charities below, or they can think of their own.

shelter for people without homes	shelter for battered women
community center that gives food to the poor	group that gives scholarships to music students
group that helps people in retirement homes	group that gives sports equipment to poor children

B. In your groups, think of reasons why people would give money to your charity. Make a list of all the good things the charity does.

C. Each group will make a presentation to the class. The group members will tell the class about the good things the charity does, and try to persuade the class to give money to the charity. Your group will only have three minutes to make your presentation.

Presentation
A. Each student in the class has $100 to give to the charities. You can't give the money to your own group's charity. Listen to the presentations, and decide how to spend your money.

B. On a piece of paper, write (1) the charities you want to give money to and (2) the amount of money for each charity. Give your paper to your teacher. Your teacher will tell the class which charities collected the most money.

GAME: Giving Christmas Presents

7 PARTNER GAME

_____
partner's name

It's Christmas. Many people in the United States give presents to friends and family members. The Sills, Chills, Bills, and Tills families exchange presents at Christmas every year. They put the presents under the tree. But this year the Chills baby pulled the name tags off the presents. The Chills now have to match the presents to the people. You will help them. Work with a partner. The winner is the *first pair* to match the presents correctly.

Play the Game

- Look at the presents on this page. Look at the people on page 6.
- When your teacher tells you, read the clues on Appendix 13 at the back of the book.
- Try to find the pattern: *Why do certain people get certain gifts?* Remember, you have to think fast! Hint: You will need to count!
- Write the name of the present for each person in the blanks on page 6.
- When you finish, raise your hand. Your teacher will check your answers.
- A pair wins if all the answers are correct. But the pair is out of the game if all the answers aren't correct. The game continues with the other pairs.

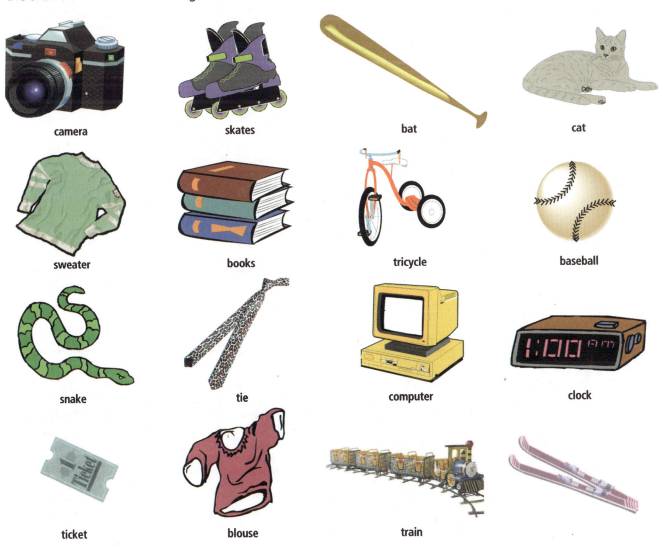

camera — skates — bat — cat
sweater — books — tricycle — baseball
snake — tie — computer — clock
ticket — blouse — train — skis

EPISODE 41 PAGE 5

GAME Giving Christmas Presents

Saul Sills

Susanna Sills

Sally Sills

Samuel Sills

Carson Chills

Cindy Chills

Caroline Chills

Cal Chills

Brian Bills

Brenda Bills

Ben Bills

Beatrice Bills

Tom Tills

Thalia Tills

Teddy Tills

Tallulah Tills

The Audition

EPISODE 42

THEMES
- Waiting
- The Importance of Education
- An Audition

SONG
- Dream Catcher

OPTIONAL PROJECT
- Dedication (Appendix 6)

THEME Waiting

1 CLASS BRAINSTORM

In this episode, Rebecca and Bill have to wait a long time for an audition. As a class, think of a list of eight common situations in which people wait. Use the pictures to get some ideas. Write your list below the pictures. (You will use the boxes in Activity 2.)

1. _____ ☐
2. _____ ☐
3. _____ ☐
4. _____ ☐
5. _____ ☐
6. _____ ☐
7. _____ ☐
8. _____ ☐

2 GROUP SURVEY

_____
group number

Find out when the members of your group hate to wait the most.

A. Divide into groups. Look at the list of situations from Activity 1.
B. Ask this question: *When do you really hate to wait?* Each person can vote for only three situations. Count the votes for each situation and write the number in the boxes in Activity 1.
C. Compare your group's answers with those of other groups. Are the answers alike? When do your classmates really hate to wait?

3 PARTNER INTERVIEW

partner's name

How long would you wait for certain things? Write the times in the chart. Then, ask your partner the questions and write his/her times.

	TIME	
How long would you wait...	You	Your partner
to get a table in a restaurant?		
to buy a ticket for a concert?		
to buy something on sale?		
for a job interview?		
for an appointment with a friend?		
for an appointment with a doctor?		

4 CLASS DATA ANALYSIS

As a class, tell the teacher your times from Activity 3. The teacher will write the numbers on the board. Find the average waiting time for the class for each item. Then, answer these questions:

- *For how many items are you above the class average?* _____
- *For how many items are you below the class average?* _____

As a class, discuss this question: *Are you surprised by how long people wait for things?*

THEME The Importance of Education

5 CLASS DISCUSSION

School is very important to Rebecca. How important do *you* think school is? Read the following sentences. Check (✔) *I agree* or *I disagree*. Discuss your answers with the class.

I've got to focus on school.

	I agree	disagree
1. Education is necessary to be successful.		
2. Education is helpful to be successful.		
3. Education doesn't help people be successful.		
4. You have to go to an expensive school to get a good education.		
5. You have to go to school to get an education.		
6. It's possible to have too much education.		

 **GROUP — ROLE-PLAY**

group number

Parents and their children sometimes have very different views on education. Many times parents want their children to get an education, while the children don't always want to continue their studies.

A. Divide into groups of three. One person should take the role of the child, and the other two will be the parents. Take the following positions:

> **Child:** *You just want to get a job. You're not interested in studying more right now. You don't know what you want to be. You want to learn about the world before you decide on a career. Persuade your parents that you're doing what's right for you.*

> **Parents:** *Money for college tuition is no problem for you. You want your child to go to school so he/she can get the best job possible. Persuade your child to go to college.*

B. When you're finished, discuss your role-play. What happened?

 **GROUP — PRESENTATION**

group number

Imagine that you're in a country where English is not the first language. You're on a parent committee at your local school. The school has to decide whether or not to offer English classes to children. Your group will make a presentation to support English classes.

A. Divide into groups. Discuss this question: *Why is it important for people to learn English?* Make a list of reasons. Be ready to explain each one.

Reasons to learn English

_____   _____
_____   _____
_____   _____
_____   _____

B. Take turns. Each group has five minutes to present its ideas.
C. As a class, discuss the best reasons you heard in the presentations.

1. Would you like to have more education?
2. What would you like to study?
3. Why are *you* studying English?

THEME **An Audition**

8   CLASS   GAME

In this episode, Bill and Rebecca go on an audition. Now it's your turn. You are auditioning for a part in the *Connect with English* video.

A. Work with a partner. Choose a scene from *Connect with English* program. You will use the scene for your audition. It can be any scene from the series. Choose the character that each of you will play. Write the scene and the characters on a piece of paper. Don't show your paper to your classmates.

EXAMPLE

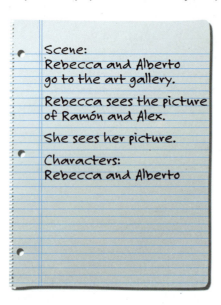

Scene:
Rebecca and Alberto go to the art gallery.

Rebecca sees the picture of Ramón and Alex.

She sees her picture.

Characters:
Rebecca and Alberto

B. With your partner, prepare a script. You don't need to use the exact words from the video, but you should present the general ideas. Also, think about the gestures and body language you will use. Your scene will need to be one minute long.

C. Rehearse your scene.

The Game

- Give your paper to your teacher.
- Each pair acts out its scene for the class.
- The other pairs will try to guess the characters and the scene. On a piece of paper, they write down their guesses. After all the auditions, they give their paper to the teacher to score.

Scoring

This is how pairs can earn points:

- Each pair gets one point for each correct scene and characters it names.
- Each pair also gets one point for every pair in the class that correctly guesses its scene.

The pair with the most points wins!

1. Have you ever had an audition?
2. If yes, what was it for?
3. Do you get nervous before auditions or interviews?

SONG Dream Catcher

9	PARTNER	SONG

partner's name

In this episode, Rebecca sings her song, "Dream Catcher."
With your group, look at the words of the song and discuss them.
Answer the questions below.

Dream catcher, catch me.

1 All the lights are shining bright down in the city,
2 Shining like a million dreams.
3 Sometimes I feel like I'm upside down—
4 All those dreams are falling right past me.
5 Everybody needs a dream catcher,
6 Someone to be there when your dreams start to fall.
7 Everybody needs a dream catcher,
8 Someone to be there when the bad dreams are all you can see.
9 Dream catcher, catch me.

Circle your answers:

1. How does the singer of this song feel?

    a. Happy.   b. Sad.   c. Angry.

2. What are the "dreams" in Rebecca's song?

    a. Good dreams at night.   b. Bad dreams during the day.   c. Hopes.

3. In line 4 the singer says, "All those dreams are falling right past me."
   What does this mean?

    a. The singer has too many dreams.   b. The singer is losing her dreams.

4. In Rebecca's song, what is a dream catcher?

    a. A thing.   b. An idea.   c. A person.

Write your answers:

5. What does the singer want the dream catcher to catch? _____

   _____

6. How can someone be a dream catcher? _____

   _____

Compare answers with another pair. Discuss the reasons for your answers.

SONG **Dream Catcher**

10 GROUP DRAWING

group number

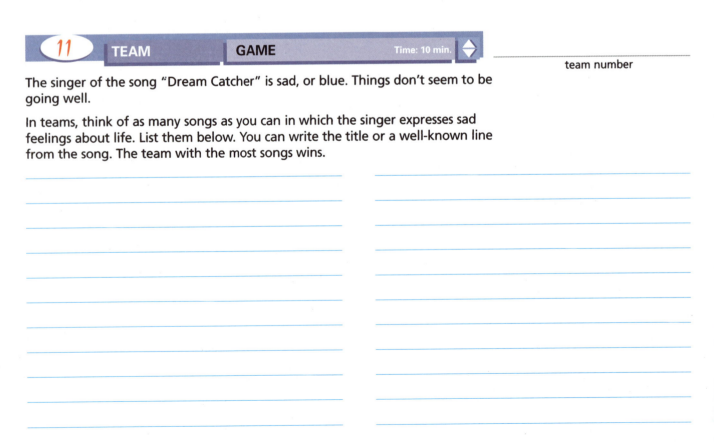

"All the lights are shining bright down in the city..."

Songs often paint pictures in your mind. The words in songs make you see special things.

A. In groups, discuss this question: *What words in "Dream Catcher" paint pictures in your mind?* Make a list.

B. Get paint, crayons, or pencils and a large sheet of paper. Draw a picture for the song "Dream Catcher." What do you "see" in your mind when you hear the song?

C. Share your picture with your group, and explain what you drew.

11 TEAM GAME Time: 10 min.

team number

The singer of the song "Dream Catcher" is sad, or blue. Things don't seem to be going well.

In teams, think of as many songs as you can in which the singer expresses sad feelings about life. List them below. You can write the title or a well-known line from the song. The team with the most songs wins.

EPISODE **42** PAGE **6**

Dream Catcher

EPISODE 43

THEMES
- Success
- Talent
  Having Confidence

INFORMATION GAP
- Taking a Message

OPTIONAL PROJECT
- Chocolates (Appendix 7)

THEME Success

 PARTNER **RANKING**

In this episode, Bill talks about success. What does "success" mean to you?

A. Look at the statements in the chart below. Decide how important each item is to your idea of success. Circle your answers.

B. Find out what your partner thinks. Ask this question: *How important is making a lot of money*? Circle your partner's answers.

```
1 = Very important
2 = Important
3 = Somewhat important
4 = Not very important
5 = Not important at all
```

partner's name

Being a success in the music business means more than just making music. It means making money.

How important is ...	You	Your partner
making a lot of money?	1 2 3 4 5	1 2 3 4 5
being famous?	1 2 3 4 5	1 2 3 4 5
living in a big house?	1 2 3 4 5	1 2 3 4 5
having an important job?	1 2 3 4 5	1 2 3 4 5
being the best at what you do?	1 2 3 4 5	1 2 3 4 5
being free to do what you like?	1 2 3 4 5	1 2 3 4 5
having a nice family?	1 2 3 4 5	1 2 3 4 5
having an expensive car?	1 2 3 4 5	1 2 3 4 5

1. Is anyone you know successful?
2. In what way is this person a success?
3. What do you think are the reasons for his or her success?
4. Would you like to have this same kind of success?

THEME Talent

2 CLASS BINGO

Who in your class has talent? Look at the squares below. You're going to try to find people with these talents.

A. Take your book and a pencil. Move around the class, and ask questions.
   For example, ask:
   ■ Are you <u>a good singer</u>?
   ■ Can you <u>swim</u>?

B. When someone says "Yes," write the person's name on the line in that square. When someone says "No," ask another question. Or you can ask someone else the same question.

C. To win, get five *different* names in a row (across, up and down, or diagonally). When you have five names, say "Bingo!" The first person to say "Bingo" is the winner.

D. The winner will do the following: Tell the class the five people and what talents they have.

_____ is a good singer.	_____ can draw.	_____ can whistle.	_____ can do gymnastics.	_____ is a good actor.
_____ can play a musical instrument.	_____ is good at math.	_____ can ride a horse.	_____ can speak languages.	_____ can tell jokes.
_____ can roller-skate.	_____ can wiggle his or her ears.	**FREE**	_____ is a good cook.	_____ can swim.
_____ can sew.	_____ can ride a bike.	_____ can repair a car.	_____ can take good pictures.	_____ can sail a boat.
_____ can do magic tricks.	_____ is good at a sport.	_____ can write computer programs.	_____ is a good dancer.	_____ can tell stories.

1. What's your best talent?
2. What talent would you like to have?
3. Is talent something a person is born with?

3 GROUP ROLE-PLAY

group number

The year is 2039. The earth is in trouble. A giant comet is going to hit the earth soon. Everyone is trying to escape to other planets.

There is room on a spaceship for one more person. The group needs a person with valuable talents.

A. You want to go on the spaceship. Try to persuade the group to take you along. On a separate piece of paper, write a list of your talents. Use the information in the box below for help.

Useful expressions:	Questions the group may ask you:
I can <u>speak two languages</u>.	Can you <u>use a computer</u>?
I am <u>strong and healthy</u>.	Are you <u>intelligent</u>?
I'm good at <u>working with others</u>.	Are you good at <u>fixing things</u>?
I'm a good <u>cook</u>.	Are you a good <u>worker</u>?
I know how to <u>fly a spaceship</u>.	Do you know how to <u>farm</u>?

B. Present your information to the group. Be ready to answer any of their questions. The group will take notes on your presentation.

C. After the presentations, talk about the most useful talents each person has. Who should be the person to get the last spot on the spaceship?

THEME Having Confidence

4 GROUP BRAINSTORM

group number

In this episode, Bill talks about his future in music. He is very confident. He also has confidence in Rebecca. Musicians need confidence to perform in front of people. Who else needs confidence?

With your group, complete the sentences below about people who need confidence. Be sure to explain why these people need confidence.

EXAMPLE	__Musicians__	need confidence because	__they perform in front of people__ .
1.	_____	need/s confidence because	_____ .
2.	_____	need/s confidence because	_____ .
3.	_____	need/s confidence because	_____ .
4.	_____	need/s confidence because	_____ .
5.	_____	need/s confidence because	_____ .

5 GROUP INTERVIEW

group number

A. Read the statements below about confidence. Are they true or false? Check (✔) your answers.

B. Divide into groups of three. How do the people in your group feel about confidence? Listen to your group members and write their answers in the chart. Ask them to explain any answers that you don't understand.

	You		Group member 1		Group member 2	
	True	False	True	False	True	False
1. Confidence is an important quality.						
2. It's better to have too little confidence than too much.						
3. Confidence helps people to succeed.						
4. Confidence comes after you are successful.						
5. Men usually have more confidence than women.						

6 TEAM GAME   Time: 10 min.

team number

Divide into teams. With your teammates, think of words or names from the *Connect with English* story that start with each of the letters below. The team with the most words wins.

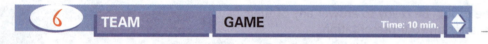

C	O	N	F	I	D	E	N	T
college	opera tickets	Nancy						

1. Are you usually a confident person?
2. In what situations do you feel most confident?
3. In what situations would you like to have more confidence?

INFORMATION GAP Taking a Message

7 PARTNER — **INFORMATION GAP**

STUDENT A Work with a partner. One of you works on this page. The other works on page 6. Don't look at your partner's page.

_____
partner's name

Part One
You're going to call a friend. Your partner will answer the phone. Your friend isn't home, so you have to leave a message.

A. Choose a name for your friend. On the phone, you'll ask to speak to him or her. Here are some ways people ask for someone on the phone:

> Hello. May I please speak to _____ ?
>   or
> Hello. This is _____ . Is _____ there?

B. Choose one of the situations below and leave this message for your friend.

> 1. You and your friend plan to see a movie. It starts at 8:00 p.m. You want him/her to meet you at 7:45 in front of the Central Square Cinema.

> 2. You want to invite your friend to a concert. It's next Saturday. You want your friend to call you back as soon as possible because you need to buy tickets.

> 3. You want your friend to pick you up at the airport. Your flight arrives next Sunday at 7:50 p.m. It's World Air flight number 2047.

Part Two
Change roles with your partner. You'll answer the phone. Your partner's friend isn't there. You will offer to take a message.

A. Here are some ways people offer to take messages:

> Would you like to leave a message?
>   or
> Can I give him/her a message?

B. Use the form at the right to write down the message.

Part Three
Show your partner the message you took in Part Two. Is it correct?

To: _____
Date: _____ Time: _____

WHILE YOU WERE OUT

Name _____
Phone _____

Message _____
_____
_____
_____
_____
_____

EPISODE 43 PAGE 5

INFORMATION GAP Taking a Message

7 PARTNER — **INFORMATION GAP**

STUDENT B Work with a partner. One of you works on this page. The other works on page 5. Don't look at your partner's page.

_____
partner's name

Part One
Your partner is going to call a friend. You answer the phone. The friend isn't there. You'll need to take a message.

A. Answer the phone. Offer to take a message. Here are some ways people offer to take messages:

> Would you like to leave a message?
>
> or
>
> Can I give him/her a message?

B. Use the form at the right to write down the message.

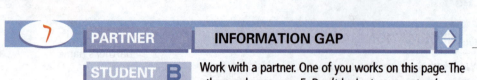

To: _____
Date: _____ Time: _____

WHILE YOU WERE OUT

Name _____
Phone _____
Message _____
_____
_____
_____
_____

Part Two
Change roles with your partner. Now you'll call a friend. Choose a name for your friend.

A. Here are some ways people ask for someone on the phone:

> Hello. May I please speak to _____?
>
> or
>
> Hello. This is _____. Is _____ there?

B. Choose one of the situations below and leave this message for your friend.

> 1. You and your friend talked about going out for dinner tonight. You want to meet at Café Brasilia at 7:15.

> 2. You want to invite your friend to a soccer game. It's next Sunday. Your friend should call you back as soon as possible.

> 3. Your friend wants to buy a bicycle. There's a big sale tomorrow at Bicycle World. It starts at 9:30 a.m.

Part Three
Show your partner the message you took in Part One. Is it correct?

Gifts

EPISODE 44

THEMES
- The Community Center
- Breaking Up
- Inspirations

GAME
- Skiing

OPTIONAL PROJECT
- Helping People in the Community (Appendix 8)

THEME **The Community Center**

1 GROUP DISCUSSION

_____
group number

In this episode, Ramón and Rebecca take food to the community center for Christmas dinner. A community center helps people in many ways.

A. You and the members of your group run a community center. Your center usually helps the community in all of the ways below. Add one more activity to the list below.

B. This year, the center doesn't have enough money to do everything. With your group, choose six of the items below for the center to do. Check (✔) your answers.

_____ give food to poor people

_____ take care of children whose parents work

_____ take care of older people who don't have anyone to help them

_____ give free medical care to poor people

_____ teach job skills and adult education classes

_____ give homeless people a place to sleep

_____ help people keep their neighborhood safe and clean

_____ hold religious services

_____ organize sports teams for neighborhood children

_____ your own idea: _____

2 CLASS POLL

Which items from the list in Activity 1 were the most popular?

A. Your teacher will copy the list from Activity 1 onto the board.

B. As your teacher reads each item, have a group leader raise his or her hand if your group checked that item.

C. Count the number of groups that put a ✔ next to each item. Your teacher will write this number on the board next to each item.

D. What were the six most popular answers?

EPISODE 44 PAGE 1

3 PARTNER PUZZLE

partner's name _____

Ramón brings food to people at the community center on Christmas. Many community centers also deliver food to people in their homes. Often the people are elderly or are too sick to leave their house.

Work with your partner. You have to deliver meals to five people in an apartment building, but the meals and the apartment numbers are mixed up. Read the clues. Match the meal to the right person. Write the letter of each meal on the correct floor.

Some of the people in the building have these special food requirements:
- One person is a vegetarian. He doesn't eat meat.
- One person can't eat sweets or cakes.
- One person won't eat beef.
- One person can't have milk products like cheese or ice cream.

The Meals
A. pizza with cheese and tomato, salad, lemonade
B. chicken, beans, cake, and coffee
C. chicken, beans, corn, tea
D. hamburger, fries, ice cream, soda
E. hamburger, fries, apple, tea

CLUES

▶ The vegetarian lives above the person who can't eat sweets. He lives below the person who can't have milk products.

▶ The person who can't eat milk products wants beef.

▶ The person who can't eat beef lives on the first floor.

▶ The person who can't eat milk products lives on the top floor.

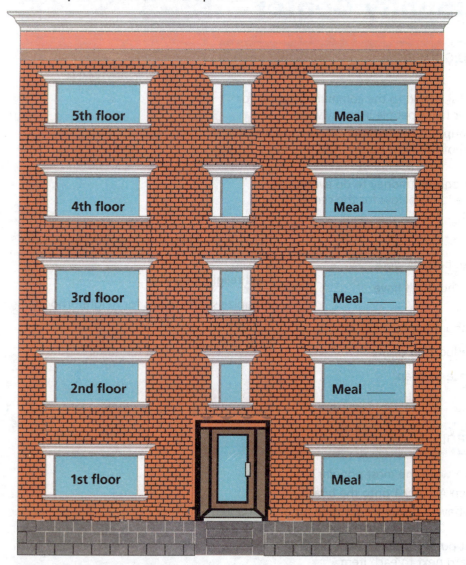

5th floor — Meal **E**
4th floor — Meal **A**
3rd floor — Meal **C**
2nd floor — Meal **D**
1st floor — Meal **B**

What About You?

1. Is there a community center close to your neighborhood? If so, where is it?
2. What services does the center offer?
3. Have you ever been to a community center? If so, what did you do there?

THEME Breaking Up

  GROUP   OPINION SURVEY

group number

In this episode, Alberto tells Rebecca that he just wants to be friends. When people break up, they often want to stay friends.

A. Circle your answers to the questions in the chart below.
B. Divide into groups. Find out how many people in your group believe it's possible to be friends after a breakup. Ask these questions:
 - Can people be friends after they break up?
 - Is it easy for people to be friends after they break up?
C. Circle your group members' answers.

Name	Sex (M/F)	Can people be friends after they break up?		Is it easy for people to be friends after they break up?	
You		Yes	No	Yes	No
1.		Yes	No	Yes	No
2.		Yes	No	Yes	No
3.		Yes	No	Yes	No
4.		Yes	No	Yes	No

  PARTNER   DATA ANALYSIS

partner's name

Work with a partner from a different group. Compare surveys from Activity 4.

1. What is the total number of *women* who answered the questions? _____
   What is the total number of *men* who answered the questions? _____
2. How many *women* thought people could be friends after a breakup? _____
   How many *men* thought people could be friends after a breakup? _____
   Who answered "Yes" to this question more often—women or men? _____
3. How many *women* thought it was easy to be friends after a breakup? _____
   How many *men* thought it was easy to be friends after a breakup? _____
   Who answered "Yes" to this question more often—women or men? _____

1. Have you ever broken up with someone?
2. If so, are you still friends with that person?
3. Do you know any people who are still friends after a breakup?
4. Why do people want to stay friends after a breakup?

THEME Inspirations

6 PARTNER WRITING

_____
partner's name

Alberto gave Rebecca a dream catcher. Rebecca told him that the dream catcher inspired her to write her song. It gave her the idea, or the *inspiration* for the song.

Inspirations can come from either people or things. For example, a good teacher might inspire you to read a book, or study a certain subject. A beautiful photograph of an island might inspire you to visit that place for a vacation.

Did a person or a thing ever "inspire" *you* to do something?

Step One
Ask your partner the questions below. They're about an inspiration. Write what your partner says.

1. What was your inspiration? Was it a person or a thing? _____

2. What did the person or thing do to inspire you? _____
3. Why was this special? _____
4. What did you do because of this inspiration? _____
5. How do you feel about this inspiration now? _____
6. Your own question: _____

Step Two
Write a short paragraph below about the inspiration that your partner described.

_____
_____
_____
_____
_____
_____
_____
_____
_____
_____
_____
_____

Step Three
When you're done writing, read what you have written to your partner. Your partner will tell you if you have understood everything correctly.

EPISODE 44 PAGE 4

GAME Skiing

| 7 | TEAM | GAME |

team number

Play this game and go skiing with Alberto. The team that hits the fewest trees wins!

Get Ready to Play

Step One
Divide into an even number of teams. The teacher will number the teams. Team 1 will play Team 2, Team 3 will play Team 4, and so on.

Step Two
With your teammates, think of five words from the *Connect with English* video. Write them below. They can be words for people, places, or things. They should be words you have discussed in class. Don't show the words to the other team.

Connect with English words:

EXAMPLE ___goggles___

1. _____ 2. _____ 3. _____ 4. _____ 5. _____

Step Three
One player from each team cuts out the trees on Appendix 13. Each team will cut out and use the game board on page 6. Now you're ready to play.

Play the Game

- On a piece of paper or the board, the other team will write spaces for each letter of their first word.

  EXAMPLE For goggles, they would write: ___ ___ ___ ___ ___ ___ ___

- Try to guess the letters in the other team's word.
- If you guess a letter that *isn't* in the word, put a tree in front of your skier on your team's gameboard. Then, guess another letter.
- If your team guesses a letter that *is* in the word, the other team will write the letter in the correct space (or spaces).

  EXAMPLE For goggles, if you guess the letter E, they will write:
  ___ ___ ___ ___ ___ E ___

- Continue to guess letters. When you know the whole word, guess it!
- If your team guesses the wrong word, put TWO trees in front of your skier. You can continue to guess letters or words.
- If you guess the correct word, your turn is finished. Don't remove your trees from the gameboard yet!
- Change roles. Now, the other team tries to guess one of your words. Your team will write the spaces for the letters that the other team will guess.
- After each team has had a turn at guessing a word, count the number of trees in front each team's skier. The team with the fewest trees wins the round. Record the winner in the chart on page 6. Remove the trees and play another round. Play five rounds in all.

GAME Skiing

Which team won the most rounds?

Round 1 _____

Round 2 _____

Round 3 _____

Round 4 _____

Round 5 _____

True Love

EPISODE 45

THEMES
- An Ekeko
- Exchanging Christmas Presents
- Falling in Love

INFORMATION GAP
- Planning a Trip

OPTIONAL PROJECT
- Legends (Appendix 9)

THEME An Ekeko

 PARTNER INTERVIEW

In this episode, Ramón gives Rebecca an ekeko. According to an old Peruvian legend, if you hang your dreams on the ekeko, they will come true. Ramón hangs an item on the ekeko for each of Rebecca's dreams.

A. Now it's your turn. Work with a partner. What three items would you put on *your* ekeko? You can choose any of the items below, or you can think of others. In the chart, write the names of the items and what they mean to you.

B. Then, interview your partner. Ask your partner these questions:
- *What items would you put on your ekeko?*
- *Why would you put a diploma on the ekeko? What does it mean to you?*

Write your partner's answers.

partner's name

a diploma   a ring   a passport   a pen   a star   a heart

	Your item	What it means	Your partner's item	What it means
EXAMPLE	a gold record	having a hit song	a ring	marriage
	1.			
	2.			
	3.			

2 TEAM GAME

team number

Play a guessing game with ekeko items.

A. Write your ekeko items from Activity 1 on a small piece of paper. Write your name on it and give it to your teacher. Don't show it to anyone else!

EXAMPLE

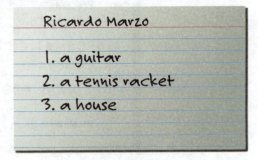

B. Divide into two teams. Your partner from Activity 1 can't be on your team.

C. Team 1 sends two players to the board. One student faces the board (*Student A*), the other student faces away from it (*Student B*).

D. The teacher will choose one of your classmates' papers and will write the three ekeko items on the board. *Student A* will try to explain the items on the board to *Student B*. *Student B* will try to guess the items. *Student A* and *Student B* have two minutes to explain and guess all three items. The team gets one point for each correct answer.

E. The teams take turns sending pairs to the board. The game is over when all students on both teams have had a turn at the board. The team with the most points wins.

3 CLASS DISCUSSION

As a class, discuss the ekeko items. Each person tells the class what her/his items are and what they mean. Then, answer the following questions:
- *What was the most common ekeko item in the class?*
- *What were the most unusual ekeko items in the class?*
- *Did any two people have the same three ekeko items?*

THEME: Exchanging Christmas Presents

 4 PARTNER — WAYS TO SAY IT

partner's name

In this episode, Rebecca and Ramón exchange Christmas presents. They're very happy with their gifts. Here are some ways to say you like a present in English:

I love it!	It's just what I wanted!	Oh, it's great/awesome!
Wow! Thank you so much!	It's just what I needed!	What a beautiful shirt!

Work with a partner. Look at the situations below. Take turns. One person chooses a situation. The other person chooses an expression from above. Then, make up your own situation.

Situations   **Expressions**

EXAMPLE   Your mother gives you a warm jacket.   Thanks, Mom! It's just what I needed!

1. Your girlfriend/boyfriend gives you a ring.
2. Your grandfather gives you a watch.
3. Your parents give you a new car.
4. Your situation:

 5 GROUP — DISCUSSION

group number

A. Divide into three groups. With your group members, you'll talk about classmates who *are not in your group*. For example, Group 1 talks about Group 2, Group 2 talks about Group 3, and Group 3 talks about Group 1.

B. For each person in the other group, discuss this question: *What are his/her likes and interests?*

C. Decide on a gift for each person. You want the present to be the best gift the person has ever received!

EXAMPLE   The person really likes music.
           Gift: The latest CD in the music style the person likes best

D. Write your gift decision for each person on a piece of paper and give it to the person.

E. As a class, discuss the gifts that each person received. Were people surprised with their gift? Were most people happy with the gift?

THEME Falling in Love

6 PARTNER DISCUSSION

partner's name

good looks	nice family	intelligence	money
kindness	talent	humor	fame
interest in children	dedication	same religion	sense of responsibility

Work with a partner. Discuss why Ramón and Rebecca are falling in love.

A. From the list above, choose the two most important reasons that Ramón is falling in love with Rebecca. Write them below.

Why Ramón is falling in love with Rebecca
1. _____
2. _____

B. From the list above, choose the two most important reasons that Rebecca is falling in love with Ramón. Write them below.

Why Rebecca is falling in love with Ramón
1. _____
2. _____

7 GROUP DISCUSSION

group number

A. Look again at the list of reasons in Activity 6. With the members of your group, answer these questions:
   Which do you think are the three "best" reasons for falling in love?
   Which do you think are the three "worst" reasons for falling in love?

B. Complete the chart.

Best reasons for falling in love	Worst reasons for falling in love
1.	1.
2.	2.
3.	3.

C. Share your answers with the class. Are there any reasons that every group listed? What are they?

What About you?
1. Do people think of reasons when they fall in love?
2. What is "love at first sight"?
3. Do you think "love at first sight" is possible?
4. How do you know when you're in love?

EPISODE 45 PAGE 4

INFORMATION GAP **Planning a Trip**

8 PARTNER — INFORMATION GAP
STUDENT A

Work with a partner. One of you works on this page. The other works on page 6. Don't look at your partner's page.

_____
partner's name

Part One

In this episode, Kevin begins planning for his trip to San Francisco. Now it's your turn to plan a trip! Talk to a travel agent. Find out the best tour for you.

You want to take a tour of Boston and the eastern part of the United States. You're interested in visiting museums and historical places. You don't want to spend more than $1,500 for the tour. You want to stay one week. Your partner is a travel agent. He/she has some tours to sell. Ask questions about the tours. Decide which one is best for you. Write its number in the space below.

Ask questions like these:
- What places does the tour go to?
- What things do you do with the tour group?
- How long is the tour?
- How much does the tour cost? What is included in the cost?

Number of the tour you will take: _____

Boston

Part Two

Read the information on these three tours to the western part of the United States. Your partner will ask you questions about the tours. Help him/her find the best tour.

1. **West Coast Adventure Tour**
   You'll go skiing in the Rocky Mountains. You'll go down the fast-moving waters of the Colorado River on a raft. You'll climb mountains in California. These are just three of the adventures you will have on this tour. You will also stay in the best hotels. The tour is for eight days. Hotel and meals are included in the price of $2,500.

2. **Western Cities Tour**
   See the cities in the western part of the United States. This tour takes you to Los Angeles, San Francisco, and Seattle. Visit the movie studios in Hollywood. See Chinatown in San Francisco. Drive through the redwood forests of Northern California. Go to the top of the Space Needle in Seattle. You'll see all the main sights of the West Coast cities. You will stay in good quality hotels. The tour is for seven days. The price includes hotel costs, but not meals. This tour is $1,400.

3. **West Coast City and Outdoors Tour**
   On this tour, you'll go skiing outside of Denver. You'll also take a ride in a helicopter over the Grand Canyon, and climb mountains in California. You will see Los Angeles, visit the movie studios in Hollywood, and take a cable car in San Francisco. The tour is for seven days. You will stay in good-quality hotels. The hotels are included in the price of $1,900, but meals are extra.

EPISODE 45 PAGE 5

INFORMATION GAP Planning a Trip

8	PARTNER	INFORMATION GAP
	STUDENT B	Work with a partner. One of you works on this page. The other works on page 5. Don't look at your partner's page.

_____
partner's name

Part One

In this episode, Kevin begins planning for his trip to San Francisco. Now your partner is planning a trip. Read the information on these three tours to the eastern part of the United States. Your partner will ask you questions about the tour. Help him/her find the best tour.

1. **East Coast Museum Tour**
   This tour takes you to the great museums of the East Coast. You'll go to museums in Boston, Philadelphia, New York, and Washington, D.C. You'll spend your entire day in museums and galleries with your guide. At night, you'll go to the best restaurants, and you'll stay at the best hotels. Hotel and meals are included in the price. The tour lasts one week. The cost is $2,500.

2. **Historic East Coast Tour**
   Visit important places in the history of the United States. You will visit Boston, Philadelphia, and Washington, D.C. with your guide. You have a free day in each place to visit museums or to shop. You'll stay in good-quality hotels. The hotel is included in the price, but meals are an additional cost. The tour lasts six days. The cost is $1,200.

3. **See the East Coast!**
   This tour takes you to historical places and museums on the East Coast. A guide takes you to the top sites. You will visit New York, Philadelphia, and Washington, D.C. You will stay in hotels that are not expensive. The price includes hotels, but meals are extra. The tour lasts 7 days. The cost is $1,000.

Part Two

Now it's your turn to plan a trip! Talk to a travel agent. Find out the best tour for you.

You want to take a tour of San Francisco and the western part of the United States. You like to do things outdoors, but you also want to visit some big cities. Your partner is a travel agent. You don't want to spend more than $2,000 for the tour. You want to stay at least one week. Your partner has some tours to sell. Ask questions about the tours. Decide which one is best for you. Write its number in the space below.

Ask questions like these:
- What places does the tour go to?
- What things do you do with the tour group?
- How long is the tour?
- How much does the tour cost? What is included in the cost?

Number of the tour you will take: _____

San Francisco

Friendship

EPISODE 46

THEMES
- Being Impressed
- Collecting Autographs
- Sharing Good News

GAME
- The Music Business

OPTIONAL PROJECT
- Languages (Appendix 10)

THEME Being Impressed

1 PARTNER RANKING

In this episode, Rebecca takes Kevin to the recording studio. He is very impressed with it. What kinds of things impress *you*?

A. Look at the choices below. Check (✔) the six things that impress you the most.

B. Then, ask your partner this question: *Which six things impress you the most?* Check (✔) your partner's answers.

partner's name _____

Oh, Rebecca, that was totally cool!

	You	Your partner
1. great art		
2. modern hospitals		
3. space travel		
4. computer technology		
5. the pyramids of Egypt		
6. the Great Wall of China		
7. people who can draw well		
8. people who can speak several languages		
9. great athletes		
10. great musicians		
11. great writers		
12. other: _____		

2 CLASS BRAINSTORM

People do many things to impress others. Discuss the list below with your classmates. Add any other ideas that you can think of. Your teacher will write a "master list" on the board.

- dress well
- talk about interesting things you have done
- talk about your family
- talk about your accomplishments
- be early for an appointment
- talk about the money you have
- talk about your hobbies or interests
- talk about the latest films, songs, and so on

_____
_____
_____
_____
_____

_____
_____
_____
_____
_____

3 PARTNER COMPARISON

_____
partner's name

A. Work with a partner. One of you will be *Partner A*, the other will be *Partner B*. Follow the directions for each partner below.

Partner A: Write four things that you would do to impress a new friend. Use the list above in Activity 2.

1. _____
2. _____
3. _____
4. _____

Partner B: Write four things that a new friend could do that would impress you. Use the list above in Activity 2.

1. _____
2. _____
3. _____
4. _____

B. Compare answers. Do any of the items match?

1. When have you impressed somebody?
2. How did you know the person was impressed?
3. When were you last impressed? What impressed you?
4. What does *not* impress you?

THEME Collecting Autographs

 4 GROUP DISCUSSION

_____
group number

In this episode, Alex is very excited to receive an autographed baseball. It has the signatures of some professional baseball players on it.

Many people like to collect autographs. Who do people usually ask for their autographs? With your group, add items to the chart below.

People who give autographs	
Category	Names
Professional athletes	Michael Jordan, Monica Seles
1.	
2.	
3.	
4.	
5.	
6.	
7.	
8.	

 5 CLASS GAME Time: 10 min.

Think of one interesting or unusual thing that you have done. Your classmates should not know about it. For example, did you ever have a small part in a movie? Did you ever meet a famous person? Did you ever win a prize?

A. On a piece of paper, write your name and what you did. Give your teacher the paper. Your teacher will choose *ten* interesting things and write them on the board. Copy any *five* of these onto a piece of paper.

B. Go around the class and try to find the person who did each of the five things on your list. Start your questions in the following way: *Did you ever. . .?* You can ask a person only one question at each exchange.

C. When you find a match, ask the person for his/her autograph. He or she will write it on your paper.

D. When you have an "autograph" for all five of the things on your paper, tell your teacher. You are the winner.

1. Are you interested in collecting autographs?
2. Have you ever asked anyone for his/her autograph? Who?
3. Whose autograph would you like to have?

THEME: Sharing Good News

6 PARTNER — WAYS TO SAY IT

partner's name

In this episode, Bill shares his good news with Rebecca. He's going to Los Angeles to work as a musician. Here are some ways to talk about good news:

A	B
To announce good news	**To react to good news**
I have some good news.	That's great!
Listen, I've got something to tell you.	What wonderful news!
Guess what?	I'm so glad to hear it!
Listen to this!	Good for you!
	Terrific!

Work with a partner. Look at the situations below. Take turns. One partner announces some good news with an expression from Column **A** above. The other partner reacts to the news with an expression from Column **B** above. Then, make up your own situation.

EXAMPLE   You passed all your exams.
           Student A: Guess what?   Student B: Good for you!
              I passed all my exams.

1. You've just won a new car.

   Student A _____

   Student B _____

2. You've just been accepted to a school.

   Student A _____

   Student B _____

3. You've just decided to get married.

   Student A _____

   Student B _____

4. Your situation:

   Student A _____

   Student B _____

7 GROUP — GAME

group number

Sit in a circle. One person begins the game by saying, "I have some good news. I won fifty thousand dollars in the lottery." The next person answers, "That's great!" He/she then repeats all the good news and adds something new: "I have some good news. I won fifty thousand dollars in the lottery and I just bought a new car." How many pieces of good news can your group list before someone forgets?

EPISODE 46 PAGE 4

GAME The Music Business

 TEAM | GAME

team number

What do you know about the music business? Play this music tic-tac-toe game and find out.

Get Ready to Play

Step One
Divide into four teams. Team 1 will play Team 2, and Team 3 will play Team 4.

Step Two
Each team will write 10 questions about songs and musicians. The questions must begin with *Who sings the song. . .?* or *Who sang the song. . .?* Then, you must give three answer choices.

EXAMPLES
Who sings the song, "Dream Catcher"?
   a. Julio Iglesias
   b. Madonna
   c. Rebecca Casey

Who sang the song, "Yesterday"?
   a. The Rolling Stones
   b. The Beatles
   c. Juan Luis Guerra

Write your questions below:

1. _____
   a. _____
   b. _____
   c. _____

2. _____
   a. _____
   b. _____
   c. _____

3. _____
   a. _____
   b. _____
   c. _____

4. _____
   a. _____
   b. _____
   c. _____

5. _____
   a. _____
   b. _____
   c. _____

6. _____
   a. _____
   b. _____
   c. _____

7. _____
   a. _____
   b. _____
   c. _____

8. _____
   a. _____
   b. _____
   c. _____

9. _____
   a. _____
   b. _____
   c. _____

10. _____
   a. _____
   b. _____
   c. _____

GAME The Music Business

Step Three
Decide which team will be the Os and which team will be the Xs. Flip a coin to see which team goes first.

Step Four
Cut out the game pieces on Appendix 13. The O team will cut out the Os and the X team will cut out the Xs. Now you're ready to play.

Play the Game
- The O team asks the X team a music question. If the X team answers the question correctly, it gets to put an X in one of the tic-tac-toe squares below.
- If the X team doesn't answer the question correctly, it doesn't get to mark a square, and it's the O team's turn.
- Take turns asking questions. The first team to get three X's or three O's in a row or diagonally wins! Play several rounds of the game. Write new questions if necessary.

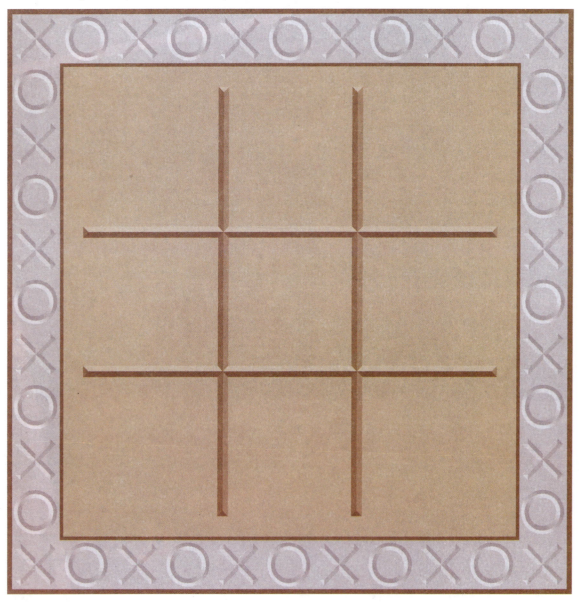

The Lost Boys

EPISODE 47

THEMES
- Changing Plans
- Baby-sitting
- Children and Money

INFORMATION GAP
- A Missing Person's Report

OPTIONAL PROJECT
- Ice Skating (Appendix 11)

THEME Changing Plans

1   PARTNER   INTERVIEW

_____
partner's name

In this episode, Alex and Vincent are lost. Kevin and Rebecca change their plans to help look for the boys. Some people can change plans more easily than others. These people are more flexible.

Read the situations below. Decide if you would change your plans. Check (✔) *Yes* or *No*. Then, ask your partner about the situations. Check (✔) your partner's answers. Who is more flexible?

	WOULD YOU CHANGE YOUR PLANS?			
	You		Your partner	
	Yes	No	Yes	No
1. You have tickets to the theater. Someone in your family is ill.				
2. You plan to take tomorrow off to visit your child's school. Your boss wants you to go to an important meeting.				
3. You're going to go to the beach for a week-long vacation. You break your leg.				
4. You're going to go shopping to buy a special present for a friend. You have a fight with this friend.				
5. You want to get to a store before it closes. You see a small child in the street. He/she looks lost.				

1. Do you change your plans often?
2. Are there any situations when you should not change plans? What are they?
3. How do you feel if a friend cancels plans to do something with you?
4. Do you like to make plans?

THEME: Baby-sitting

2 GROUP — WRITING INSTRUCTIONS

group number

In this episode, a baby-sitter comes to take care of Alex.

Parents need to give baby-sitters clear instructions. You have a four-year-old child named John. Look at the picture. Work with your group. Use the clues in it to complete the list of instructions for the baby-sitter. Continue the list on a separate piece of paper if you need to. Add any other instructions you think are important.

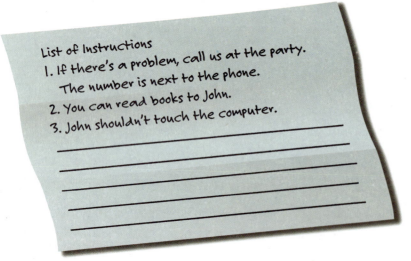

List of Instructions
1. If there's a problem, call us at the party. The number is next to the phone.
2. You can read books to John.
3. John shouldn't touch the computer.

1. In the United States, teenagers often baby-sit to make money. Do teenagers do this in your country?
2. If yes, how much money do baby-sitters earn in your country?
3. Did you ever baby-sit to make money?

EPISODE 47 PAGE 2

THEME **Children and Money**

3 PARTNER PUZZLE

partner's name

In this episode, Vincent takes the money out of his piggy bank. Mrs. Wang finds his empty bank. Children in the United States often have piggy banks. They put money they want to save into their piggy banks.

In this puzzle, you need to figure out the kinds of coins in each piggy bank. Work with a partner. Write your answers in the boxes.

1¢
penny

5¢
nickel

10¢
dime

25¢
quarter

50¢
half dollar

Alex has 6¢ in his piggy bank.
He has two coins.

Answer 1 nickel, 1 penny
5¢ + 1¢ = 6¢

1. Marta has 77¢ in her piggy bank.
   She has five coins.

   Answer

2. Lisa has 95¢ in her piggy bank.
   She has 11 coins.

   Answer

3. Motoi has 53¢ in his piggy bank.
   He has seven coins.

   Answer

4. Peter has 66¢ in his piggy bank.
   He has four coins.

   Answer

Bonus Question

Alex has 51¢ in his piggy bank. He only has one penny. How many coin combinations are possible?
Think of as many as you can.
Use a separate piece of paper if necessary.

Combinations

1. one half dollar + one penny
2. two quarters + one penny

EPISODE 47 PAGE 3

4 PARTNER INTERVIEW

partner's name

In the United States and Canada, children often have their own money to spend. What is usual in your country? Did you have your own money as a child? Check (✔) your answers to the questions below. Then, ask your partner, and check (✔) your partner's answers.

	You	Your partner
1. In your country, how many children have their own money?	❑ most ❑ some ❑ few	❑ most ❑ some ❑ few
2. Where do children get money?	❑ from their parents ❑ as gifts ❑ from working ❑ other _____	❑ from their parents ❑ as gifts ❑ from working ❑ other _____
3. What do children usually do with their money?	❑ spend it for fun ❑ use it for necessities ❑ save it for the future	❑ spend it for fun ❑ use it for necessities ❑ save it for the future
4. How much spending money did you have as a child?	❑ lots ❑ some ❑ little	❑ lots ❑ some ❑ little
5. Who decided how you used your money?	❑ I did. ❑ My parents did. ❑ other _____	❑ I did. ❑ My parents did. ❑ other _____

5 PARTNER ROLE-PLAY

partner's name

A. With your partner, act out a conversation between a child and a parent. One of you takes the role of the child. The other takes the role of the parent. Read your positions in the boxes below.

B. Do one conversation. Then, change roles.

C. Volunteer to perform your role-play in front of the class.

Child

Your parent gives you a little money each week. This is your allowance. You would like a bigger allowance. Try to persuade your parent to increase your allowance. You can:
- explain why you need the money
- offer to earn the money
- tell how much your friends get each week

Parent

You give your child some money every week. You want your child to learn the value of money. You want your child to learn not to spend more money than he/she has. Also, you yourself are trying to save money to buy a new car. Listen to your child. Make a decision.
- Does your child have a real need for the money?
- Does your child offer to earn the money?
- Does your child show he/she is learning the value of money?

INFORMATION GAP A Missing Person's Report

6 PARTNER — **INFORMATION GAP**
STUDENT A — Work with a partner. One of you works on this page. The other works on page 6. Don't look at your partner's page.

_____
partner's name

Someday, you may have to describe someone who is missing. How well can you describe a person? To do this activity, bring a photo of a person to class. It may be from a magazine. It may be someone you know. The teacher will collect the photos and place them face down on a table or a desk. Before you begin, pick a photo. Make sure it isn't the one you brought in. Don't show it to anyone else.

Part One
Study the photo for one minute. Then turn it over. Your partner needs to get a description of the "missing person." Describe the person in the photo as carefully as you can, but don't look at the photo again! Talk about what the person is wearing and what he/she looks like. Your partner will take notes. He/she will also ask questions.

Part Two
Your partner will look at a photo of a "missing person" for one minute. You need to get information about the missing person. Fill in the form below. First, your partner will give a description. Then, ask questions about the person.

MISSING PERSON'S REPORT

Age	Sex (M/F)
Height	Weight
Hair color	Eye color

Clothing _____

Other information _____
_____
_____
_____

Part Three
Return your photo to the teacher. The teacher will number all of the photos and put them on display. Can you find the missing person your partner described? Check your guess with your partner. Then, compare your missing person's report with your partner's. Answer these questions:
- _Who remembered the most about his/her photo?_
- _What kinds of things did you notice about the person in the photo?_
- _What kinds of things didn't you notice?_

EPISODE 47 PAGE 5

INFORMATION GAP A Missing Person's Report

6 PARTNER INFORMATION GAP

STUDENT B Work with a partner. One of you works on this page. The other works on page 5. Don't look at your partner's page.

_____
partner's name

Someday, you may have to describe someone who is missing. How well can you describe a person? To do this activity, bring a photo of a person to class. It may be from a magazine. It may be someone you know. The teacher will collect the photos and place them face down on a table or a desk. Before you begin, pick a photo. Make sure it isn't the one you brought in. Don't show it to anyone else.

Part One

Your partner will look at a photo of a "missing person" for one minute. You need to get information about the missing person. Fill in the form below. First, your partner will give a description. Then, ask questions about the person.

MISSING PERSON'S REPORT

Age _____   Sex (M/F) _____

Height _____   Weight _____

Hair color _____   Eye color _____

Clothing _____

Other information _____

_____

_____

_____

Part Two

Study the photo you have for one minute. Then turn it over. Your partner needs to get a description of the "missing person." Describe the person in the photo as carefully as you can, but don't look at the photo again! Talk about what the person is wearing and what he/she looks like. Your partner will take notes. He/she will also ask questions.

Part Three

Return your photo to the teacher. The teacher will number all of the photos and put them on display. Can you find the missing person your partner described? Check your guess with your partner. Then, compare your missing person's report with your partner's. Answer these questions:
- Who remembered the most about his/her photo?
- What kinds of things did you notice about the person in the photo?
- What kinds of things didn't you notice?

A Very Good Year

EPISODE 48

THEMES
- New Year's Resolutions
- Trust
- Parenting

GAME
- Grounding

OPTIONAL PROJECT
- New Year's Eve (Appendix 12)

THEME New Year's Resolutions

1 PARTNER INTERVIEW

_____
partner's name

read   exercise   get organized   learn to dance   travel

At New Year's time, people often make promises about what they will do during the new year. These promises are called **New Year's resolutions**. Here are some examples:

I will get organized.	I will learn to dance.	I will eat less junk food.
I will travel.	I will exercise more.	I will read more.

Work with a partner. Pretend it's New Year's Eve.

A. Write three New Year's resolutions in the spaces below. You can use the examples in the box above, or you can think of others.

B. Ask your partner the question: *What are your New Year's resolutions?* Write your partner's answers.

Your New Year's resolutions
1. _____
2. _____
3. _____

Your partner's New Year's resolutions
1. _____
2. _____
3. _____

2 CLASS GAME Time: 10 min.

A. Write one of your three New Year's resolutions from Activity 1 on a small piece of paper. Don't write your name on it, and don't show it to anyone.

B. Give your paper to the teacher. The teacher will number each resolution by writing a number in the corner of each paper. Then, he/she will put them on a table or desk.

C. With your classmates, look at all the cards. Try to guess who wrote each resolution. Write your guesses below.

Resolution number	Person	Resolution number	Person
1.		11.	
2.		12.	
3.		13.	
4.		14.	
5.		15.	
6.		16.	
7.		17.	
8.		18.	
9.		19.	
10.		20.	

D. When the time is up, each person tells which is his/her resolution. The person with the most correct guesses wins.

3 CLASS DISCUSSION

Your English class is a good place for a New Year's resolution!

Each person in the class will make one resolution about learning English. Your teacher can help you with your resolution.

Here are some examples of good resolutions:
I will speak English outside of class with classmates.
I will read English on my own at least two hours a week.

Write your resolution here. Then share it with the class.

1. Do you ever make New Year's resolutions?
2. Do you always *keep* your resolutions?
3. How many resolutions do you think a person should make?

THEME Trust

4 PARTNER — TRUST TEST

partner's name

Take this "Trust Test." Read the situations. Check (✔) *Yes* or *No*. Then ask your partner the questions, and check (✔) your partner's answers. Discuss the results.

	You		Your partner	
	Yes	No	Yes	No
1. You sometimes lend things to a friend. She doesn't give them back. Then she asks to borrow your new CD and promises to give it back. Do you trust her?				
2. Your mechanic promised to fix your car yesterday. Now he says it will be ready today. Do you trust him?				
3. Someone you just met didn't keep an appointment with you. You waited an hour. Now he wants to make another appointment. Do you trust him to keep it?				
4. You have a new car. Your brother, who is very careful, asks to borrow it. Do you trust him enough to let him use it?				
5. Your boyfriend/girlfriend asks you to lend him/her some money. Do you trust him/her to return it?				
6. The television repair person has promised to come and fix your TV today. Do you believe her?				
7. You have some valuable jewelry. You don't want to leave it in your apartment when you are away on vacation. Do you trust a friend to keep it for you?				
8. Someone on the street offers to sell you gold jewelry at a low price. Do you trust him?				
9. Someone calls you on the phone and says you have won a boat. Do you trust him?				

SCORING: *Yes answers are worth 1 point.*
No answers are worth 0 point.

If your score is 1 point or lower: You aren't very trusting.

If your score is between 2–6 points: You're in the middle. You trust some people, but you don't believe everything people tell you.

If your score is 7 points or more: You're too trusting. You shouldn't believe everything people tell you.

THEME Parenting

5 PARTNER SURVEY

_____
partner's name

Pretend you have an eight-year-old child.

A. What answers do you give in the following situations? Circle them in the chart below. Note: "I'll think about it" means you may or may not agree. Often it suggests you won't say yes.

B. Find out your partner's answers. Ask this question: *What would you say?* Circle your partner's answers.

C. Who is more strict—you or your partner? If you're strict, you'll say no more often.

You			Situation	Your partner		
Yes	No	I'll think about it.	1. Your child asks for $20 for a video.	Yes	No	I'll think about it.
Yes	No	I'll think about it.	2. Your child asks for an expensive game. He/she says everyone in the school has it.	Yes	No	I'll think about it.
Yes	No	I'll think about it.	3. Your child wants to go with a 10-year-old friend to an ice-skating rink across town.	Yes	No	I'll think about it.
Yes	No	I'll think about it.	4. Your child asks to go on a ride at an amusement park. The ride isn't recommended for children under 10.	Yes	No	I'll think about it.
Yes	No	I'll think about it.	5. Your child asks to go to a movie. All his/her friends have seen it. The newspaper says it's scary for children under 10.	Yes	No	I'll think about it.

6 CLASS DEBATE

A. Read the two opinions below. If you agree with Opinion 1, join group 1. If you agree with Opinion 2, join Group 2.

B. With your group members, make a list of reasons to support your opinion. Be ready to explain each one. Use a separate piece of paper.

C. Take turns. Each group has five minutes to present its ideas.

D. Discuss the opinion most of the class agrees with.

Opinion 1
It's better to be strict with your children. If you're too relaxed, there'll be trouble.

Opinion 2
It's better to be relaxed, with your children. If you're too strict, there'll be trouble.

Write your reasons on a separate piece of paper.

GAME Grounding

7 TEAM GAME

team number

"You know you're grounded, right?"

In this episode, Ramón **grounds** his son. This means that Alex can't go out and play with his friends for a period of time. It's a common way to punish children in the United States. Play this game and decide how *you* would punish *your* children.

Play the Game

- Form a team of four people. Then divide your team into two sets of partners.
- Work with your partner. Look at the list of bad behaviors on page 6. Discuss each behavior, and decide on one of five punishments. Check (✓) your answers in the chart on page 6. Don't show your answers to the other half of your team!

EXAMPLE   Your child fought at school.

	Grounding for two weeks	Grounding for one week	Extra house work	No dessert after dinner	No punishment
Bad behavior 1		✓			
Bad behavior 2					

You think your child should be grounded for one week for fighting in school.

- When you've finished, join the other half of your team. Compare answers. Your team gets a point if both parts of a team have checked the same punishment for the same bad behavior.
- A total of 12 points is possible. The team with the most points wins. Keep track of your points in the chart below.

Game Rules

- Groups cannot change any answers after they have checked them. After you check all 12 answers, put down your pens and pencils.
- Don't talk to the other group in your team until after you both have finished all 12 answers.

	Points
Bad behavior 1	
Bad behavior 2	
Bad behavior 3	
Bad behavior 4	
Bad behavior 5	
Bad behavior 6	
Bad behavior 7	
Bad behavior 8	
Bad behavior 9	
Bad behavior 10	
Bad behavior 11	
Bad behavior 12	

GAME Grounding

> **Bad Behaviors**
> 1. Your child got bad grades in school.
> 2. Your child cheated at school.
> 3. Your child fought at school.
> 4. Your child lied to you.
> 5. Your child hit his/her brother/sister.
> 6. Your child ran away.
> 7. Your child stole money from you.
> 8. Your child stole money from a store.
> 9. Your child used bad language.
> 10. Your child was mean to the dog.
> 11. Your child broke a window with a ball.
> 12. Your child spilled milk on your favorite book.

Check (✔) your answers.

	Grounding for two weeks	Grounding for one week	Extra house work	No dessert after dinner	No punishment
Bad behavior 1					
Bad behavior 2					
Bad behavior 3					
Bad behavior 4					
Bad behavior 5					
Bad behavior 6					
Bad behavior 7					
Bad behavior 8					
Bad behavior 9					
Bad behavior 10					
Bad behavior 11					
Bad behavior 12					

Keep track of your points on page 5.

EPISODE 37

PROJECT Computer Classes

1 GROUP RESEARCH

_____
group number

In this episode, Kevin talks to Michael about computer classes.

A. Divide into groups. Call or visit a college, university, or computer institute in your area. Each group should try to choose a different school. Ask the questions below. Write the answers on a separate piece of paper.
  1. How many computer classes does the school offer?
  2. What kinds of computer classes are they?
  3. How much do the classes cost?

B. Compare your answers with the class. List the four most common types of classes. Then, vote on the best place to take computer classes.

  1. _____   3. _____
  2. _____   4. _____

2 GROUP SURVEY

_____
group number

Work in the same groups from Activity 1. Your group wants to open a computer school. You need to get some information. Who would come to your school? Which classes would be most popular?

A. Each person in the group needs to talk to three people outside the class. Complete an interview card like the one below for each person. List the four kinds of courses from Activity 1.

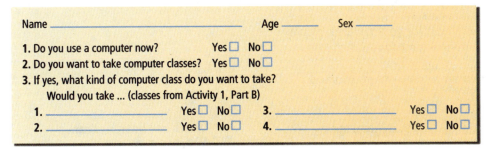

```
Name _____  Age _____  Sex _____
1. Do you use a computer now?        Yes ☐  No ☐
2. Do you want to take computer classes?  Yes ☐  No ☐
3. If yes, what kind of computer class do you want to take?
     Would you take ... (classes from Activity 1, Part B)
   1. _____  Yes ☐ No ☐   3. _____  Yes ☐ No ☐
   2. _____  Yes ☐ No ☐   4. _____  Yes ☐ No ☐
```

B. Compare the surveys in your group. Complete the information below.
  1. Who gave more "Yes" answers, men or women? _____
  2. How many "Yes" answers did the following age groups have?

     10–20 years _____   21–29 years _____   30–49 years _____   50+ years _____

  3. Which classes would be the most popular at your school? _____

1. Do you use a computer regularly?
2. If so, why do you use the computer?
3. If not, would you like to use a computer? Why or why not?
4. What kinds of computer classes would you like to take?

APPENDIX 1 EPISODE 37 PROJECT

EPISODE **38**

PROJECT **Sports for Children**

partner's name

1 PARTNER SURVEY

In this episode, we see Alex and his friends kicking a soccer ball. The children are playing sports in their after-school program.

You're going to help your local community center. It wants to start an after-school sports program for children. Because of money, it can start the program with only two sports. You're getting information to help the center choose the two sports. Your teacher will divide the class into an even number of pairs. Half of the pairs will do Activity A and half of the pairs will do Activity B.

Activity A

With your partner, interview at least three children from the ages of 6–12. Ask the following questions and write their answers in the chart. Continue the chart on a separate piece of paper if necessary.
- *What team sport do you like to play the most?*
- *What individual sport do you like to play the most?*

Child	Team sport	Individual sport
1		
2		
3		

Activity B

With your partner, interview at least three parents of children of the ages of 6–12. Ask the following questions and write their answers in the chart. Continue the chart on a separate piece of paper if necessary.
- *What team sport do you think is best for your children to play?*
- *What individual sport do you think is best for your children to play?*
- *Which are better for your children to play—team sports or individual sports?*

Parent	Team sport	Individual sport	Which are better—team or individual sports?
1			
2			
3			

A. Join a pair that did a different activity from the one you did. Discuss the answers to both surveys. What conclusions can you make?

B. Share your information with the rest of the class. What sports will you recommend to the community center?

EPISODE 39

PROJECT Opera

 PARTNER **RESEARCH**

_____
partner's name

In this episode, Alberto wants Rebecca to go to the opera with him.

In operas, singing and music tell a story. Grand opera is sung in opera houses around the world. Great composers like Mozart, Verdi, and Wagner wrote grand opera in the 1700s and 1800s.

There are other musical styles used to tell stories. For example, there are rock operas. In English-speaking countries, there is a popular form of storytelling through songs. It's called a musical. You may have heard of musicals like "Cats" or "Phantom of the Opera." Many cultures have their own special forms of musical storytelling.

Work with a partner. Find the name of an opera or a musical. Pick one you would like to know more about. To get names and information, you can interview people, look at music encyclopedias, or go to a music store. Complete the following chart. Be prepared to tell the story of the musical to the class.

Name of opera or musical _____

Who wrote it _____ When it was written _____

The main characters _____

The main story _____

What happens at the end _____

 CLASS **STORYTELLING**

A. With your partner from Activity 1, make a presentation to the class. Write the name of the opera or musical on the board. Share your information about it. If possible, play parts of it to the class.

B. When all the presentations are finished, discuss these questions:
- _Which was the most unusual fact you learned?_
- _Which story seems the most interesting?_

C. Have the class members vote for the opera or musical that they would like to see the most. They can also vote on the opera or musical that they would _not_ want to see.

EPISODE 40

PROJECT Using the Library

1 GROUP RESEARCH

_____
group number

A. Divide into groups. Work together to answer the questions below about your local or school libraries. If possible, each group should call or visit a different library. Use a separate piece of paper to write your answers.
   1. When is the library open?
   2. What do you have to do to borrow books?
   3. How do you find the books you want?
   4. How do you find the magazines the library has?
   5. What does the library have besides books and magazines?
   6. Does the library have Internet access?
   7. What are three magazines you can read at the library?
   8. What are three reference books you can use at the library?

B. When each group is finished, compare answers as a class. Which library would be the best place to do research?

2 PARTNER RESEARCH GAME

_____
partner's name

A. Work with a partner. Do library research to answer the following questions. Write your answers in the chart. Write where you found the information and how long it took you to find it. Don't forget to try the Internet.

Questions	Answers	Where you found the information	Time
1. What is the capital city of Niger?			
2. Who was the fourth president of the United States? When did he become president?			
3. Who are two actors who played in the movie *Star Wars*?			
4. What was the first year that women were allowed to compete in the Olympic Games?			
5. Where is the Rock and Roll Hall of Fame? When did it open?			

B. Compare answers as a class. Which pairs found the most correct answers most quickly? Which sources did they use?

EPISODE 41

PROJECT Vacations

1 PARTNER RESEARCH

partner's name

In this episode, Alberto is planning a ski vacation in Colorado. Where would you like to go on vacation?

A. With a partner, decide on a place you would like to visit.

B. Find out about the place. You can go to a travel agent and get information and brochures. Or you can go to the library to look at travel books and magazines. You can also get information on the Internet. Try to find some pictures.

C. Answer the following questions.

1. Where would you like to go? _____
2. How would you get there? _____
3. Where would you stay? _____
4. What kind of weather should you expect? _____
5. How much would your vacation cost? _____
6. What would you do there? _____

2 PARTNER PRESENTATION

partner's name

A. With your partner from Activity 1, make a presentation to the class. Write the name of the vacation place on the board. Share your information about this place. Tell why you want to go there. Try to show your classmates that this is a great place to visit. Show pictures of your place if you can.

B. When all the presentations are finished, take a class vote. Each person will answer the question: *Which place would you like to visit?* Vote for one place—it can't be the one that you researched. The teacher will write the results of the vote on the board.

1. What do you usually do on vacation?
2. What is your favorite vacation memory?
3. Have you ever taken a ski vacation? If yes, where did you go? If no, would like to take a ski vacation?

EPISODE 42

PROJECT Dedication

1 PARTNER RESEARCH

partner's name _____

Rebecca is dedicated to her music. She will do anything necessary to be a songwriter and performer.

A. Work with a partner. Choose any dedicated person in the history of the world. This person can be alive or dead, famous or not famous. Here are some examples:

Nelson Mandela	Louis Pasteur
Dian Fossey	Maria Taglioni
Leo Tolstoy	Mahatma Gandhi
Katharine Hepburn	Elizabeth Cady Stanton
Simón Bolívar	

B. Complete the information below. You can use your school library, a biographical dictionary, an encyclopedia, the Internet, and so on.

Name of the dedicated person _____

Where the person was/is from _____

What the person was dedicated to _____

What the person accomplished _____

C. Present the information to the class. Show a picture of the person if possible.

1. If you could meet one of the people from Activity 1, who would it be?
2. Why would you want to meet this person?
3. What are you dedicated to?
4. What have you accomplished?

APPENDIX 6 EPISODE 42 PROJECT

EPISODE 43

PROJECT Chocolates

 PARTNER — RESEARCH

partner's name

In this episode, Nancy and Rebecca eat chocolate. What do you know about chocolate?

A. With your partner, find the answers to the following questions. You can use your school library, an encyclopedia, the Internet, and so on. You can also go to a candy store to get some help! Write your answers on a separate piece of paper.

1. From what tree is chocolate made?
2. Which cultures first used chocolate?
3. In which country do people eat the most chocolate?
4. What are four kinds of chocolate?

When you finish, compare your answers as a class. How many different kinds of chocolate can the class list?

 GROUP — SURVEY

group number

In the United States and Canada, giving boxes of chocolates is a tradition on Valentine's Day. This holiday celebrates love and romance. People give gifts of chocolates and other candies on other holidays, too, such as Christmas, Easter, and Halloween.

A. Find out about customs in other countries. Interview people in your group and people outside of class. Ask these questions:
- Are gifts of chocolates or other candies popular on holidays?
- What is the name of the holiday?
- What is the custom that has to do with the chocolates or candies?

(Copy the chart below onto another piece of paper, and add extra lines.)

B. Share your findings with the class.

Country	Holiday	The custom
1. the United States	Halloween	Children dress in costumes. They go to friends' or neighbors' doors and say, "Trick or treat." They usually get some candy.
2.		
3.		

1. In your country, are chocolates a popular treat?
2. Do people give chocolates as gifts?
3. Do you like to eat chocolates?

EPISODE 44

PROJECT Helping People in the Community

1 GROUP RESEARCH

group number

In this episode, Ramón and Rebecca help people in their community. They help serve food at the community center. How can you help people in your community?

A. With your group members, find out about a local program/organization that helps your community in one of the following areas:

Education	Housing
Food and Nutrition	The Environment
Parenthood and Family	Services for the Elderly
Disease and Disability	Sports and Athletics
Services for Immigrants	Bad Weather/Natural Disasters

B. Use your school library, a newspaper, the Internet, and so on. You can also call or visit local government offices, community centers, or volunteer organizations. Answer the following questions about your program/organization. Use a separate piece of paper.
  1. What's the name of the program/organization?
  2. Where is it located?
  3. What services does the program/organization offer?
  4. What can volunteers do there?

C. Present your information to the class. Explain why your program/organization is important to the community. Also, explain why it would be fun to volunteer there.

D. As a class, choose one of the programs/organizations from the presentations. Plan a volunteer activity for the whole class with that program/organization. Take a lot of of photos! After the volunteer activity, show the photos to the principal/director of your school and tell him/her about what you did.

1. Besides this project, have you ever helped people in your community? What did you do?
2. Have people in your community ever helped you? What did they do?
3. What do you think the most helpful community program is in your area?

EPISODE 45

PROJECT Legends

1 GROUP RESEARCH

group number

In this episode, Ramón tells Rebecca about the legend of the ekeko. A legend is a kind of story from the past. Usually the stories in legends never happened. Often legends contain magic or mysterious events. Most cultures have legends. Some legends are about how the world began. Some legends are about heroes. Some are about lovers.

Atlantis	El Dorado	The Holy Grail
King Arthur	The Flying Dutchman	Pandora's Box
Quetzalcóatl	Paul Bunyan	John Henry
	El Cid	

Your legend _____

Legend has it that he can bring you good luck and fulfill your dreams. You hang all your dreams on the ekeko, and they'll come true.

Divide into groups. Choose a person, event, object, or place from the list above, or think of your own. Find out about its legend. Write about the legend below. Tell the story of the legend. You can use your school library, an encyclopedia, the Internet, and so on.

Legend _____
_____
_____
_____
_____
_____
_____
_____
_____

2 GROUP POSTER

group number

Work in the same groups from Activity 1. If possible, get colored paper, colored pencils, markers, and so on. Make a poster of your legend. Write a description of your legend on your poster. Present it to the class and tell the story of the legend.

1. Why do people like legends?
2. What was the first legend you ever learned about?
3. What's your favorite legend?

EPISODE 46

PROJECT Languages

1 GROUP RESEARCH

group number

In this episode, Vincent and Alex talk about the languages of Taiwan (Mandarin) and Mexico (Spanish). What do you know about the languages of the world?

Work with a partner. Answer the questions below about languages. You can use the school library, an encyclopedia, an almanac, the Internet, and so on. When you finish, compare your answers with those of another group.

1. How many languages (and dialects) are there in the world? Check (✔) your answer.

    A. under 10,000 _____   B. 10,000–20,000 _____   C. over 20,000 _____

2. Put the following languages in order from 1–10. Write *1* next to the language that the most people speak, write *2* next to the language that is the second most commonly spoken, and so on.

    _____ Arabic   _____ Chinese (Mandarin)   _____ German   _____ Japanese   _____ Russian
    _____ Bengali   _____ English   _____ Hindi   _____ Portuguese   _____ Spanish

3. Over one billion people (1,000,000,000) speak Chinese! How many people speak the language(s) in the list below?

    French _____   Urdu   _____
    Thai   _____   Tagalog _____

① Do they speak English there?

② I don't know. I think they speak Mandarin.

2 TEAM GAME

team number

How many words from different languages can you find?

A. Divide into teams. Copy the chart below onto a separate piece of paper. Add more lines.
B. Walk around your school, campus, or neigborhood. Find words from as many different languages as you can. Look at signs, posters, and books. Write the words below. Next to these words, write what language they are from, and what they mean in English. *(Note: Use each language only once.)*
C. Share your answers with your classmates. The team with the longest list wins.

	Word	Language	Definition in English
EXAMPLE	adiós	Spanish	goodbye
	1.		
	2.		
	3.		

EPISODE 47

PROJECT Ice Skating

1 PARTNER RESEARCH

_____
partner's name

What do you know about ice skating? Work with a partner. Your teacher will assign you one of the questions below. Find the answers using your school library, an encyclopedia, the Internet, and so on. Write your answers on a separate piece of paper. Share your answers with the class.

1. What are the differences between speed skating and figure skating?
2. When was speed skating first included in the Olympics?
3. When was figure skating first included in the Olympics?
4. Who is a famous speed skater? Who is a famous figure skater?

2 PARTNER RESEARCH

_____
partner's name

Do one of the following activities. Present your findings to the class.

Activity A

Work with a partner. Choose one of the Olympic figure skaters from the list below. Find out the following information about this person.

1. What year did this person win a medal in the Olympics? _____
2. How old was this person when he/she won the medal? _____
3. What country is/was this person from? _____

| Karl Schaefer | Sonja Henie | Oksana Baiul | Richard Button |
| Viktor Petrenko | Elizabeth Manley | Katarina Witt | Scott Hamilton |

Activity B

Work with a partner. How fast is a speed skater? Find the Olympic records. Then, answer the questions below. Note: You will compare the speeds in different sports. You will compare the speeds over different distances. You may have to do some math! Write the speeds on a separate piece of paper.

1. How fast can an Olympic speed skater travel 100 meters? 500 meters? 1,000 meters?
2. How fast can Olympic runners complete these distances? How fast do swimmers go? Find the speeds for various sports.

EPISODE 48

PROJECT New Year's Eve

PARTNER RESEARCH

_____
partner's name

In this episode, Ramón, Rebecca, Kevin, and Alex celebrate New Year's Eve together.

Work with a partner. Find out about New Year's Eve celebrations for a country, culture, or religion that neither of you is familiar with. You can use your school library, an encyclopedia, the Internet, and so on. You can also interview people. Find out the answers to the following questions. Try to answer as many as you can.

New Year's Celebration

Place, Culture, or Religion _____

1. When is it celebrated? _____
2. Why is it celebrated on this date? _____
3. What do people do? _____
4. What are the reasons for these traditions? _____
5. What do people eat and drink? _____
6. Why do they eat these things? _____

CLASS PRESENTATION

With your partner from Activity 1, make a presentation to the class. Write the name of your place, culture, or religion on the board. Share your information about New Year's Eve.

When all the presentations are finished, discuss these questions as a class:
- *How are some of the New Year's celebrations alike?*
- *Which was the most unusual fact you learned?*
- *Which celebration would you like to join in the most?*

1. What do you usually do on New Year's Eve?
2. What's the most unusual thing you've ever done on New Year's Eve?
3. Have you ever spent New Year's Eve alone?

APPENDIX 13 Manipulatives

Episode 39

Episode 41

Clues
1. Susanna Sills's present is a sweater.
2. Carson Chills's present is a camera.
3. Ben Bills's present is a bat.
4. Thalia Tills's present is a ticket.

Episode 44

Episode 46

全新版新世纪走遍美国

视频理解 4

Pamela McPartland-Fairman
Michael Berman
Linda Butler
Maggie Sokolik

北京市版权局著作权合同登记号　图字 01-2008-1460

图书在版编目(CIP)数据

全新版新世纪走遍美国. 视频理解 4/Pamela McPartland-Fairman 等编著. —北京：北京大学出版社, 2008.11

ISBN 978-7-301-14380-3

Ⅰ. 全… Ⅱ. P… Ⅲ. 英语—听说教学—教材 Ⅳ. H319.9

中国版本图书馆 CIP 数据核字(2008)第 164900 号

Pamela McPartland-Fairman　Michael Berman　Linda Butler　Maggie Sokolik
Connect with English, Video Comprehension Book 4
ISBN: 0-07-292762-3
Copyright © 1998 by the WGBH Educational Foundation and the Corporation for Public Broadcasting. All rights reserved. Printed in the United States of America. Except as permitted under the United States Copyright Act of 1976, no part of this publication may be reproduced or distributed in any form or by any means, or stored in a data base or retrieval system, without the prior written permission of the publisher.

All rights reserved. This edition is authorized for sale in the People's Republic of China only, excluding Hong Kong, Macao SARs and Taiwan.

此书只限在中华人民共和国境内(不包括中国香港、澳门特别行政区及台湾地区)销售。未经出版者预先书面许可，不得以任何方式复制或抄袭本书的任何部分。

本书封面贴有 McGraw-Hill 公司防伪标签，无标签者不得销售。

书　　　名：	全新版新世纪走遍美国·视频理解 4
著作责任者：	Pamela McPartland-Fairman　等编著
责 任 编 辑：	张建民
标 准 书 号：	ISBN 978-7-301-14380-3/H · 2089
出 版 发 行：	北京大学出版社
地　　　址：	北京市海淀区成府路 205 号　100871
网　　　址：	http://www.pup.cn
电 子 信 箱：	zbing@pup.pku.edu.cn
电　　　话：	邮购部 62752015　发行部 62750672　编辑部 62755217　出版部 62754962
印 刷 者：	世界知识印刷厂
经 销 者：	新华书店
	889 毫米×1194 毫米　16 开本　7 印张　170 千字
	2008 年 11 月第 1 版　2008 年 11 月第 1 次印刷
定　　　价：	98.00 元(包括视频理解、会话练习、学习指导及光盘)

未经许可，不得以任何方式复制或抄袭本书之部分或全部内容。
版权所有，侵权必究
举报电话：(010)62752024　电子信箱：fd@pup.pku.edu.cn

TABLE OF CONTENTS

To the Teacher v
A Visual Tour vi
How to Use this Book x
The Story So Far xi

EPISODE 37

Thanksgiving
**The Caseys celebrate Thanksgiving on the farm.
Rebecca learns a family secret.**

Culture Focus: Thanksgiving

EPISODE 38

Starting Over
**Rebecca returns to San Francisco.
She goes to see Emma Washington and gets some bad news.**

Culture Focus: Men and Emotion

EPISODE 39

The Pressure's On
Rebecca talks to Professor Thomas at the San Francisco College of Music. She makes an important decision about her classes.

Culture Focus: Ways to Spend the Holidays

EPISODE 40

Sharing Feelings
**Ramón and Alberto have an honest talk about their personal lives.
Bill asks Rebecca to go to an audition.**

Culture Focus: Family Relationships

EPISODE 41

Unexpected Offers
**Mr. and Mrs. Wang receive an important letter from Taiwan.
Rebecca is surprised by an invitation from Ramón.**

Culture Focus: Christmas in the United States and Canada

EPISODE 42

The Audition
Nancy and Rebecca talk about the Mendoza brothers.
Bill and Rebecca go to a music audition.

Culture Focus: The Entertainment Business

EPISODE 43

Dream Catcher
Alberto has something important to tell Rebecca.
Bill talks about Rebecca and the music business.

Culture Focus: Final Exams

EPISODE 44

Gifts
Alberto and Rebecca talk about their relationship.
Rebecca spends Christmas with Ramón at the community center.

Culture Focus: Volunteer Work

EPISODE 45

True Love
Rebecca and Ramón exchange Christmas presents.
Rebecca gets an exciting telephone call from Kevin.

Culture Focus: Smoking

EPISODE

Friendship
Kevin visits Rebecca in San Francisco.
Alex and Vincent make plans for New Year's Eve.

Culture Focus: Changing Jobs and Homes

EPISODE

The Lost Boys
Alex and Vincent spend New Year's Eve together.
Their parents don't know where they are.

Culture Focus: Outdoor Activities

EPISODE 48

A Very Good Year
Ramón and the Wangs find Alex and Vincent.
Everyone celebrates New Year's Eve together.

Culture Focus: New Year's Eve Traditions

Discussion Group Index
Character Index

TO THE TEACHER

The primary goal of each *Video Comprehension Book* is to help students build listening comprehension skills and gain a clear understanding of the characters and story line in the *Connect with English* video series.

This Introduction and the following Visual Tour provide important information on how each *Video Comprehension Book* and the corresponding video episodes can be successfully combined to teach English as a second or foreign language.

PROFICIENCY LEVEL:
The comprehension exercises found in each *Video Comprehension Book* are accessible to high-beginning through intermediate students. While the majority of the activities are written at the high-beginning level, special *What About You?* features found throughout the books allow teachers to raise or lower the level of difficulty of the materials according to their students' abilities. These *What About You?* activities encourage students to share their personal opinions and ideas related to the characters and the story. Many times, students are asked to predict what they think will happen next. Because of the open-ended nature of these activities, there are numerous opportunities for classroom discussion and debates. The *What About You?* feature can also be used as the basis for writing and journal activities, creating further possibilities for exploration of themes related to the *Connect with English* story.

LANGUAGE SKILLS:
The primary skill emphasized in each *Video Comprehension Book* is listening, along with recognition skills related to facial expressions, body language, and cultural nuances. Additional language skills/topics covered in each book include reading, oral communication, and vocabulary development.

OPTIONS FOR USE:
Each *Video Comprehension Book* can be used in a variety of different learning environments, including classroom, distance learning, tutorial, and/or independent study situations. Instructors may choose to show the video during class time, while simultaneously using the *Video Comprehension Book*. If access to televisions or VCRs is not possible, teachers can assign students to watch the video episodes in a library, language lab, or at home. Class time can then be used for review of the activities found in the *Video Comprehension Book*.

The *Video Comprehension Books* can easily be combined with other corresponding texts in the *Connect with English* print program. For classes with an emphasis on oral communication skills, *Conversation Books 1-4* contain a variety of multi-level pair, group, team, and whole-class activities based on important themes and events from each episode. For classes with a focus on grammatical structures, *Grammar Guides 1-4* provide multi-level practice in grammar and vocabulary and also include various options for reading and writing activities. Finally, there are 16 *Connections Readers* which offer students graded reading practice based on the *Connect with English* story. For additional information about the *Connect with English* print program, please refer to the inside back cover of this book.

A Visual Tour of this Text

This visual tour is designed to introduce the key features of *Video Comprehension Book 4*. The primary focus of each *Video Comprehension Book* is to help students develop listening and story comprehension. *Video Comprehension Book 4* corresponds to episodes 37–48 of *Connect with English,* and it presents an assortment of activities dealing with various aspects of comprehension, including understanding main points, comprehending details, ordering, decoding, inference, analysis, and more.

The Opening Page
The first page of each chapter introduces key characters and themes from the corresponding video episode and builds on students' prior knowledge to help them predict upcoming events.

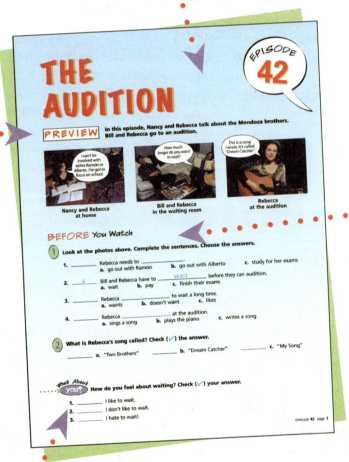

PREVIEW
This section presents a brief summary of the video episode. The three photos highlight key events from each of the three parts of the episode. The **Preview** section builds students' confidence as it gives them a base of contextualized clues about the characters and story line before they watch the video.

BEFORE You Watch
Activities in this section help students further identify the characters and story line. This particular example is a multiple-choice activity which utilizes students' prior knowledge and calls upon their ability to make inferences about the information presented in the photos, captions, and speech bubbles on this page.

What About You? activities provide open-ended questions that encourage students to express their personal feelings, opinions, and reactions to the events and characters in the story. Whenever possible, language prompts or cues are used to provide linguistic support for lower-level students. At the same time, these activities create a springboard for more sophisticated discussions among students who are at higher levels of oral proficiency. The **What About You?** activities can also be used as optional writing assignments.

WATCH FOR MAIN IDEAS
This first viewing activity asks students to watch the entire episode with the purpose of focusing on major story highlights.

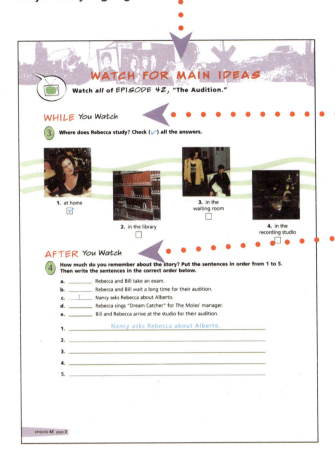

WHILE You Watch
The **While You Watch** section provides a focused viewing activity dealing with specific people, places, things, and/or events central to the development of the story.

AFTER You Watch
Activities in the **After You Watch** section ask students to recall specific information about the story. The first activity is usually a sequencing exercise dealing with the order of the major events in the episode. Many of the activities in this section also include an emphasis on recognition skills for facial expressions, body language, and cultural nuances.

Variety of Activity Types
A variety of different types of activities are included in each chapter, including multiple-choice, sentence completion, true/false, circling, and checking activities. The numbered activities are designed to be accessible to students engaged in independent study — at home, in a language lab, or any place where they have access to a TV and VCR. However, instructors can modify most of these activities into much more elaborate conversation and/or writing topics. For example, in the first sentence in Activity 5, we learn that Nancy thinks that Ramón wants to date Rebecca. In a classroom setting, instructors can start a discussion by simply asking the question, *"Why?"*

A VISUAL TOUR vii

WATCH FOR DETAILS

The **Watch for Details** section helps students develop a more specific understanding of the video story. Each video episode is divided into three viewing sections, labeled on-screen as Part 1, Part 2, and Part 3. In this section of the book, students are asked to view one part at a time, and comprehension is checked with more detailed activities regarding the characters and their experiences.

WHILE You Watch

Many of the **While You Watch** activities in *Video Comprehension Book 4* require students to listen and watch carefully in order to identify speakers, key vocabulary, or completed actions or events. In this example, students listen for specific lines spoken by each character, giving them practice in listening for details.

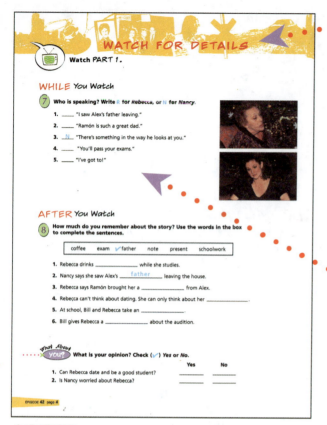

AFTER You Watch

The **After You Watch** activities continue to check students' comprehension of the story and help to solidify their understanding of the subtle nuances related to the characters' feelings and emotions.

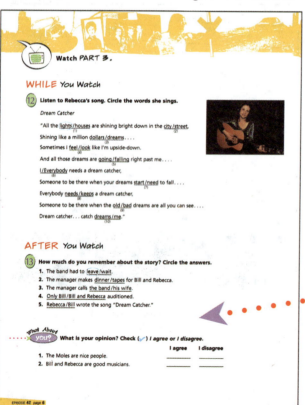

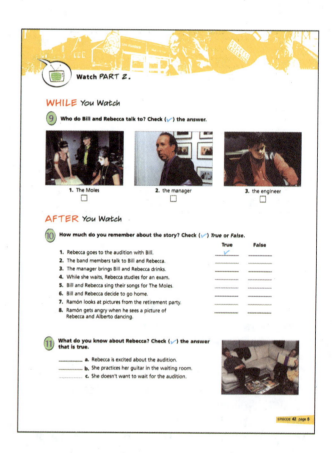

Discussion Topics Encourage Conversation

The **What About You?** activity shown here asks students to share their opinions on certain issues occurring in this episode. These questions can be used as a basis for in-class discussions in which students discuss and compare their impressions of the events in the story.

HIGHLIGHTS

The **Highlights** page offers students an opportunity to explore various cultural and language points from the story.

CULTURE

These boxes expand on subject matter found in the video by providing cultural information about life in the United States and Canada. In this example, students learn that the entertainment business is very important. This topic is explored because two of the main characters in the story go to a music audition for a popular band. An open-ended **What About You?** activity always follows the culture point and encourages students to compare and contrast their understanding of this new information with the corresponding cultural situation in their own countries.

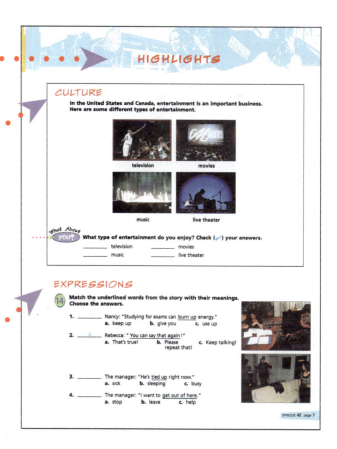

EXPRESSIONS

In this section, students have an opportunity to work with some of the key idioms and expressions from the episode. Only those expressions which were presented in the context of the video story are included in this section. Care has been taken to ensure that the vocabulary features high-frequency items that students might encounter in conversational American English.

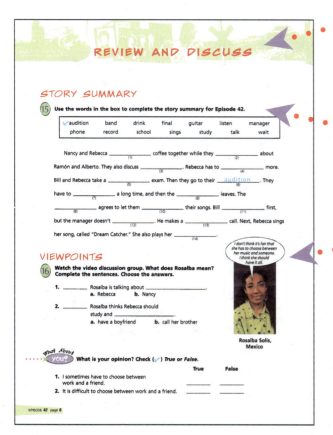

REVIEW AND DISCUSS

This final page of each chapter gives students the opportunity to review the entire episode and offers a chapter-culminating discussion topic.

STORY SUMMARY

In this section, students summarize the episode by selecting and inserting key vocabulary used in the video or earlier in the chapter. As in every exercise in the chapter, a sample answer is provided.

VIEWPOINTS

Activities found in the **Viewpoints** section are based on the final review portion of the video episode. In this part of the video, various non-native English speakers from around the world talk about the episode and share their personal feelings about things that happened. Students using *Video Comprehension Book 4* are asked to interpret and react to these comments and ideas in a final **What About You?** activity.

A VISUAL TOUR ix

HOW TO USE THIS BOOK

CONNECT WITH ENGLISH is a story to help you learn English. Watch the program by yourself, in a classroom, or with family or friends. Record the program so you can watch it again. The episodes are closed-captioned. Turn on your captioning system to see the words on the screen and get extra help in following the story.

This book will help you understand the story. Each episode has three parts. Before you watch the episode, look at the pictures in the *Preview* section. These pictures will show you some of the most important events from each part of the episode. The activities underneath the pictures will also help you get ready to watch.

Watch the episodes as many times as you need to. If you can, watch the whole episode one time through. Then you can go back and watch each part of the episode again. As you watch, you will see on-screen labels that say Part 1, Part 2, and Part 3. At the end of each episode, you will also see a group of students talk about the story.

The activities in the *Watch for the Main Ideas* and the *Watch for the Details* sections will help you learn the most important things that happen in each episode.

When you see a *What About You?* activity, you have a chance to talk about your own ideas and opinions about the **Connect with English** story. Discuss the questions and answers with your friends, family, or classmates. Your teacher might even ask you to write about your ideas.

In the *Highlights* section, a *Culture* box will tell you about life in the United States and Canada. In this section, you will also have a chance to talk about your country and how it is similar to or different from what you have learned about the United States and Canada. The *Expressions* section will help you understand some common American English phrases and expressions that the characters say in the episode.

On the last page of every chapter, a *Story Summary* reviews everything that happened in the episode. Look back through the activities you have already completed for help in doing the summary. The *Viewpoints* section gives you a chance to hear what some other English students think about **Connect with English**.

Remember, as you use this book, here's how you can *connect* with English: watch and record the episodes, read the book, and talk about the program with your family, friends, or classmates. Most of all, have fun and enjoy the story!

THE STORY SO FAR

1. Rebecca Casey is a singer. She leaves Boston and goes to music school in San Francisco.

2. In San Francisco, Rebecca stays with her godmother, Nancy Shaw. She meets many new friends.

3. Rebecca goes on a date with Alberto Mendoza. She meets Alberto's parents and his brother, Ramón.

4. Rebecca gets a job at an after-school program. Ramón's son, Alex, and Alex's friend Vincent both go to the program.

5. Ramón and Rebecca become very good friends.

6. Rebecca gets bad news about her father's health. She goes home to Boston.

7. Rebecca's father had a serious heart attack.

8. Rebecca and Kevin meet their uncle Brendan for the first time. He comes to Boston to see his brother, Patrick.

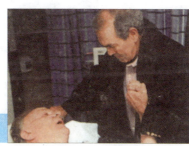
9. Patrick Casey dies. Friends and family go to his funeral.

10. Rebecca and Kevin find some important things in their father's safe deposit box.

11. Rebecca and Kevin talk about the future. Kevin is very upset about his father.

12. Uncle Brendan and Aunt Anne want to help. They invite Kevin and Rebecca to visit their farm in Illinois.

13. Rebecca and Kevin help their friend Sandy. Sandy's boyfriend hits her, and she wants to leave him.

14. The police arrest Sandy's boyfriend Jack. Sandy goes to stay in a shelter—a safe place.

15. Rebecca and Kevin decide to leave Boston and go to Uncle Brendan's farm for a while.

LOOKING AHEAD

In this part of the story, Kevin decides where he will live. Rebecca goes back to her life in San Francisco. The Mendozas and the Wangs solve some family problems, and everyone celebrates a very happy New Year.

What About you?

What is your opinion? Check (✓) *I agree* or *I disagree*.

	I agree	I disagree
1. Patrick Casey was a good father.	_____	_____
2. It is a good idea for Rebecca and Kevin to go to the farm.	_____	_____
3. Sandy should try to help Jack.	_____	_____
4. Rebecca should go back to music school.	_____	_____

THANKSGIVING

EPISODE 37

PREVIEW In this episode, Rebecca and Kevin meet their cousin, Michael, and his family. Rebecca learns a family secret.

The Casey family at the table

Kevin and Michael in the family room

Brendan and Rebecca in the truck

BEFORE You Watch

1 Look at the photos above. Use the words in the box to complete the sentences.

| cousins | dinner | question | ✓son | teacher |

1. The Caseys eat a big _____.
2. Rebecca and Kevin are Michael's _____.
3. Michael is a _____.
4. Michael is Brendan's ___son___.
5. Rebecca has a _____ for Brendan.

2 What do you know about the Casey family? Check (✓) the sentence that *is not* true.

_____ a. They welcome Kevin and Rebecca to the farm.
_____ b. They are glad to spend Thanksgiving together.
_____ c. They want Kevin and Rebecca to go back to Boston.

What About you? How big is your family? Write the number.

_____ brothers _____ sisters _____ uncles _____ aunts
_____ cousins _____ sons _____ daughters

WATCH FOR MAIN IDEAS

Watch *all* of EPISODE 37, "Thanksgiving."

WHILE You Watch

3 Who are these people? Circle their names.

1. Anne / Peggy

2. Kevin / Michael

3. Michael / Brendan

4. (Erin and Katie) / Peggy and Anne

AFTER You Watch

4 How much do you remember about the story? Check (✓) *True* or *False*.

	True	False
1. The Caseys have Thanksgiving dinner.	✓	____
2. Kevin decides to return to Boston.	____	____
3. Rebecca decides to return to school.	____	____
4. Brendan tells Rebecca a family secret.	____	____
5. Anne takes Rebecca to the airport.	____	____

5 What does Rebecca do on Thanksgiving? Check (✓) all the answers.

1. She helps cook dinner.

✓

2. She plays soccer.

☐

3. She sings a song.

☐

4. She eats dinner.

☐

6 What do you know about these people? Circle the answers.

1. (Kevin)/ Michael plays soccer with Erin and Katie.
2. Michael / Brendan teaches a computer class.
3. Kevin / Rebecca is going back to San Francisco.
4. Rebecca / Brendan talks to Kevin about their parents.
5. Rebecca / Kevin talks to Brendan about Patrick.

7 What does Kevin decide to do? Circle the answer.

a. ...return to Boston
b. ...go to San Francisco
c. ...stay on the farm

What About you? What do you think will happen? Check (✓) *Yes* or *No*.

	Yes	No
1. Will Kevin like living on the farm?	_____	_____
2. Will Kevin go to college?	_____	_____
3. Will Rebecca be happy in San Francisco?	_____	_____

Watch PART 1.

WHILE You Watch

8 What do the Caseys cook for their Thanksgiving dinner? Check (✓) all the answers.

1. bread
   ✓

2. hamburgers
   ☐

3. turkey
   ☐

4. sweet potatoes
   ☐

5. spaghetti
   ☐

AFTER You Watch

9 How much do you remember about the story? Put the photos in order from 1 to 5.

a. _____
b. _____
c. ___1___
d. _____
e. _____

① Welcome to the Casey farm.
② He's doing a darn good job.
a.

Mom, where are the girls?
b.

…and this is Erin, and this is Katie.
c.

Let's eat!
d.

Kevin has decided to put up with us so that his sister can go back to college.
e.

10 How does Michael feel about his cousins? Check (✓) the sentence that *is not* true.

1. _____ He is glad to meet Rebecca and Kevin.
2. _____ He is happy that Kevin is working in the barn.
3. _____ He thinks that Kevin should get a job.

Watch PART 2.

WHILE You Watch

11 **Listen to Rebecca's song. Circle the words she sings.**

'Tis the Gift to Be Simple

"'Tis the gift to be simple,

'tis the gift to be alive / (free)
(1)

'tis the gift to come through / down
(2)

where we ought to be.

And when we are in the house / place just right,
(3)

we'll be in the valley of love / friends and delight.
(4)

When our / true simplicity is gained,
(5)

to bow and to bend / walk we will not be ashamed.
(6)

To turn, to turn

will be our delight,

till by turning, turning,

we stop / come round right."
(7)

AFTER You Watch

12 **How much do you remember about the story? Use the words in the box to complete the conversation.**

| class | college | computer | ✓ field | learn |

1. Kevin: "Your dad tells me you teach a _____ course."

2. Michael: "Yeah. I teach at a community _____ in town."

   Kevin: "I'm into computers."

3. Michael: "Good for you. It's a great ___field___ —something new happening all the time."

4. Kevin: "Oh, yeah, there's a lot to _____."

5. Michael: "Hey, maybe you could enroll in my _____."

What About you? **Check (✓) Yes or No.**

	Yes	No
1. Do you use a computer?	_____	_____
2. Do you take computer classes?	_____	_____

Watch PART **3**.

WHILE You Watch

13 Who is speaking? Write **B** for *Brendan*, or **R** for *Rebecca*.

1. __B__ "Are you excited about going back to school?"
2. _____ "Why didn't you and my father talk for so many years?"
3. _____ "Are you sure you want to know?"
4. _____ "It was my mother, wasn't it?"
5. _____ "Things never were the same between your father and me."

AFTER You Watch

14 How much do you remember about the story? Circle the answers.

1. Brendan and Rebecca go to the airport / bus station .
2. Rebecca asks Brendan a (personal) / funny question.
3. Brendan tells Rebecca a story about her father / brother .
4. A long time ago, Brendan got a letter / telephone call from Patrick.
5. Brendan is sorry / happy he didn't talk to Patrick for so long.

15 Complete the conversations with the sentences below. Choose the answers.

✓ a. "Sure . . . go ahead."
    b. "It was my mother, wasn't it?"
    c. "Your father never told you?"

1. __a__

2. _____

3. _____

What About you? How do you think Rebecca feels when Brendan tells her what happened?

I think Rebecca feels _____.

HIGHLIGHTS

CULTURE

Thanksgiving is a traditional holiday in the United States. It is a day to be thankful for all that we have. The Pilgrims and the Native Americans shared the first Thanksgiving dinner hundreds of years ago. Today, people do many different things on Thanksgiving. They . . .

 visit with family and friends.
 eat turkey.
 watch football.
 give thanks.
 have a big meal.

In the U.S., Thanksgiving is celebrated on the last Thursday in November. In Canada, it is celebrated on the second Monday in October.

What About you? Check (✓) *Yes* or *No*.

	Yes	No
1. Do you have Thanksgiving dinner?	_____	_____
2. Do you like to eat turkey?	_____	_____
3. In your country, do you have a family holiday?	_____	_____

EXPRESSIONS

 Match the underlined words from the story with their meanings. Check (✓) the answers.

1. "Kevin has decided to put up with us."
   ___✓___ a. Kevin will stay with us.   _____ b. Kevin doesn't like us.

2. "My father passed away."
   _____ a. My father went away.   _____ b. My father died.

3. "I'll give it a shot."
   _____ a. I'll try.   _____ b. I won't try.

4. "We had a lot of friends in common."
   _____ a. We had different friends.   _____ b. We had the same friends.

REVIEW AND DISCUSS

STORY SUMMARY

17 Use the words in the box to complete the story summary for Episode 37.

| airport | computer | ✓dinner | farm | football | learn |
| meet | says | song | tells | wife |

Rebecca and Kevin _____(1)_____ their cousin Michael. Peggy is Michael's _____(2)_____, and his daughters are Erin and Katie. Everyone helps make a large __dinner__(3). The men watch _____(4)_____ on television. Brendan _____(5)_____ a word of thanks before dinner. The family is thankful that Kevin will stay on the _____(6)_____. Michael tells Kevin about a _____(7)_____ course. Kevin wants to _____(8)_____ more about computers. Rebecca sings a _____(9)_____, "'Tis the Gift to Be Simple." She and Kevin talk about their parents. Finally, Rebecca goes to the _____(10)_____ with Brendan. Brendan _____(11)_____ Rebecca that he was in love with her mother many years ago.

VIEWPOINTS

...people look back and are thankful for all the good things that they got during the year.

18 Watch the video discussion group. What does Laura mean? Complete the sentences. Check (✓) *True* or *False*.

	True	False
1. Laura is talking about Thanksgiving.	_____	_____
2. She says the Caseys celebrate Thanksgiving in a traditional way.	_____	_____

Laura Eastment, Argentina

What are you thankful for?

I am thankful for _____
_____.

...my job   ...my family   ...my health   ...living in this country

STARTING OVER

EPISODE 38

PREVIEW In this episode, Rebecca returns to San Francisco. She speaks to Professor Thomas and Emma Washington.

I've missed my life here.
Rebecca and Nancy at home

1. *I would like to get together and talk about my courses.*
2. *Why don't you come by at 5 o'clock?*
Rebecca and Professor Thomas on the phone

1. *I had to replace you.*
2. *I understand.*
Rebecca and Emma at the after-school program

BEFORE You Watch

1 Look at the photos above. Complete the sentences. Choose the answers.

1. __a__ Rebecca is __happy__ to be home.
   a. happy   b. sad   c. angry

2. _____ Rebecca makes an appointment with _____.
   a. Nancy   b. Alberto   c. Professor Thomas

3. _____ Professor Thomas _____ see Rebecca.
   a. can   b. can't   c. doesn't want to

4. _____ Rebecca _____ her old job.
   a. wants   b. hates   c. forgets

5. _____ Emma has _____ for Rebecca.
   a. good news   b. bad news   c. a letter

What About you? How do you feel when you have to start over with something? Check (✓) your answers.

I feel _____.

_____ excited   _____ sad   _____ tired
_____ frustrated   _____ angry   _____ worried

WATCH FOR MAIN IDEAS

 Watch *all* of EPISODE 38, "Starting Over."

WHILE You Watch

2 Who does Rebecca talk to? Check (✓) all the answers.

1. Nancy ✓

2. Alberto ☐

3. Professor Thomas ☐

4. Emma ☐

5. Ramón ☐

AFTER You Watch

3 How much do you remember about the story? Put the photos in order from 1 to 5.

a. _____
b. _____
c. _____
d. _____
e. __1__

a.

b.

c.

d.

e.

EPISODE 38 page 2

What do these people do? Check (✓) *True* or *False*.

	True	False
1. Alberto talks about Rebecca.	✓	
2. Rebecca calls her adviser.	___	___
3. Rebecca gets her old job back.	___	___
4. Ramón sees Rebecca.	___	___
5. Alberto and Rebecca go to the opera.	___	___

 How do these people feel? Use the words in the box to complete the sentences. You may use a word more than once.

1.

   Alberto and Pete are
   _____.

2.

   Rebecca is
   _____.

3.

   Nancy is
   _____.

4.

   Rebecca is
   sad.

5.

   Ramón is
   _____.

What About you? **What do you think will happen? Check (✓) *True* or *False*.**

	True	False
1. Rebecca will get a new job.	___	___
2. Rebecca will go back to school.	___	___
3. Alberto will give Rebecca a present.	___	___

WATCH FOR DETAILS

 Watch PART 1.

WHILE You Watch

6 Which people have a photograph? Check (✓) their names.

1. ___✓___ Alberto
2. _____ Pete
3. _____ Nancy
4. _____ Rebecca
5. _____ Professor Thomas

AFTER You Watch

7 How much do you remember about the story? Circle the answers.

1. Memorial Day / (Christmas) is coming soon.
2. Alberto wants to take Rebecca / Pete to the opera.
3. Rebecca still feels sad about her adviser / father.
4. Nancy is sad about Professor Thomas / Edward.
5. Edward wants to come home / stay at the nursing home.
6. Rebecca missed a lot of television shows / schoolwork.
7. Rebecca has a photograph of her family / boyfriend with her.

 What About you? Are photographs important to you? Check (✓) Yes or No.

	Yes	No
1. Do you carry any photographs with you?	_____	_____
2. Do you have any photographs in your home?	_____	_____
3. Do you have any old family photographs?	_____	_____

Watch PART 2.

WHILE You Watch

 Who is speaking? Write R for *Rebecca*, T for *Professor Thomas*, or N for *Nancy*.

1. __R__ "I would like to get together and talk about my courses."
2. ____ "I'm planning to be in my office late today."
3. ____ "Did you hear anything from Emma Washington?"
4. ____ "And that's why your father and I never got along."
5. ____ "They had a chance to talk."

AFTER You Watch

 How much do you remember about the story? Circle the answers.

1. Rebecca telephones Alberto / **Professor Thomas**.
2. Rebecca will meet Professor Thomas at 5:00 / 3:00.
3. Nancy tells Rebecca not to cry / worry.
4. Nancy told Rebecca's mother to marry Brendan / Patrick.
5. Rebecca's mother married Brendan / Patrick.

10 **What do Nancy and Rebecca talk about? Check (✔) the answers.**

1. Why didn't Nancy get along with Patrick Casey?
   _____ a. Nancy didn't like Rebecca's mother.
   _____ b. Nancy wanted Brendan to marry Rebecca's mother.
   _____ c. Nancy loved Brendan.

2. What does Rebecca tell Nancy about Brendan and Patrick?
   _____ a. They didn't like Nancy.
   _____ b. They both loved Nancy.
   _____ c. They talked before Patrick died.

EPISODE 38 page 5

Watch PART 3.

WHILE You Watch

11 What does Emma tell Rebecca? Check (✓) the sentences she says.

1. __✓__ "I had to find someone for your old job."
2. _____ "There might be an opening after the new year."
3. _____ "Please keep me in mind."
4. _____ "I have so much catching up to do."
5. _____ "I'll put a notice on the bulletin board."

AFTER You Watch

12 How much do you remember about the story? Check (✓) the sentences about Rebecca that are true.

1. _____ She keeps her job at the after-school program.
2. _____ She doesn't want to go back to college.
3. _____ She works well with children.
4. _____ She wants to give guitar lessons.
5. __✓__ She sees Ramón.
6. _____ She sees Professor Thomas.

What About you? What is your opinion? Check (✓) *I agree* or *I disagree*.

	I agree	I disagree
1. Rebecca should get a new job.	_____	_____
2. Rebecca should only worry about school.	_____	_____

HIGHLIGHTS

CULTURE

In the United States and Canada, some men don't like to show their emotions. They think it is weak to be emotional.

 What is your opinion? Check (✓) *True* or *False*.

	True	False
1. Men in my country like to show their emotions.	_____	_____
2. A man is weak if he shows his emotions.	_____	_____

EXPRESSIONS

13 Match the expressions from the story with their meanings. Check (✓) the answers.

1. Nancy tells Rebecca, "Take one step at a time." She means. . .

   _____ a. Walk around the house a little.
   ✓ b. Do things slowly.

2. Nancy says, "Your mother had a mind of her own." She means. . .

   _____ a. Your mother was independent.
   _____ b. Your mother was smart.

3. Emma tells Rebecca, "We're so shorthanded." She means. . .

   _____ a. We need more workers.
   _____ b. We're so late.

4. Rebecca says, "Please keep me in mind." She means. . .

   _____ a. Please don't forget about me.
   _____ b. Please teach me.

REVIEW AND DISCUSS

STORY SUMMARY

 Use the words in the box to complete the story summary for Episode 38.

| calls | courses | father | filled | ✓house | marry |
| meet | returns | sees | talks | tickets | uncle |

Alberto gets two opera _____(1)_____. Rebecca _____(2)_____ to San Francisco. She arrives at Nancy Shaw's __house__(3). They talk about Rebecca's _____(4)_____ and Nancy's _____(5)_____, Edward. Rebecca _____(6)_____ Professor Thomas. They decide to _____(7)_____ at 5:00 to talk about Rebecca's _____(8)_____. Nancy tells Rebecca that she wanted her mother to _____(9)_____ Brendan. Rebecca _____(10)_____ with Emma. Emma tells Rebecca that she has _____(11)_____ her position. Rebecca _____(12)_____ Ramón at the after-school program.

VIEWPOINTS

 Watch the video discussion group. What does Ventha mean? Circle the answers.

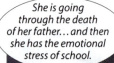
She is going through the death of her father...and then she has the emotional stress of school.

1. Ventha is talking about Rebecca / Nancy .

2. Ventha thinks Rebecca's situation is easy / difficult .

Ventha Danapalan, India

What About you? **What do you think Rebecca needs to do now? Check (✓) your answers.**

1. _____ Get a job.
2. _____ Study hard.
3. _____ Go out with Alberto.
4. _____ Go back to the farm.

THE PRESSURE'S ON

EPISODE 39

PREVIEW In this episode, Rebecca talks with Ramón and Alex. She goes to see Professor Thomas. Alberto visits Rebecca at home.

"The letter from you and Alex meant a lot to me."

Ramón and Rebecca at the after-school program

"If you don't pass, you risk losing your partial scholarship."

Professor Thomas at the music school

1. I sure have missed you.
2. This is such a suprise.

Rebecca and Alberto at Nancy's house

BEFORE You Watch

1 Look at the photos above. Circle the answers.

1. Ramón and Alex sent Rebecca a **letter** / photograph.
2. Rebecca thinks that Alex and Ramón's letter is **important** / not important.
3. Professor Thomas and Rebecca **meet** / talk on the phone.
4. Rebecca might lose her job / **scholarship**.
5. Alberto **visits** / calls Rebecca.

2 What is Rebecca worried about? Check (✓) the answer.

_____ a. passing her exams
_____ b. visiting Alberto
_____ c. writing letters to Ramón and Alex

 What is your opinion? Check (✓) Yes or No.

	Yes	No
1. Is Rebecca happy to see Ramón?	_____	_____
2. Is Rebecca happy to see Alberto?	_____	_____

EPISODE **39** page 1

WATCH FOR MAIN IDEAS

Watch *all* of EPISODE 39, "The Pressure's On."

WHILE You Watch

3 Where does Rebecca go? Check (✓) all the answers.

1. __✓__ the after-school program
2. _____ Professor Thomas' office
3. _____ the library
4. _____ Nancy's house
5. _____ the opera

AFTER You Watch

4 How much do you remember about the story? Put the photos in order from 1 to 5.

a. _____
b. _____
c. _____
d. _____
e. __1__

a. "I'll be in my room studying."

b. "Tickets to the San Francisco Opera."

c. "Get together with your classmates. Study with them."

d. "Alberto really seems to care about you."

e. "Rebecca! You're back!"

EPISODE 39 page 2

5. Use the words in the box to complete the conversations.

| ✓appointment | sorry | study | take | tickets |

1. Ramón: "Where are you going?"
   Rebecca: "I have an __appointment__ at school."

2. Ramón: "Are we going to see you around here?"
   Rebecca: "Emma had to hire someone to _____ my place."

3. Angela: "I am so _____ about your father."
   Rebecca: "It was a total shock."

4. Alberto: "I have something to cheer you up."
   Rebecca: "They're _____ to the San Francisco Opera."

5. Angela: "Maybe you'll spend the holidays with Alberto."
   Rebecca: "I don't think so. I have to _____."

6. What does Rebecca decide to do? Circle the answer.

a. ...go to the opera with Alberto
b. ...study for her exams
c. ...visit Kevin

What About you? What do you think Rebecca should do? Check (✓) *I agree* or *I disagree*.

	I agree	I disagree
1. Rebecca should go to the opera with Alberto.	_____	_____
2. She shouldn't go to the opera.	_____	_____
3. She should study hard and take her exams now.	_____	_____
4. She should wait and take her exams later.	_____	_____

WATCH FOR DETAILS

Watch PART 1.

WHILE You Watch

7 Listen to Ramón. Check (✓) the sentences he says.

1. __✓__ "It's great to have you back!"
2. _____ "How are you doing?"
3. _____ "The pain will go away."
4. _____ "Alex doesn't have time for guitar lessons."
5. _____ "We need you badly."
6. _____ "Maybe Alberto and I can buy you a hamburger."

AFTER You Watch

8 How much do you remember about the story? Complete the sentences. Choose the answers.

1. __b__ Rebecca thanks Alex for the ___letter___ and drawing.
   a. phone call   b. letter   c. photo

2. _____ Ramón tells Rebecca that _____ will go away.
   a. her job   b. her exams   c. the pain

3. _____ Rebecca has an appointment at the _____.
   a. opera   b. college   c. restaurant

4. _____ Rebecca tells Ramón that she _____ job.
   a. has a new   b. doesn't want a   c. lost her

5. _____ Ramón wants Rebecca to _____.
   a. continue Alex's guitar lessons   b. work in the restaurant   c. be Alex's soccer coach

9 How does Rebecca feel? Check (✓) all the answers.

1. _____ She is happy to be back in San Francisco.
2. __✓__ She is sad that her father died.
3. _____ She is sad to see Ramón.
4. _____ She is happy to see Alex.
5. _____ She is unhappy about losing her job.

Watch PART 2.

WHILE You Watch

10 Who is speaking? Write **R** for *Rebecca*, **T** for *Professor Thomas*, or **A** for *Angela*.

1. __T__ "I don't want to frighten you."
2. _____ "I'd like to try to take the exams."
3. _____ "It's last year's exam."
4. _____ "Rebecca, you're back!"
5. _____ "You won't see much of me for a while."
6. _____ "I'm going home to see my parents."

AFTER You Watch

11 How much do you remember about the story? Circle the answers.

1. Who talks to Rebecca about studying?   Professor Thomas / Angela
2. Who gives Rebecca an old music exam?   Melaku / (Professor Thomas)
3. Who will stay in San Francisco for Christmas? Rebecca / Melaku
4. Who will visit friends for Christmas?   Melaku / Angela
5. Who will spend the holidays with her parents? Angela / Nancy

12 What do you know about Rebecca? Check (✓) the sentences that *are not* true.

1. _____ She will take her final exams.
2. ___✓___ Her exams will be easy.
3. _____ She doesn't need to study.
4. _____ San Francisco is her home now.
5. _____ She will be with Nancy for Christmas.

 How do you spend your holidays?

I spend my holidays _____
_____.

Watch PART 3.

WHILE You Watch

13 Listen to Rebecca and Alberto's conversation. Circle the words they say.

1. Rebecca: "Tickets to the San Francisco Ballet /(Opera)."
2. Alberto: "Best / Most expensive seats in the house."
3. Rebecca: "That's very smart / nice of you."
4. Alberto: "I'm sure you'll see / enjoy it."
5. Rebecca: "I'm sure I would, too, but I can't make any plans / phone calls."
6. Alberto: "A ton of school / office work, huh?"

AFTER You Watch

14 How much do you remember about the story? Put the sentences in order from 1 to 5.

a. _____ Alberto says he'll call Rebecca.

b. _____ Rebecca goes to study.

c. ___1___ Alberto visits Rebecca.

d. _____ Rebecca says she has to study.

e. _____ Alberto asks Rebecca to the opera.

15 How does Rebecca feel? Check (✓) *True* or *False*.

	True	False
1. She is surprised to see Alberto.	✓	
2. She wants to go to the opera.		
3. She is worried about school.		
4. She feels very tired.		
5. She gets angry at Angela.		

What About you?
What is your opinion? Check (✓) *Yes* or *No*.

	Yes	No
1. Is Rebecca happy to see Alberto?		
2. Do Rebecca and Alberto have a good relationship?		
3. Does Alberto listen to Rebecca?		

HIGHLIGHTS

CULTURE

Not everyone in the United States and Canada spends the holidays with his or her family. Here are some other things people do.

go to parties   take a vacation   do volunteer work   visit friends

What About you? Check (✓) *Yes* or *No*.

	Yes	No
1. Do you like parties?	___	___
2. Do you take a vacation during the holidays?	___	___
3. Do you volunteer when you have free time?	___	___

EXPRESSIONS

16 Match the underlined words from the story with their meanings.

a. try hard
✓ b. waiting for you
c. good for you
d. make you happy
e. going

1. _____   2. _____

3. __b__   4. _____   5. _____

REVIEW AND DISCUSS

STORY SUMMARY

17 Use the words in the box to complete the story summary for Episode 39.

death	exams	goes	✓ happy	invites	lessons
plans	room	study	talk	team	tired

Ramón and Rebecca are __happy__ (1) to see each other again. Alex tells Rebecca his _____ (2) won a game. Ramón and Rebecca talk about her father's _____ (3). Ramón and Rebecca decide to continue Alex's guitar _____ (4). Rebecca meets her professor to _____ (5) about her courses. She decides to take her _____ (6). Rebecca _____ (7) home, where Angela and Melaku greet her. They ask her about her holiday _____ (8). Alberto visits and _____ (9) Rebecca to the opera. Rebecca says she has to _____ (10). Rebecca feels _____ (11) and worried. She goes to her _____ (12).

VIEWPOINTS

18 Watch the video discussion group. What does Boris mean? Complete the sentences. Choose the answers.

She will always pick work over having fun.

1. _____ Boris is talking about _____.
   a. Angela   b. Rebecca

2. _____ Boris thinks Rebecca wants to _____.
   a. go to the opera   b. study

Boris Levitin, Russia

What About you?

What is your opinion? Check (✓) *True* or *False*.

	True	False
1. Work is more important than having fun.	_____	_____
2. My family is more important than my career.	_____	_____

SHARING FEELINGS

EPISODE 40

PREVIEW In this episode, Bill and Rebecca study for their final exams. Ramón and Alberto talk about their problems.

Come with me to the audition.

Bill and Rebecca at the music school

I went to the opera.

Alberto and Ramón at the restaurant

① *Rebecca is a very dedicated student.* ② *Maybe too dedicated.*

Ramón and Alberto at the restaurant

BEFORE You Watch

1 Look at the photos above. Use the words in the box to complete the sentence.

opera	student	✓ studies	working

1. Rebecca ____studies____ with Bill at the music school.
2. Alberto went to the _____.
3. Ramón is _____ in the restaurant.
4. Ramón thinks Rebecca is a good _____.

2 What does Bill want? Check (✓) the sentence that is true.

_____ a. Bill wants Rebecca to practice the guitar more.
_____ b. He wants Rebecca to go to a music audition with him.
_____ c. He wants Rebecca to go to the opera.

What is your opinion? Check (✓) *Yes* or *No*.

	Yes	No
1. Do you like to study with other people?	_____	_____
2. Do you like to study alone?	_____	_____

EPISODE **40** page 1

WATCH FOR MAIN IDEAS

Watch *all* of EPISODE 40, "Sharing Feelings."

WHILE You Watch

3 Who talks to Rebecca? Check (✓) all the answers.

1. __✓__ Bill
2. _____ Mr. Mendoza
3. _____ Alberto
4. _____ Ramón
5. _____ Alex

AFTER You Watch

4 How much do you remember about the story? Put the sentences in order from 1 to 6.

a. _____ Bill asks Rebecca to go to a music audition.
b. __1__ Bill helps Rebecca study in the music lab.
c. _____ Rebecca tells Alberto she can't go to the opera.

d. _____ Alberto invites Ramón to go skiing.
e. _____ Ramón tells Alberto to be patient with Rebecca.
f. _____ Alberto goes to the opera alone.

EPISODE **40** page 2

5 What do you know about these people? Use the names in the box to complete the sentences.

| Alberto | Bill | Ramón | ✓Rebecca |

1. __Rebecca__ isn't going to the opera.
2. _____ has to work at the restaurant.
3. _____ is going skiing.
4. _____ and Rebecca are going to an audition.

6 How much do you remember about Rebecca's day? Circle the answers.

1. Rebecca is at <u>the music school / Nancy's house</u>.
2. Rebecca and Bill study for their <u>(music)/ computer</u> exam.
3. Rebecca and Bill talk about their <u>brothers / parents</u>.
4. Bill asks Rebecca to go to <u>a party / an audition</u>.
5. Rebecca <u>calls / visits</u> Alberto.
6. She tells Alberto that she can't go to the <u>music school / opera</u>.

What About you? What do you think will happen? Circle the answers.

1. Where will Alberto spend the holidays?
   a. skiing   b. in the restaurant   c. with Rebecca

2. Where will Ramón spend the holidays?
   a. skiing   b. in the restaurant   c. with his parents

3. Where will Rebecca spend the holidays?
   a. skiing   b. in the library   c. with Kevin

WATCH FOR DETAILS

Watch PART 1.

WHILE You Watch

7 What does Bill tell Rebecca? Check (✓) the sentences he says.

1. __✓__ "All I want to do is play my music, not go to school."
2. _____ "They don't know what they're talking about."
3. _____ "Money isn't all that important to me."
4. _____ "I'm serious. I have to make music."
5. _____ "Hey, it might even be fun."

AFTER You Watch

8 How much do you remember about the story? Circle the answers.

1. Rebecca (studies)/talks with Alberto all day.
2. Bill and Rebecca talk about the after-school program/music.
3. Both Bill's and Rebecca's parents think it's hard to make friends/money in the music business.
4. Rebecca will go/won't go to the audition with Bill.
5. The audition is with a study group/rock group called The Moles.

9 How does Rebecca feel about music? Check (✓) the answer.

_____ a. It isn't important.

_____ b. It's all she cares about.

_____ c. It's too hard.

EPISODE 40 page 4

Watch PART 2.

WHILE You Watch

10 Where does Alberto go? Check (✓) all the answers.

1. ___✓___ his office
2. _____ Rebecca's house
3. _____ the opera
4. _____ the library
5. _____ the restaurant

AFTER You Watch

11 How much do you remember about the story? Choose the answers.

1. _____ Where are Ramón and Alberto's parents?
   a. They are in Mexico.   b. They are in Los Angeles.

2. _____ Why is Alex going to Los Angeles?
   a. He is going to see friends.   b. He is going to visit his mother.

3. ___b___ Who went to the opera with Alberto?
   a. Rebecca went with him.   b. Nobody went with him.

4. _____ Why is Alberto going to Aspen?
   a. He is going skiing.   b. He is going to visit his friends.

 What is your opinion? Check (✓) *True* or *False*.

	True	False
1. I need a vacation now.	_____	_____
2. I can't take a vacation right now.	_____	_____

Watch PART 3.

WHILE You Watch

12 Who is speaking? Write **R** for *Ramón*, or **A** for *Alberto*.

1. __R__ "Oh, now I get it. Woman trouble."
2. _____ "Thanks for the sympathy, brother."
3. _____ "Pictures from the retirement party."
4. _____ "You know, Rebecca is a very dedicated student."
5. _____ "I have to get up early in the morning. It's time to go home."

AFTER You Watch

13 How much do you remember about the story? Use the words in the box to complete the conversation.

interested	miss	patient	simple	✓talking	woman

1. Ramón: "This was good . . . __talking__, I mean. We haven't done that for a long time."
2. Alberto: "So, do you _____ having someone in your life?"
3. Ramón: "I liked being married. But the next time, she's going to have to be the right _____. It's not so simple."
4. Alberto: "Things are never as _____ as they might appear."
5. Alberto: "Let's just say at the moment, Rebecca doesn't seem to be very _____."
6. Ramón: "Well, if that's what you want, you have to be _____."

14 What does Alberto think? Check (✓) the sentence that is true.

_____ a. Rebecca loves him.
_____ b. Rebecca doesn't want to be with him.
_____ c. Having a relationship is easy.

What About you? What is your opinion? Check (✓) *I agree* or *I disagree*.

                                                                   I agree   I disagree

1. Alberto should be patient with Rebecca. _____ _____
2. Alberto should find a new girlfriend. _____ _____

HIGHLIGHTS

CULTURE

In the United States and Canada, there are many different kinds of family relationships. In some families, brothers and sisters do not have close relationships. In other families, brothers and sisters talk to each other often. They depend on each other.

 Describe your relationship with your brothers and sisters. Check (✓) *Yes* or *No*.

	Yes	No
1. Do you have a good relationship with your brothers and sisters?	_____	_____
2. Do you talk with them often?	_____	_____
3. Do you want to talk to them more?	_____	_____

EXPRESSIONS

 Match the underlined words from the story with their meanings.

1. __b__ "I can't keep up with you!"
2. _____ "I thought I'd drop by."
3. _____ "What's with you?"
4. _____ "Cut it out!"
5. _____ "Now I get it!"

a.

b.

c.

d.

e.

REVIEW AND DISCUSS

STORY SUMMARY

16 Use the words in the box to complete the story summary for Episode 40.

alone	audition	calls	exams	future	interested	✓ library
music	patient	restaurant	says	star	study	wants

Rebecca is studying at the __library__ (1). Bill asks her to go to the _____ (2) lab. Bill helps Rebecca study for her _____ (3). They talk about their _____ (4) plans. Bill wants to be a rock and roll _____ (5). Bill asks Rebecca to go to an _____ (6). She says yes. Rebecca _____ (7) Alberto to cancel their opera date. She _____ (8) she has to _____ (9). Alberto goes to the opera _____ (10). Alberto goes to the _____ (11) after the opera. He _____ (12) to go skiing in Aspen, Colorado, for the holidays. Ramón can't go. Alberto says Rebecca isn't _____ (13) in him anymore. Ramón tells Alberto to be _____ (14) with her.

VIEWPOINTS

17 Watch the video discussion group. What does Roberto mean? Check (✓) *True* or *False*.

I think he's searching for love.

	True	False
1. Roberto is talking about Ramón.	_____	_____
2. Roberto thinks Alberto will marry Rebecca.	_____	_____

Roberto Arévalo, Colombia

What About you? What do you think will happen? Check (✓) *I agree* or *I disagree*.

	I agree	I disagree
1. Alberto and Rebecca will end their relationship.	_____	_____
2. Ramón and Rebecca will date.	_____	_____
3. Rebecca and Bill will date.	_____	_____

UNEXPECTED OFFERS

PREVIEW In this episode, Alex visits his mother. Mr. and Mrs. Wang talk about an important plan. Ramón and Alberto talk about Rebecca.

Alex and Ramón
on the plane

Mr. and Mrs. Wang
at home

Ramón and Alberto
at Alberto's office

BEFORE You Watch

1 Look at the photos above. Check (✓) *True* or *False*.

	True	False
1. Alex will spend Christmas with Ramón.		✓
2. Alex will be in San Francisco for New Year's Eve.		
3. Mr. and Mrs. Wang get an important letter.		
4. Ramón visits Alberto at work.		
5. Ramón talks to Rebecca about Christmas.		

 What is your opinion? Check (✓) *Yes* or *No*.

	Yes	No
1. Does Alex want to go to Los Angeles?		
2. Does Ramón want to go with Alex?		
3. Are holidays difficult for Alex?		

EPISODE **41** page 1

WATCH FOR MAIN IDEAS

Watch *all* of EPISODE 41, "Unexpected Offers."

WHILE You Watch

Who gets a present? Check (✓) all the answers.

1. ___✓___ Vincent
2. _____ Ramón
3. _____ Rebecca
4. _____ Mrs. Wang
5. _____ Alberto

AFTER You Watch

How much do you remember about the story? Put the photos in order from 1 to 5.

a. ___1___
b. _____
c. _____
d. _____
e. _____

a. "You promise to call me on Christmas Day?"

b. ① "They want me to work for them." ② "In Taiwan?"

c. "I asked Rebecca to join me for Christmas."

d. "Would you spend Christmas with me?"

e. "A gift from Alex!"

4 How do these people feel? Check (✓) *True* or *False*.

	True	False
1. Alex wants to go to Los Angeles.	___	___
2. Mrs. Wang wants to go to Taiwan.	___	___
3. Mr. Wang wants to stay in San Francisco.	___	___
4. Ramón wants to spend Christmas with Rebecca.	✓	___
5. Ramón feels lonely.	___	___

5 What do they say? Complete the conversations with the sentences below.

a. "We'll go very soon."
b. "Don't worry. I'll do it right away."
c. "Not now. We both have work to do."
d. "Many times, we must do things we don't want to."
✓ e. "I'll miss Alex this Christmas."

1. _____ Alex: "You have to give Vincent, Rebecca, and Uncle Alberto their presents."

   Ramón: _____

2. _____ Vincent: "Alex doesn't want to go to Los Angeles."

   Mrs. Wang: _____

3. _____ Mrs. Wang: "When do we go to Taiwan?"

   Mr. Wang: _____

4. ___e___ Rebecca: "Are you all right, Ramón?"

   Ramón: ___I'll miss Alex this Christmas.___

5. _____ Ramón: "We should talk about Rebecca."

   Alberto: _____

What About you? What do you think will happen? Check (✓) your answer.

Rebecca will spend the holidays with _____.

_____ Ramón   _____ Bill   _____ Alberto   _____ Nancy

WATCH FOR DETAILS

 Watch PART 1.

WHILE You Watch

6 Who is speaking? Write **R** for *Ramón*, **W** for *Mrs. Wang*, or **V** for *Vincent*.

1. _____ "Don't act like that."
2. _____ "You'll have a great time."
3. _____ "A gift from Alex!"
4. _____ "Alex will be in Los Angeles for Christmas."
5. _____ "He didn't want to go to L.A. No way."
6. __W__ "Vincent has a good life here."

AFTER You Watch

7 How much do you remember about the story? Complete the sentences. Choose the answers.

1. ___a___ Alex will come back for ___New Year's___.
   a. New Year's   b. Christmas   c. his birthday

2. _____ Alex asks Ramón to deliver _____ presents.
   a. two   b. three   c. four

3. _____ Ramón will call Alex on _____.
   a. Christmas Day   b. New Year's Eve   c. his birthday

4. _____ Vincent's father gets a _____ from Taiwan.
   a. letter   b. call   c. photo

5. _____ Mr. Wang has a _____ in Taiwan.
   a. brother   b. house   c. new job

8 Why does Mrs. Wang think her family should stay in San Francisco? Check (✓) all the answers.

1. __✓__ They have a good business.
2. _____ They have a nice house.
3. _____ Vincent has friends.
4. _____ San Francisco is their home.
5. _____ Their relatives live in San Francisco.

Watch PART 2.

WHILE You Watch

9 Listen to Rebecca and Ramón's conversation. Circle the words they say.
1. Rebecca: "Ramón! What a nice present /(surprise)!"
2. Ramón: "I just dropped by to give you this. It's a Christmas / New Year's present from Alex."
3. Rebecca: " Alberto / Alex is so sweet. He's a great kid."
4. Ramón: "I just put him on a plane to Mexico / L.A. He's visiting his mother."
5. Rebecca: "It must be difficult / quiet not having Alex around for Christmas."

AFTER You Watch

10 How much do you remember about the story? Circle the answers.
1. Who is Rebecca's present from?   (Alex)/ Alberto
2. Who does Ramón put on a plane?   Rebecca / Alex
3. Who is going skiing for the holidays?   Alberto / Rebecca
4. Who will be alone for Christmas?   Kevin / Ramón
5. Who has a family Christmas tradition?   Rebecca / Ramón

11 What are Ramón's Christmas traditions? Use the words in the box to complete the sentences.

| Christmas ✓ | eat | food | house | Mexican | songs | story |

Ramón's family has a tradition. On _____ day, they
                                          (1)
bring _____ to the community center. It's like a "posada."
        (2)

The posada is a _____ tradition. People go from _____
                    (3)   (4)

to house. They _____eat_____, sing _____, and share
                    (5)   (6)

the Christmas _____.
                    (7)

 What is your opinion? Check (✓) *I agree* or *I disagree*.

	I agree	I disagree
1. Rebecca wants to spend Christmas alone.	_____	_____
2. She doesn't want to cause a problem for Ramón and Alberto.	_____	_____

EPISODE **41** page **5**

Watch PART 3.

WHILE You Watch

12 What does Ramón tell Alberto? Check (✓) the sentences he says.

1. _____ "I think I'd like to go skiing with you."
2. ___✓___ "I think I did something out of line."
3. _____ "I had to deliver Alex's present to Rebecca."
4. _____ "I asked her to join me for Christmas."
5. _____ "I was smart to ask her."

AFTER You Watch

13 How much do you remember about the story? Circle the answers.

1. Alberto made a reservation at a (ski lodge)/ restaurant.
2. Ramón can / can't go with Alberto.
3. Ramón feels good / bad about his talk with Rebecca.
4. Ramón wants to talk to / fight with Alberto.
5. Alberto wants to discuss it now / later.

14 Check (✓) all the words that describe Ramón.

1. ___✓___ lonely
2. _____ bored
3. _____ excited
4. _____ sad

 What is your opinion? Check (✓) *Yes* or *No*.

	Yes	No
1. Is Ramón wrong to invite Rebecca for Christmas?	_____	_____
2. Is Alberto angry at his brother?	_____	_____

HIGHLIGHTS

CULTURE

Christmas is a Christian holiday celebrated by many people in the U.S. and Canada. Christmas is on December 25th.
These are some Christmas traditions.

singing Christmas songs

giving presents

Christmas trees

 Check (✓) *Yes* or *No*.

	Yes	No
1. Do you celebrate Christmas?	_____	_____
2. Do you enjoy . . .		
having a Christmas tree?	_____	_____
giving presents?	_____	_____
singing songs?	_____	_____

EXPRESSIONS

 Match the underlined words from the story with their meanings. Circle the answers.

1. *I'll do it right away.*

now / later

2. *Would you care for anything to drink?*

get / like

3. *Alex made me promise to drop this off.*

(deliver this) / find this

4. *I need a break.*

present / rest

REVIEW AND DISCUSS

STORY SUMMARY

16 Use the words in the box to complete the story summary for Episode 41.

| ✓airplane | Christmas | gives | go | have | house | mother |
| moving | parents | present | say | spend | talk | unhappy |

Ramón and Alex are on an __airplane__ (1). Alex is going to spend Christmas with his _____(2), but he doesn't want to _____(3) to Los Angeles. Ramón takes a _____(4) to Vincent. Vincent doesn't _____(5) a present for Alex. Later, Vincent hears his _____(6) talking. They talk about _____(7) to Taiwan. Ramón goes to Rebecca's _____(8). He _____(9) her a present from Alex. They talk about _____(10). Ramón asks Rebecca to _____(11) Christmas with him. She doesn't know what to _____(12). Ramón leaves, and Rebecca is _____(13). Ramón visits Alberto, and they _____(14) about Rebecca.

VIEWPOINTS

17 Watch the video discussion group. What does Rosalba mean? Complete the sentences. Choose the answers.

1. _____ Rosalba is talking about _____.
   a. Mrs. Wang   b. Rebecca

2. _____ Rosalba thinks Rebecca is _____.
   a. surprised by Ramón's invitation   b. angry at Ramón

I think she felt very stunned.

Rosalba Solís, Mexico

What About you? What is your opinion? Check (✓) *True* or *False*.

	True	False
1. I always like to be surprised.	_____	_____
2. I sometimes like to be surprised.	_____	_____
3. I don't like surprises.	_____	_____

THE AUDITION

PREVIEW In this episode, Nancy and Rebecca talk about the Mendoza brothers. Bill and Rebecca go to an audition.

I can't be involved with either Ramón or Alberto. I've got to focus on school.

Nancy and Rebecca at home

How much longer do you want to wait?

Bill and Rebecca in the waiting room

This is a song I wrote. It's called "Dream Catcher."

Rebecca at the audition

BEFORE You Watch

1 Look at the photos above. Complete the sentences. Choose the answers.

1. _____ Rebecca needs to _____.
   a. go out with Ramón   b. go out with Alberto   c. study for her exams

2. __a__ Bill and Rebecca have to ____wait____ before they can audition.
   a. wait   b. pay   c. finish their exams

3. _____ Rebecca _____ to wait a long time.
   a. wants   b. doesn't want   c. likes

4. _____ Rebecca _____ at the audition.
   a. sings a song   b. plays the piano   c. writes a song

2 What is Rebecca's song called? Check (✔) the answer.

_____ a. "Two Brothers"   _____ b. "Dream Catcher"   _____ c. "My Song"

What About you? How do you feel about waiting? Check (✔) your answer.

1. _____ I like to wait.
2. _____ I don't like to wait.
3. _____ I hate to wait!

WATCH FOR MAIN IDEAS

 Watch *all* of EPISODE 42, "The Audition."

WHILE You Watch

3 Where does Rebecca study? Check (✓) all the answers.

1. at home
   ✓

2. in the library
   ☐

3. in the waiting room
   ☐

4. in the recording studio
   ☐

AFTER You Watch

4 How much do you remember about the story? Put the sentences in order from 1 to 5. Then write the sentences in the correct order below.

a. _____ Rebecca and Bill take an exam.
b. _____ Rebecca and Bill wait a long time for their audition.
c. ____1____ Nancy asks Rebecca about Alberto.
d. _____ Rebecca sings "Dream Catcher" for The Moles' manager.
e. _____ Bill and Rebecca arrive at the studio for their audition.

1. __Nancy asks Rebecca about Alberto.__
2. _____
3. _____
4. _____
5. _____

5 Who does these things? Circle the answers.

1. Who thinks Ramón wants to date Rebecca?   Nancy / Bill
2. Who thinks Rebecca only has time for school?   (Rebecca) / Nancy
3. Who gives an exam?   The Moles / Professor Thomas
4. Who wants to leave the audition early?   Rebecca / Bill
5. Who leaves the music studio early?   Rebecca / The Moles
6. Who calls home?   Bill / the manager

6 Where are Bill and Rebecca? Match the sentences with the pictures.

1. _____ They are in the studio.
2. _____ They are in the waiting room.
3. _____ They are at the music school.

a.

b.

c.

 What do you think will happen? Check (✓) *Yes* or *No*.

	Yes	No
1. Will Rebecca pass her exams?	_____	_____
2. Will The Moles call Bill?	_____	_____
3. Will The Moles call Rebecca?	_____	_____

WATCH FOR DETAILS

 Watch PART 1.

WHILE You Watch

7 Who is speaking? Write **R** for *Rebecca*, or **N** for *Nancy*.

1. _____ "I saw Alex's father leaving."
2. _____ "Ramón is such a great dad."
3. __N__ "There's something in the way he looks at you."
4. _____ "You'll pass your exams."
5. _____ "I've got to!"

AFTER You Watch

8 How much do you remember about the story? Use the words in the box to complete the sentences.

| coffee | exam | ✓father | note | present | schoolwork |

1. Rebecca drinks _____ while she studies.
2. Nancy says she saw Alex's __**father**__ leaving the house.
3. Rebecca says Ramón brought her a _____ from Alex.
4. Rebecca can't think about dating. She can only think about her _____.
5. At school, Bill and Rebecca take an _____.
6. Bill gives Rebecca a _____ about the audition.

 What About you? What is your opinion? Check (✓) *Yes* or *No*.

	Yes	No
1. Can Rebecca date and be a good student?	_____	_____
2. Is Nancy worried about Rebecca?	_____	_____

Watch PART 2.

WHILE You Watch

9 Who do Bill and Rebecca talk to? Check (✓) the answer.

1. The Moles □   2. the manager □   3. the engineer □

AFTER You Watch

10 How much do you remember about the story? Check (✓) *True* or *False*.

	True	False
1. Rebecca goes to the audition with Bill.	✓	___
2. The band members talk to Bill and Rebecca.	___	___
3. The manager brings Bill and Rebecca drinks.	___	___
4. While she waits, Rebecca studies for an exam.	___	___
5. Bill and Rebecca sing their songs for The Moles.	___	___
6. Bill and Rebecca decide to go home.	___	___
7. Ramón looks at pictures from the retirement party.	___	___
8. Ramón gets angry when he sees a picture of Rebecca and Alberto dancing.	___	___

11 What do you know about Rebecca? Check (✓) the answer that is true.

_____ a. Rebecca is excited about the audition.
_____ b. She practices her guitar in the waiting room.
_____ c. She doesn't want to wait for the audition.

EPISODE 42 page 5

 Watch PART 3.

WHILE You Watch

12 **Listen to Rebecca's song. Circle the words she sings.**

Dream Catcher

"All the (lights)/houses are shining bright down in the city/street,
        (1)   (2)

Shining like a million dollars/dreams. . . .
                        (3)

Sometimes I feel/look like I'm upside-down.
             (4)

And all those dreams are going/falling right past me. . . .
                         (5)

I/Everybody needs a dream catcher,
   (6)

Someone to be there when your dreams start/need to fall. . . .
                                    (7)

Everybody needs/keeps a dream catcher,
           (8)

Someone to be there when the old/bad dreams are all you can see. . . .
                          (9)

Dream catcher. . . catch dreams/me."
                      (10)

AFTER You Watch

 How much do you remember about the story? Circle the answers.

1. The band had to (leave)/wait.
2. The manager makes dinner/tapes for Bill and Rebecca.
3. The manager calls the band/his wife.
4. Only Bill/Bill and Rebecca auditioned.
5. Rebecca/Bill wrote the song "Dream Catcher."

What About you? What is your opinion? Check (✓) *I agree* or *I disagree*.

	I agree	I disagree
1. The Moles are nice people.	_____	_____
2. Bill and Rebecca are good musicians.	_____	_____

HIGHLIGHTS

CULTURE

In the United States and Canada, entertainment is an important business. Here are some different types of entertainment.

television

movies

music

live theater

What about you? What type of entertainment do you enjoy? Check (✓) your answers.

_____ television   _____ movies
_____ music   _____ live theater

EXPRESSIONS

14 Match the underlined words from the story with their meanings. Choose the answers.

1. _____ Nancy: "Studying for exams can <u>burn up</u> energy."
   a. keep up   b. give you   c. use up

2. ___a___ Rebecca: "<u>You can say that again</u>!"
   a. That's true!   b. Please repeat that!   c. Keep talking!

3. _____ The manager: "He's <u>tied up</u> right now."
   a. sick   b. sleeping   c. busy

4. _____ The manager: "I want to <u>get out of here</u>."
   a. stop   b. leave   c. help

REVIEW AND DISCUSS

STORY SUMMARY

15 Use the words in the box to complete the story summary for Episode 42.

✓audition	band	drink	final	guitar	listen	manager
phone	record	school	sings	study	talk	wait

Nancy and Rebecca ____(1)____ coffee together while they ____(2)____ about Ramón and Alberto. They also discuss ____(3)____. Rebecca has to ____(4)____ more. Bill and Rebecca take a ____(5)____ exam. Then they go to their __audition__(6). They have to ____(7)____ a long time, and then the ____(8)____ leaves. The ____(9)____ agrees to let them ____(10)____ their songs. Bill ____(11)____ first, but the manager doesn't ____(12)____. He makes a ____(13)____ call. Next, Rebecca sings her song, called "Dream Catcher." She also plays her ____(14)____.

VIEWPOINTS

16 Watch the video discussion group. What does Rosalba mean? Complete the sentences. Choose the answers.

1. _____ Rosalba is talking about _____.
   a. Rebecca   b. Nancy

2. _____ Rosalba thinks Rebecca should study and _____.
   a. have a boyfriend   b. call her brother

I don't think it's fair that she has to choose between her music and someone. I think she should have it all.

Rosalba Solís, Mexico

What About you? What is your opinion? Check (✓) *True* or *False*.

	True	False
1. I sometimes have to choose between work and a friend.	_____	_____
2. It is difficult to choose between work and a friend.	_____	_____

DREAM CATCHER

EPISODE 43

PREVIEW In this episode, Rebecca finishes her audition. Alberto calls Rebecca. Bill talks about Rebecca and the music business.

Don't call us—we'll call you.

Rebecca, Bill, and the manager at the studio

Alberto wants you to call him. It's important.

Nancy and Rebecca at home

Rebecca only has one thing on her mind—her exams.

Rebecca and Bill in the library

BEFORE You Watch

1 What does Rebecca need to do? Check (✓) all the answers.

1. _____ She needs to call the manager.
2. _____ She needs to call Alberto.
3. _____ She needs to call Bill.
4. ___✓___ She needs to study for her exams.
5. _____ She needs to go to another audition.

2 Which sentence about Rebecca is true? Check (✓) the answer.

_____ a. Rebecca isn't worried about her exams.
_____ b. Rebecca is waiting for Alberto to call her.
_____ c. Rebecca is only thinking about her exams.

What About you? What do you think Alberto has to tell Rebecca?

I think that Alberto _____.

WATCH FOR MAIN IDEAS

Watch *all* of EPISODE 43, "Dream Catcher."

WHILE You Watch

3 What places do you see in this episode? Check (✓) all the answers.

1. _____ the recording studio
2. _____ the music school
3. _____ Ramón's house
4. ___✓___ Nancy's house
5. _____ the Casa Mendoza restaurant
6. _____ Alberto's office

AFTER You Watch

4 How much do you remember about the story? Put the photos in order from 1 to 5.

a. ___1___
b. _____
c. _____
d. _____
e. _____

a. *Dream Catcher, catch me.*

b. *They probably won't even listen to the tapes.*

c. *No, Rebecca isn't here.*

d. *Rebecca's kind of success isn't mine.*

e. *You deserve a special treat.*

EPISODE **43** page **2**

5 What do you know about these people? Complete the sentences with the phrases below.

a. wants Rebecca to call him about something important
b. gives tapes to Bill and Rebecca
✓ c. thinks music is a business
d. asks Rebecca about her exams
e. doesn't want to call Alberto right away

1. _____ The manager of the recording studio _____.
2. _____ Nancy _____.
3. _____ Rebecca _____.
4. ___c___ Bill ___thinks music is a business_____.
5. _____ Alberto _____.

6 What does Nancy think Rebecca has to do? Circle the answer.

What About you? What do you think will happen? Check (✓) all your answers.

1. _____ Rebecca will call Alberto.
2. _____ Rebecca will break up with Alberto.
3. _____ Rebecca will pass her final exams.
4. _____ Bill will make a lot of money.

WATCH FOR DETAILS

 Watch PART 1.

WHILE You Watch

7 Who is speaking? Write **B** for Bill, **M** for the manager, or **R** for Rebecca.

1. __M__ "I have to get going."
2. ____ "Here's a copy of your performance."
3. ____ "Some audition, huh?"
4. ____ "I'd love to orchestrate it for you."
5. ____ "Don't overdo it . . . ."
6. ____ "Relax! Just leave everything to me."

AFTER You Watch

8 How much do you remember about the story? Circle the answers.

1. Who sings "Dream Catcher"? — Bill / Rebecca
2. Who talks to Alberto? — Nancy / Rebecca
3. Who has to call Alberto? — Rebecca / Bill
4. Who is in a hurry to get home? — Bill / the manager
5. Who doesn't want Rebecca or Bill to call him? — Alberto /(the manager)
6. Who likes Rebecca's song? — Nancy / Bill
7. Who wants to help Rebecca with her song? — Bill / Alberto

9 What do Bill and Rebecca think? Circle the answers.

1. They are positive /(negative) about the audition.
2. Rebecca thinks / doesn't think The Moles will listen to her tape.
3. Bill thinks Rebecca's song is long / beautiful.
4. Rebecca thinks "Dream Catcher" is a simple / short song.

Watch PART 2.

WHILE You Watch

 10 What does Nancy tell Rebecca? Check (✓) the sentences she says.

1. ___✓___ "I couldn't sleep."
2. _____ "When will you get your grades?"
3. _____ "You had a phone call."
4. _____ "It's too late to call him now."
5. _____ "I think you should date both brothers."

AFTER You Watch

 11 How much do you remember about the story? Put the sentences in order from 1 to 5.

a. _____ Nancy gives Rebecca a message.
b. _____ Nancy asks about Rebecca's exams.
c. _____ Rebecca thinks about calling Alberto.
d. ___1___ Rebecca comes home.
e. _____ Nancy gives Rebecca some chocolates.

12 What are Nancy and Rebecca saying? Circle the answers.

Sorry to put my nose in your business, but…

I know what I have to do.

1. Nancy is saying that . . .
   a. she is sorry for hurting Rebecca.
   b. she is sorry for asking about Rebecca's personal life.

2. Rebecca is saying that . . .
   a. she has to pass her exams.
   b. she has to talk to Alberto about her feelings.

 What is your opinion? Should Rebecca choose Ramón or Alberto?

I think Rebecca should choose _____.

EPISODE **43** page **5**

Watch PART 3.

WHILE You Watch

13 What people do you see? Check (✓) their names.

1. Professor Thomas ✓
2. The Moles ☐
3. Kevin ☐
4. Alex ☐
5. Ramón ☐
6. Alberto ☐

AFTER You Watch

14 What does Bill say about Rebecca? Check (✓) all the answers.

1. _____ She's a serious person.
2. _____ She doesn't study enough.
3. __✓__ She only thinks about her exams.
4. _____ She has a good voice.
5. _____ She has an easy life.
6. _____ She wants the same kind of success as I do.

15 What does Bill think? Complete the sentences. Choose the answers.

1. __b__ The library is too __quiet__.
   a. busy   b. quiet

2. _____ Rebecca needs to _____.
   a. relax   b. quit school

3. _____ _____ are part of learning.
   a. Parties   b. Auditions

4. _____ Making money is _____.
   a. important   b. not important

What About you? What is your opinion? Check (✓) *I agree* or *I disagree*.

	I agree	I disagree
1. Musicians should try to make a lot of money.	_____	_____
2. Musicians should think about music, not money.	_____	_____

HIGHLIGHTS

CULTURE

In the United States and Canada, university students take final exams at the end of each semester. In certain courses, students write a final paper instead of taking a test. Usually students must wait for their grades to be sent to them at home. Teachers will sometimes tell students their scores ahead of time, if they have finished the grading.

studying

taking exams

 Check (✓) *Yes* or *No*.

	Yes	No
1. Do you study before you take a test?	_____	_____
2. Do tests make you nervous?	_____	_____
3. Is it hard for you to wait for your test grade?	_____	_____

EXPRESSIONS

16 Match the underlined words from the story with their meanings.

a. decide
b. nice
c. leave
✓ d. misunderstand me
e. relax

1. _____ The manager: "Lets <u>get going</u>."

2. _____ Nancy: "You have to <u>make up your mind</u>."

3. _____ Bill: "I want her to <u>lighten up</u> a little."

4. _____ Bill: "I think Rebecca's very <u>cool</u>."

5. ___d___ Bill: "Don't <u>get me wrong</u>."

EPISODE **43** page **7**

REVIEW AND DISCUSS

STORY SUMMARY

 17 Use the words in the box to complete the story summary for Episode 43.

✓audition	calls	different	exams	help	home	late	manager
serious		song	tapes	tells		wants	voice

Rebecca and Bill finish the __audition__ (1). The _____ (2) gives Bill and Rebecca their _____ (3). Bill wants to _____ (4) Rebecca with her _____ (5), "Dream Catcher." Alberto _____ (6) Rebecca and leaves a message. Rebecca goes _____ (7). Nancy _____ (8) her to call Alberto, but Rebecca thinks it's too _____ (9). Bill says Rebecca is too _____ (10). She only thinks about her _____ (11). He likes her because she knows what she _____ (12). He also thinks she has a great _____ (13). Bill says that he and Rebecca are very _____ (14), but that they will both find success.

VIEWPOINTS

 18 Watch the Reflections segment. What does Bill mean? Check (✓) *True* or *False*.

I think we'll both make it—each in our own way.

	True	False
1. Bill is talking about himself and Alberto.	_____	_____
2. Bill thinks he and Rebecca will both get what they want from their music.	_____	_____

 What is your opinion? Check (✓) *I agree* or *I disagree*.

To be successful in the music business, you need to . . .

	I agree	I disagree
1. be positive.	_____	_____
2. have famous friends.	_____	_____
3. have a lot of money.	_____	_____
4. love making music.	_____	_____

GIFTS

PREVIEW In this episode, Alberto and Rebecca talk about their feelings. Rebecca and Ramón spend Christmas together.

Rebecca and Alberto at the music studio

Rebecca at the restaurant

Rebecca and Ramón at the restaurant

BEFORE You Watch

1 Look at the photos above. Check (✓) *True* or *False*.

	True	False
1. Rebecca and Alberto talk in his office.	_____	✓
2. Rebecca and Alberto want to be friends.	_____	_____
3. Rebecca wants to work at the community center.	_____	_____
4. Rebecca spends Christmas alone.	_____	_____
5. Rebecca goes to the restaurant.	_____	_____
6. Rebecca and Ramón are happy to be together.	_____	_____

 What do you like to do on a holiday?

I like to _____.

WATCH FOR MAIN IDEAS

 Watch all of EPISODE 44, "Gifts."

WHILE You Watch

2 Where does Rebecca go? Check (✔) all the answers.

1. to recording studio ☐
2. to Alberto's office ☐
3. to the community center ☐
4. to the restaurant ✔

AFTER You Watch

3 How much do you remember about the story? Check (✔) the answers.

1. _____ a. Alberto gives Rebecca a letter.
   ___✔___ b. Alberto gives Rebecca a photograph.

2. _____ a. Ramón gives Alberto a present.
   _____ b. Alberto gives Ramón a present.

3. _____ a. Rebecca tells Nancy about Alberto's present.
   _____ b. Rebecca gives Nancy a present.

4. _____ a. Ramón and his friends eat Christmas dinner.
   _____ b. Ramón and his friends work at the community center.

5. _____ a. Ramón and Rebecca talk to Alex.
   _____ b. Ramón and Rebecca talk to Alberto.

④ **What do you know about these people? Complete the sentences with the phrases below. Choose the answers.**

a. helps Rebecca at the music studio
b. spends Christmas with Rebecca
c. goes to the community center with Ramón
d. talks to Ramón and Rebecca on Christmas day
✓ e. visits Rebecca at the music studio

1. _____ Ramón _____.
2. ___e___ Alberto ___visits Rebecca at the music studio___.
3. _____ Alex _____.
4. _____ Rebecca _____.
5. _____ Bill _____.

⑤ **Who helps to prepare food for the community center? Check (✓) all the answers.**

1. Rebecca
☐

2. Ramón

3. Alberto
☐

4. Ramón's employees
☐

What About you? What do you think will happen? Check (✓) *Yes* or *No*.

	Yes	No
1. Will Rebecca begin a relationship with Ramón?	_____	_____
2. Will Alberto forget about Rebecca?	_____	_____

WATCH FOR DETAILS

Watch PART 1.

WHILE You Watch

6 Who is speaking? Write **R** for Rebecca, or **A** for Alberto.

1. __A__ "Could you tell me where the studio is?"
2. ____ "I'm leaving town for a while."
3. ____ "It was your photography, I'm sure."
4. ____ "You can see in Ramón's eyes how much he loves his son."
5. ____ "I should probably get back to rehearsal, too."

AFTER You Watch

7 How much do you remember about the story? Put the sentences in order from 1 to 5.

a. _____ Rebecca and Alberto decide to be friends.
b. _____ Rebecca says goodbye to Alberto.
c. ___1___ Alberto looks for Rebecca at the studio.
d. _____ Alberto gives Rebecca a present.
e. _____ Alberto tells Rebecca about his ski trip.

8 Why did Rebecca write "Dream Catcher"? Check (✓) the answer.

_____ a. She sees a photo of Ramón and Alex.
_____ b. She thinks about her father.
_____ c. She gets the idea from a present from Alberto.

Everybody needs a dream catcher.

What About you?

What is your opinion? Check (✓) *I agree* or *I disagree*.

	I agree	I disagree
1. Rebecca is glad Alberto wants to be friends.	_____	_____
2. Alberto knows how Rebecca feels about Ramón.	_____	_____

EPISODE 44 page 4

Watch PART 2.

WHILE You Watch

9 What presents do you see? Check (✓) all the answers.

1. __✓__ goggles
2. _____ tickets
3. _____ a gift from Rebecca
4. _____ a photo

AFTER You Watch

10 How much do you remember about the story? Circle the answers.

1. Who gives Alberto ski goggles?   Rebecca /(Ramón)
2. Who tells Ramón that Rebecca isn't going skiing?   Rebecca / Alberto
3. Who is wrapping presents?   Nancy / Rebecca
4. Who gave Rebecca a picture of Ramón and Alex?   Alberto / Nancy

11 What are Alberto and Nancy saying? Circle the answers.

1. *She didn't want to go with you?*
2. *She might want to spend the holidays with someone else.*

I think that young man may have been trying to tell you something.

1. Alberto is saying that . . .
   a. Rebecca wants to spend the holidays with Bill.
   b. Rebecca wants to spend the holidays with Ramón.

2. Nancy is saying that . . .
   a. Alberto is angry at Rebecca.
   b. Alberto thinks Rebecca and Ramón should be together.

Watch PART 3.

WHILE You Watch

 12 Listen to Ramón and Rebecca talk to Alex. Check (✓) the sentences they say.

1. ___✓___ Ramón: "Merry Christmas."
2. _____ Ramón: "You have some presents here, too."
3. _____ Rebecca: "Your dad and I had a terrific day."
4. _____ Ramón: "You'll be back in a few weeks."
5. _____ Ramón: "I'm glad she's here, too."

AFTER You Watch

13 How much do you remember about the story? Put the sentences in order from 1 to 5.

a. _____ Ramón and Rebecca go back to the restaurant.
b. _____ Everyone at the community center sings a Christmas song.
c. ___1___ Rebecca brings food to the restaurant.
d. _____ Ramón and Rebecca talk to Alex.
e. _____ Rebecca helps Ramón at the community center.

14 What happens? Check (✓) the sentences that *are not* true.

1. _____ Ramón gives Christmas bonuses to his employees.
2. _____ Rebecca wants to be with Alberto on Christmas.
3. _____ Rebecca doesn't like helping at the community center.
4. _____ Ramón is happy to have Rebecca with him.
5. ___✓___ Alex is angry that his father is with Rebecca.

What About you? What do people do on holidays in your country? Check (✓) your answers.

In my country, many people _____ on holidays.

_____ sing   _____ eat a lot
_____ help other people   _____ are happy
_____ call friends and family _____ are sad

HIGHLIGHTS

CULTURE

In the United States and Canada, many people do volunteer work. They . . .

visit hospitals.

help at schools.

clean up parks and beaches.

answer telephones.

What About you? What volunteer work do people do in your country? Check (✓) your answers.

_____ visit hospitals   _____ help at schools
_____ clean up parks and beaches   _____ answer telephones
_____ collect money for special projects

EXPRESSIONS

 Match the underlined words from the story with their meanings. Circle the answers.

1.
   What's up?
   (What's happening?) / How are you?

2.
   Well, I have to get going.
   leave / stay

3.
   Skiing isn't my thing.
   I don't like skiing. / I don't have skis.

4.
   I have a hunch she might want to spend the holidays with someone else.
   think / hope

REVIEW AND DISCUSS

STORY SUMMARY

16 Use the words in the box to complete the story summary for Episode 44.

| airport | calls | dinner | drink | food | friends | gives |
| good | office | photo | presents | ski | song | ✓visits |

Alberto ___visits___ (1) Rebecca at school. He tells her that he's leaving for a _____ (2) trip. They talk and decide to be _____ (3). Alberto listens to Rebecca's _____ (4) and remembers the _____ (5) times. Ramón goes to Alberto's _____ (6). He will drive Alberto to the _____ (7). He _____ (8) Alberto some goggles. Rebecca wraps _____ (9). Nancy sees the _____ (10) of Ramón and Alex. Rebecca brings _____ (11) to the restaurant. She and Ramón go to the community center to serve Christmas _____ (12). They go back to the restaurant and _____ (13) champagne. Ramón _____ (14) Alex.

VIEWPOINTS

17 Watch the video discussion group. What does Hai mean? Complete the sentences. Choose the answers.

"I think it's very difficult for a man and a woman to stay friends."

Hai B. Pho, Vietnam

1. _____ Hai is talking about _____.
   a. Ramón and Rebecca
   b. Alberto and Rebecca

2. _____ Hai thinks that _____.
   a. it will be easy for Alberto and Rebecca to be friends
   b. it will be hard for Alberto and Rebecca to be friends

What About you? What is your opinion? Check (✓) *Yes* or *No*.

	Yes	No
1. Can Alberto and Rebecca be friends?	____	____
2. Do you think Alberto will find another girlfriend soon?	____	____

TRUE LOVE

PREVIEW In this episode, Ramón asks Rebecca to spend New Year's Eve with him. Rebecca talks to Kevin on the phone.

Rebecca and Ramón by the Christmas tree

Rebecca and Ramón at the door

Rebecca on the telephone

BEFORE You Watch

1 Look at the photos above. Circle the answers.

1. Who opens a present? **Rebecca** / Ramón
2. Who gives Rebecca a present? Ramón / Rebecca
3. Who doesn't have plans for New Year's Eve? Rebecca / Ramón
4. Who talks on the telephone? Rebecca / Ramón
5. Who gives Kevin a present? Rebecca / Uncle Brendan and Aunt Anne

2 What did Uncle Brendan and Aunt Anne do? Check (✓) the answer.

_____ a. They gave Kevin a plane ticket.
_____ b. They called Rebecca.
_____ c. They came to San Francisco.

 What presents do you like?

I like _____.

WATCH FOR MAIN IDEAS

 Watch all of EPISODE 45, "True Love."

WHILE You Watch

3 Who talks to Rebecca? Check (✓) all the answers.

1. __✓__ Ramón   4. _____ Kevin
2. _____ Alex   5. _____ Uncle Brendan
3. _____ Nancy   6. _____ Aunt Anne

AFTER You Watch

4 How much do you remember about the story? Put the photos in order from 1 to 5.

a. _____
b. _____
c. _____
d. __1__
e. _____

a.

b.

c.

d.

e.

5 What do you know about these people? Check (✓) *True* or *False*.

	True	False
1. Rebecca likes her present from Ramón.	✓	___
2. Rebecca gives Ramón a cassette of Moles' songs.	___	___
3. Alex will be home on New Year's Eve.	___	___
4. Kevin calls Rebecca with bad news.	___	___

6. What do these people do? Complete the sentences with the names below.

a. Kevin
b. Nancy
c. Nancy and Rebecca
d. Ramón
✓ e. Uncle Brendan and Aunt Anne
f. Rebecca

1. _____ visits Uncle Edward at the retirement home.
2. _____ invites Rebecca to spend New Year's Eve with him.
3. _____ give each other presents.
4. __Uncle Brendan and Aunt Anne__ give Kevin an airline ticket.
5. _____ will visit Rebecca in San Francisco.
6. _____ gives Ramón a cassette tape.

7. Check (✓) the sentences about Rebecca that are true.

1. __✓__ She wants to spend New Year's Eve with Ramón.
2. _____ Nancy wants to know about her relationship with Ramón.
3. _____ Rebecca doesn't want her brother to visit her.
4. _____ She doesn't care about her music anymore.
5. _____ Ramón likes her tape.
6. _____ Rebecca gives Ramón a present for Alex.

What do you think will happen? Check (✓) Yes or No.

	Yes	No
1. Will Rebecca spend New Year's Eve with Ramón?	_____	_____
2. Will Rebecca spend New Year's Eve with Kevin?	_____	_____
3. Will Kevin stay in San Francisco?	_____	_____

WATCH FOR DETAILS

 Watch PART 1.

WHILE You Watch

8 What does Ramón give Rebecca? Check (✓) all the answers.

1. a photograph
☐

2. a statue

3. an ekeko
☐

4. a tape
☐

AFTER You Watch

9 How much do you remember about the story? Put the sentences in order from 1 to 5.

a. _____ Nancy comes home.
b. ___1___ Ramón takes Rebecca home.
c. _____ Ramón burns his hand.
d. _____ Ramón and Rebecca give each other presents.
e. _____ Ramón and Rebecca kiss.

10 What does the ekeko do? Complete the sentences. Choose the answers.

1. ___b___ The ekeko brings good luck and makes ___dreams___ come true.
   a. stories   b. dreams   c. ideas

2. _____ Rebecca's ekeko has a diploma. This means she'll finish _____.
   a. school   b. work   c. singing

3. _____ There is also a photo of Kevin, so Rebecca will see her _____ soon.
   a. aunt   b. brother   c. uncle

4. _____ There is a gold record, so Rebecca's _____ will be a big hit.
   a. book   b. job   c. song

 What would you hang on an ekeko?

I would hang _____.

Watch PART 2.

WHILE You Watch

11 Who is speaking? Write **N** for *Nancy*, or **R** for *Ramón*.

1. __N__ "Oh, yes, I remember. We met at your parents' retirement party."
2. ____ "A glass of warm cider would be perfect!"
3. ____ "I hope the legend is real and your dreams do come true!"
4. ____ "I'll play your tape on my way home."
5. ____ "It's a big night at the restaurant. I have to be there."

AFTER You Watch

12 How much do you remember about the story? Circle the answers.

1. Nancy (surprises)/calls Rebecca and Ramón.
2. It will be a quiet / big night at the restaurant on New Year's Eve.
3. Rebecca says yes / no to Ramón's invitation for New Year's Eve.
4. Nancy eats Christmas dinner with Rebecca / Edward.
5. Rebecca and Ramón tell Nancy about dinner at the restaurant / community center.

13 How do these people feel? Circle the answers.

1. Nancy likes / doesn't like Ramón.
2. Nancy has a (good)/ bad time at the retirement home.
3. Ramón and Rebecca feel happy / sad about the dinner at the community center.
4. Rebecca feels happy / confused about her evening with Ramón.

 Watch PART 3.

WHILE You Watch

 14 Listen to Rebecca talk to Kevin on the phone. Circle the words she says.

1. "I'm ready for the (news)/vacation."
2. "Uncle Brendan/Michael and Aunt Anne did what?"
3. "When are you working/coming?"
4. "The day after tomorrow/New Year's?"
5. "Well, I'll show you the school/town."

AFTER You Watch

 15 How much do you remember about the story? Put the sentences in order from 1 to 5.

a. _____ Nancy gives Rebecca a present.
b. _____ Brendan tells Kevin to visit Rebecca in San Francisco.
c. ___1___ Rebecca tells Nancy about her New Year's Eve plans.
d. _____ Rebecca and Kevin talk on the phone.
e. _____ Kevin plays a game with his aunt and uncle.

16 What do Anne, Brendan, and Kevin say? Use the words in the box to complete the conversation.

| airplanes | Christmas | long | miss | visit | ✓wish |

1. Kevin: "This has been a great _____."
2. Kevin: "I just ___wish___ Rebecca were here."
3. Anne: "You _____ her, don't you."
4. Brendan: "Why don't you go out and _____ her?"
5. Kevin: "It's a _____ way."
6. Brendan: "That's what _____ were made for, Kevin."

 What is your opinion? Check (✓) Yes or No.

	Yes	No
1. Do you have to travel far to see your family?	_____	_____
2. Do you like to spend vacations with your family?	_____	_____

HIGHLIGHTS

CULTURE

In the United States and Canada, smoking is not popular. It is polite to ask other people if you can smoke. Usually you can't smoke inside public buildings. Many people think smoking is bad for your health.

no-smoking sign

warning label

 Check (✔) *Yes* or *No*.

	Yes	No
1. Are there no-smoking rules in your country?	_____	_____
2. Do you agree with no-smoking rules?	_____	_____

EXPRESSIONS

17 Match the underlined words from the story with their meanings.

a. fun
b. happen
 c. think
d. difficult

1. ___c___ Ramón: "I guess he'll smoke outside."

2. _____ Rebecca: "What a riot!"

3. _____ Ramón: "Her uncle is in a retirement home? That's rough."

4. _____ Nancy: "I hope your dreams do come true."

EPISODE **45** page **7**

REVIEW AND DISCUSS

STORY SUMMARY

18 Use the words in the box to complete the story summary for Episode 45.

game	give	✓ house	kiss	luck	phone	present
see	smoke	song	spend	tape	ticket	uncle	visit

Ramón and Rebecca go to Rebecca's __house__ (1) and _____ (2) each other presents. Rebecca opens Alex's _____ (3) first. Next, Rebecca gives Ramón a _____ (4) of her _____ (5), "Dream Catcher." Then, Ramón gives Rebecca an ekeko, to bring her good _____ (6). But, for her dreams to come true, the ekeko must _____ (7) once a day. Ramón and Rebecca have their first _____ (8). Then, Nancy comes home from a _____ (9) with her _____ (10). Ramón asks Rebecca to _____ (11) New Year's Eve with him. On the farm, Anne, Brendan, and Kevin play a _____ (12). Anne and Brendan give Kevin a _____ (13) to San Francisco. Kevin and Rebecca talk on the _____ (14). Kevin tells Rebecca that he'll _____ (15) her soon.

VIEWPOINTS

19 Watch the video discussion group. What does Nina mean? Check (✓) *True* or *False*.

I think they'll get married.

	True	False
1. Nina is talking about Ramón and Rebecca.	_____	_____
2. Nina thinks they will only be friends.	_____	_____

Nina Chen, China

What About you? What is your opinion? Who will Rebecca marry? Check (✓) your answer.

Rebecca will marry _____.

_____ Ramón   _____ Alberto   _____ no one

EPISODE 45 page 8

FRIENDSHIP

PREVIEW In this episode, Kevin visits Rebecca. Alex comes home from Los Angeles. He and Vincent make plans for New Year's Eve.

Kevin and Rebecca at the studio

1. This is so exciting.
2. I've been dreaming about this for years.

Ramón and Alex at home

1. How does it feel to be home?
2. Great! Are my other presents under the tree?

Alex and Vincent at Vincent's house

Let's make it the best New Year's we've ever had!

BEFORE You Watch

1 Look at the photos above. Use the words in the box to complete the sentences.

| ✓ dream | happy | house | make | presents | song | visits |

1. Rebecca goes to the studio to record her _____.
2. Recording a song is Rebecca's ___**dream**___.
3. Kevin _____ the studio with Rebecca.
4. Alex is _____ to be home.
5. Ramón takes Alex's _____ out of the car.
6. Alex goes to Vincent's _____.
7. Alex and Vincent _____ plans for New Year's Eve.

 **What About you?** What New Year's custom do you enjoy?

I enjoy _____.

...going to parties ...celebrating with my family ...eating at a restaurant

WATCH FOR MAIN IDEAS

Watch *all* of EPISODE 46, "Friendship."

WHILE You Watch

   Who listens to Rebecca's song? Check (✓) all the answers.

1. __✓__ Ramón
2. _____ Alex
3. _____ Kevin
4. _____ Bill
5. _____ Vincent
6. _____ Mrs. Wang

AFTER You Watch

   How much do you remember about the story? Put the photos in order from 1 to 5.

a. _____
b. _____
c. __1__
d. _____
e. _____

   What do you know about Ramón? Check (✓) the sentences that are true.

1. __✓__ Ramón is happy that Alex is back in San Francisco.
2. _____ He is thinking a lot about Rebecca.
3. _____ He forgot to get presents for Alex.
4. _____ He takes Alex to visit Vincent.
5. _____ He talks to Rebecca on the phone.

5 How do these people feel? Circle the answers.

1. Kevin is **surprised**/not surprised at Rebecca's talent.
2. Vincent is happy/sad about going to Taiwan.
3. Rebecca is happy/not happy with her new tape.
4. Rebecca is surprised/angry that Bill is going to Los Angeles.
5. Bill is excited/worried about going to Los Angeles.

6 What do these people do? Complete the sentences. Choose the answers.

1. __a__ Kevin __listens to Rebecca__ in the studio.
   a. listens to Rebecca   b. sings with Rebecca   c. calls Ramón

2. _____ Ramón _____ with Alex.
   a. plays baseball   b. listens to a tape   c. watches TV

3. _____ Rebecca _____.
   a. visits Kevin   b. calls Ramón   c. gives a guitar lesson

4. _____ Alex and Vincent _____.
   a. open presents   b. watch TV   c. count Vincent's money

5. _____ Bill gives Rebecca her new _____.
   a. tape   b. guitar   c. dream

 What do you think will happen? Check (✓) *Yes* or *No*.

	Yes	No
1. Will Bill quit school?	_____	_____
2. Will Vincent and his family move to Taiwan?	_____	_____
3. Will Alex move to Los Angeles?	_____	_____

WATCH FOR DETAILS

Watch PART 1.

WHILE You Watch

7 Listen to Rebecca and Kevin talk in the studio. Circle the words they say.

1. Kevin: "I didn't know you could write words /(songs) like that!"
2. Rebecca: "It was there. It just never had the chance / money to come out before."
3. Kevin: "I'm glad I was here to see you / this."
4. Rebecca: "I'm glad they / you were too."
5. Kevin: "I wish Ramón / Dad could have been here."
6. Rebecca: "Yeah. So do I. / Me too."

AFTER You Watch

8 How much do you remember about the story? Circle the answers.

1. Who is the studio engineer? Bill / Jay
2. Who brings Alex home? Vincent /(Ramón)
3. Who gets a lot of presents? Alex / Vincent
4. Who gets a baseball? Ramón / Alex
5. Who calls Ramón from the studio? Rebecca / Kevin

9 Check (✓) all the sentences about Kevin that are true.

1. __✓__ He loves Rebecca's song.
2. _____ He is happy about Rebecca's success.
3. _____ He doesn't like Ramón.
4. _____ He misses his father.
5. _____ He wants to go home.
6. _____ He is excited to watch Rebecca record her song.

Watch PART 2.

WHILE You Watch

10 Who is speaking? Write **R** for *Ramón*, **V** for *Vincent*, or **A** for *Alex*.

1. _____ "That's right, Rebecca's brother is in town."
2. _____ "I'll pick you up in an hour, Alex."
3. _____ "Come on, let's go practice in my room."
4. _____ "Do you really have to go to Taiwan?"
5. __V__ "Next year I'll be in Taiwan, and you'll be in L.A."

AFTER You Watch

11 How much do you remember about the story? Put the sentences in order from 1 to 5. Then write the sentences in the correct order below.

a. _____ Vincent tells Alex he has to go to Taiwan.
b. _____ Alex asks Vincent about money.
c. __1__ Ramón takes Alex to Vincent's house.
d. _____ Alex thinks he and Vincent could live together.
e. _____ Alex wants Vincent to spend New Year's Eve with him.

1. Ramón takes Alex to Vincent's house.
2. _____
3. _____
4. _____
5. _____

12 How much money does Vincent have? Check (✓) the answer.

_____ a. 52 cents
_____ b. $35.52
_____ c. $352.50

Thirty-five dollars and fifty-two cents.

 What do you think Alex and Vincent will do for New Year's Eve? Check (✓) your answer.

1. _____ They will buy something.
2. _____ They will go somewhere.

EPISODE **46** page **5**

Watch PART 3.

WHILE You Watch

13 What does Bill tell Rebecca? Check (✓) the sentences he says.

1. ___✓___ "I'm not coming back to school next term."
2. _____ "I'm heading to New York."
3. _____ "You have your dream and I have mine."
4. _____ "You have a great voice, girl."
5. _____ "You should come with me."

AFTER You Watch

14 How much do you remember about the story? Check (✓) *True* or *False*.

1.  Jay says Rebecca's song needs some more work.

    True _____ **False** ___✓___

2.  Kevin says he wants to go to music school.

    True _____ **False** _____

3.  Rebecca is proud of her tape.

    True _____ **False** _____

4.  Bill will miss Rebecca when he leaves.

    True _____ **False** _____

15 Who thinks these things? Check (✓) *Bill*, *Rebecca*, or *Bill and Rebecca*.

	Bill	Rebecca	Bill and Rebecca
1. I need to go to Los Angeles.	✓	___	___
2. I need to stay in school.	___	___	___
3. I want to be a success in music.	___	___	___
4. I like the song "Dream Catcher."	___	___	___

 What is your opinion? Check (✓) *I agree* or *I disagree*.

	I agree	I disagree
1. It is a bad idea for Bill to quit school.	___	___
2. It is a good idea for Bill to go to Los Angeles.	___	___
3. Bill is a good musician.	___	___

HIGHLIGHTS

CULTURE

In the United States and Canada, many people change homes and jobs often. This can sometimes cause problems.

What About you? Check (✓) Yes or No.

	Yes	No
1. Do you change jobs often?	_____	_____
2. Do you like to move?	_____	_____
3. Do you have to move often?	_____	_____

EXPRESSIONS

16 Match the underlined words from the story with their meanings.

a. . . . you're crazy!
b. That is terrible!
c. that was wonderful
✓ d. Sit down.
e. I must go.

1. __d__

2. _____

3. _____

4. _____

5. _____

REVIEW AND DISCUSS

STORY SUMMARY

17 Use the words in the box to complete the story summary for Episode 46.

| airport | baseball | family | good | likes | meets | miss |
| money | plans | play | present | quit | recording | ✓studio |

Rebecca is at the ___studio___ (1) to record her song. Kevin _____ (2) her friend Bill. Kevin listens to the _____ (3) session. He really _____ (4) Rebecca's song. Ramón meets Alex at the _____ (5). Alex says it feels _____ (6) to be home. Alex opens his _____ (7) from Rebecca—it's a _____ (8). Ramón takes Alex to Vincent's house, so they can _____ (9) their guitars. Vincent tells Alex that his _____ (10) will move to Taiwan. He doesn't want to go. Vincent and Alex make _____ (11) for New Year's Eve. They count Vincent's _____ (12)—he has $35.52. Bill tells Rebecca he is going to _____ (13) school. Rebecca will _____ (14) Bill.

> *It's very important to keep the family together.*

VIEWPOINTS

18 Watch the video discussion group. What does Nela mean? Complete the sentences. Choose the answers.

1. _____ Nela is talking about _____.
   a. the Mendozas
   b. the Wangs

2. _____ Nela thinks _____.
   a. Mr. Wang should go to Taiwan alone.
   b. all the Wangs need to stay or go.

Nela Hosic, Bosnia

What About you?

What is your opinion? Check (✓) *I agree* or *I disagree*.

	I agree	I disagree
1. Jobs are more important than family.	_____	_____
2. A family should always stay together.	_____	_____

EPISODE 46 page 8

THE LOST BOYS

PREVIEW In this episode, Vincent and Alex go skating without telling their parents. Ramón, Rebecca, and the Wangs worry about them.

"Three dollars to rent the skates. Do you have some money?"

Alex and Vincent in Chinatown

① "Are you all right? Come on, Alex."
② "I can't skate."

Alex and Vincent at the skating rink

"I'm going to drive around and try to find them."

Mr. Wang at the restaurant

BEFORE You Watch

1 Look at the photos above. Complete the sentences. Choose the answers.

1. _____ Alex and Vincent go to _____.
   a. the movies   b. a store   c. a skating rink

2. __b__ Alex ___falls___ on the ice.
   a. smiles   b. falls   c. yells

3. _____ Mr. Wang is _____.
   a. worried   b. happy   c. tired

4. _____ He _____ where the boys are.
   a. knows   b. doesn't know   c. doesn't care

5. _____ Mr. Wang tries to _____ Alex and Vincent.
   a. call   b. go with   c. find

What About you? What is your opinion? Check (✓) Yes or No.

	Yes	No
1. The boys are in danger.	____	____
2. The boys were wrong to go skating.	____	____
3. The boys should have asked their parents.	____	____

WATCH FOR MAIN IDEAS

Watch *all* of EPISODE 47, "The Lost Boys."

WHILE You Watch

2 What places do you see? Check (✓) all the answers.

1. the Wangs' house ✓
2. Chinatown ☐
3. Ramón's house ☐
4. the skating rink ☐
5. Nancy's house ☐

AFTER You Watch

3 How much do you remember about the story? Put the photos in order from 1 to 5.

a. __1__
b. _____
c. _____
d. _____
e. _____

a. Vincent, where are you going?

b. Wait till I get my hands on that kid!

c. You heard from them?

d. Are you all right?

e. No, Vincent's not here.

EPISODE 47 page 2

What do you know about these people? Circle the answers.

1. Alex and Vincent are excited / unhappy about going skating.
2. Mrs. Wang is worried / happy because she can't find Vincent.
3. Mr. Wang decides to look for the boys / stay at home.
4. Ramón is angry at / happy with Alex.
5. Alex hurts his ankle / arm.
6. A baby-sitter / police officer comes to Ramón's house.

 Where are Alex and Vincent? Circle the answer.

a. ...at the restaurant
b. ...at the hospital
c. ...at the library

 What do you think will happen? Check (✓) Yes or No.

	Yes	No
1. Will the boys be in trouble?	_____	_____
2. Will their parents stay angry at them?	_____	_____

WATCH FOR DETAILS

Watch PART 1.

WHILE You Watch

6 Who is speaking? Write **A** for *Alex,* **R** for *Ramón,* or **V** for *Vincent.*

1. __V__ "Out. I'll be back soon."
2. _____ "How much does it cost?"
3. _____ "I'd be honored to have Kevin here for our New Year's party."
4. _____ "This can't be. Alex is home."
5. _____ "Are you all right?"
6. _____ "I can't skate!"

AFTER You Watch

7 How much do you remember about the story? Check (✓) *True* or *False*.

	True	False
1. Vincent takes his money.	✓	
2. Mrs. Wang calls her husband.		
3. Mr. Wang is at work.		
4. The boys go to the library.		
5. Rebecca and Kevin are working at the restaurant.		
6. Ramón invites Kevin to the party.		
7. Vincent visits his cousins.		

8 Read what these people say. How do they feel? Check (✓) the answers.

1. Vincent says, "Let's go!"
   He is _____ **a.** angry   __✓__ **b.** excited

2. Mr. Wang asks, "Where else could they be?"
   He is _____ **a.** worried   _____ **b.** sad

3. Ramón says, "Forgive me. There is so much to do."
   He is _____ **a.** worried   _____ **b.** busy

4. Rebecca says, "Wait. Something is wrong."
   She is _____ **a.** angry   _____ **b.** worried

Watch PART 2.

WHILE You Watch

9 Who stays at home to answer the telephone? Check (✓) all the answers.

1. __✓__ Mrs. Wang
2. _____ Rebecca
3. _____ Ramón
4. _____ Kevin
5. _____ Alex

AFTER You Watch

10 How much do you remember about the story? Put the sentences in order from 1 to 5. Then write the sentences in the correct order below.

a. _____ Kevin will stay at Ramón's house.
b. _____ Ramón calls home, but no one is there.
c. _____ Ramón, Kevin, and Rebecca go to Ramón's house.
d. _____ Mr. Wang says he will drive around and look for the boys.
e. __1__ Mr. Wang asks Ramón if he has seen Vincent.

1. __Mr. Wang asks Ramón if he has seen Vincent.__
2. _____
3. _____
4. _____
5. _____

11 How does Ramón feel about Alex? Check (✓) the sentence that *is not* true.

_____ a. He is worried about Alex.
_____ b. He is very angry at Alex.
_____ c. He doesn't care about Alex.

What About you? Who do you think will find the boys? Check (✓) your answer.

_____ Ramón   _____ Rebecca   _____ Mr. Wang
_____ Mrs. Wang _____ Kevin

Watch **PART 3.**

WHILE You Watch

12 What does Kevin say? Circle the words you hear.

1. "Mr. Wang went to the (police)/restaurant."
2. "There is someone at the door / in the car."
3. "It was Mrs. Wang / the baby-sitter."
4. "You were going to baby-sit Alex and his friend / neighbor."
5. "They're at the restaurant / hospital."

AFTER You Watch

13 How much do you remember about the story? Complete the sentences with the phrases below.

   a. tells Kevin where Vincent and Alex are
   ✓ b. answers the telephone at Ramón's house
   c. fills out a report at the police station
   d. talks to Ramón about Alex's feelings

   1. _____ Rebecca _____.
   2. ___b___ Kevin answers the telephone at Ramón's house .
   3. _____ Mr. Wang _____.
   4. _____ Mrs. Wang _____.

14 What does Ramón say? Use the words in the box to complete the sentences.

   driving   ✓ scare   upset

1. "This is ridiculous, _____ around on New Year's Eve!"

2. "I guess he is more _____ than I realized."

3. "But still, that's no reason to __scare__ us."

HIGHLIGHTS

CULTURE

In the United States and Canada, adults and children enjoy many outdoor activities.

skating

playing baseball

swimming

camping

What outdoor activities do you enjoy? Check (✓) your answers.

_____ skating   _____ playing baseball   _____ swimming
_____ camping   _____ biking   _____ walking
_____ playing soccer   _____ hiking   _____ other

EXPRESSIONS

15 Match the underlined words from the story with their meanings.

   a. a lot
 ✓ b. take care of
   c. a very good
   d. stay at

1. _____   The boys plan <u>an awesome</u> New Year's Eve.

2. ___b___   The baby-sitter comes to <u>keep an eye on</u> the boys.

3. _____   Kevin is happy to <u>stick around</u> the house.

4. _____   The boys have <u>tons</u> of money.

REVIEW AND DISCUSS

STORY SUMMARY

16 Use the words in the box to complete the story summary for Episode 47.

| bag | calls | falls | finds | home | hospital | hurt |
| ice skating | | parents | phone | photo | ✓restaurant | worried |

Vincent and Alex go _____(1)_____ without telling their _____(2)_____. Mrs. Wang is _____(3)_____ when she can't find Vincent. Mr. Wang goes to the __restaurant__(4) to talk to Ramón. Rebecca and Kevin are there. Ramón goes _____(5)_____ to look for Alex, but he isn't there. Ramón _____(6)_____ an ad for ice skating in Alex's _____(7)_____. Rebecca and Ramón go to look for Alex. Kevin stays at the house to answer the _____(8)_____. At the skating rink, Alex _____(9)_____ on the ice. When Rebecca and Ramón get there, they show a _____(10)_____ of Alex. A man says he saw Alex and Vincent leave. Alex was _____(11)_____. Mrs. Wang _____(12)_____ Kevin at the house. She says the boys are at the _____(13)_____.

VIEWPOINTS

 17 Watch the video discussion group. What does Hai mean? Check (✓) *True* or *False*.

	True	False
1. Hai is talking about Kevin and Melissa.	____	____
2. Hai thinks children must obey their parents.	____	____

If they break the rules, they have to expect some kind of punishment.

Hai B. Pho, Vietnam

What About you? What is your opinion? Check (✓) *I agree* or *I disagree*.

	I agree	I disagree
1. Children should always obey their parents.	____	____
2. Children should have some freedom.	____	____

A VERY GOOD YEAR

EPISODE 48

PREVIEW In this episode, the boys get home safely. Alex and Ramón have a serious talk. Everyone celebrates New Year's Eve together.

We just wanted to do something special before I have to go to Taiwan.

The Wangs and Alex at the hospital

1. *I can't… manage a restaurant, Alex, **and** a personal life.*
2. *I can't believe that.*

Ramón and Rebecca in the park

This is going to be a very good year.

Rebecca and Ramón at the party

BEFORE You Watch

1 Look at the photos above. Check (✓) *True* or *False*.

	True	False
1. Rebecca and Ramón pick up Alex and Vincent at the hospital.		✓
2. Vincent explains why they went skating.		
3. Ramón thinks he has too much to do.		
4. Rebecca thinks Ramón has too much to do.		
5. Rebecca and Ramón go to a New Year's party.		

2 What does Ramón think? Check (✓) the answer.

_____ a. He will be sad this year.
_____ b. The restaurant will make money this year.
_____ c. He will be happy this year.

…▸ What About you? What is your opinion? Check (✓) *Yes* or *No*.

	Yes	No
1. Can a person have a job, a child, and a personal life?		
2. Do you have a lot to manage in your life?		

WATCH FOR MAIN IDEAS

Watch *all* of EPISODE 48, "A Very Good Year."

WHILE You Watch

 Where does Alex go? Check (✓) all the answers.

1. to the hospital
   ☑

2. to the park
   ☐

3. to his home
   ☐

4. to the New Year's party
   ☐

AFTER You Watch

 How much do you remember about the story? Circle the answers.

1. Ramón and Rebecca look for the boys in the (park) / hospital.
2. Vincent says that he knows his family is moving to Taiwan / Los Angeles.
3. Mrs. Wang tells Vincent about their family's plans / house.
4. Rebecca tells Ramón that he is a good worker / father.
5. Mr. Wang takes the boys home / to the hospital.
6. Ramón and Rebecca call / help Kevin.
7. At home, Ramón and Alex talk / watch TV.
8. The evening ends with a party at the restaurant / Ramón's house.

5 How does Ramón feel? Complete the sentences. Choose the answers.

1. __a__ Ramón hopes Alex is __safe__.
   a. safe   b. alone   c. sad

2. _____ Ramón thinks Alex is very _____.
   a. happy   b. excited   c. important

3. _____ Ramón thinks it's _____ to manage his life.
   a. easy   b. boring   c. hard

4. _____ Ramón _____ the Wangs.
   a. feels thankful for   b. feels angry at   c. doesn't want to talk to

5. _____ Ramón is _____ to have Rebecca with him.
   a. scared   b. happy   c. sad

6 What do their parents say will happen to Vincent and Alex? Check (✔) all the answers.

1. __✔__ They will be punished.
2. _____ They will never see each other again.
3. _____ Vincent will stay in San Francisco.
4. _____ Vincent and Alex will continue their friendship.
5. _____ Alex will have to move to Los Angeles.

7 What do you know about these people? Check (✔) Yes or No.

	Yes	No
1. Is Alex sorry for what he did?		
2. Does Ramón understand Alex's feelings?		
3. Is Rebecca angry at Alex?		
4. Does Alex go to the party with his father and Rebecca?		

What About you? What do you think will happen? Check (✔) I agree or I disagree.

	I agree	I disagree
1. Alex will stay with his father.		
2. Alex will get into trouble again.		
3. Ramón will ask Rebecca to marry him.		

WATCH FOR DETAILS

Watch PART 1.

WHILE You Watch

8 Listen to the Wangs' discussion in the hospital. Circle the words they say.

1. Mr. Wang: "Vincent, how do you know about (Taiwan)/Los Angeles?"
2. Vincent: "I heard you and Mr. Mendoza/Mom talking. . . ."
3. Mrs. Wang: "We think to stay/work in San Francisco is best for you."
4. Mrs. Wang: "You and I/Alex will stay here, and your father will go and work in Taiwan."
5. Vincent: "Why/Really?"
6. Mrs. Wang: "Your father will go for one year/two years."

AFTER You Watch

9 How much do you remember about the story? Put the sentences in order from 1 to 5.

a. _____ The Wangs find the boys at the hospital.
b. _____ Ramón decides to call home.
c. _____ Mrs. Wang tells Vincent that they won't go to Taiwan.
d. ___1___ Rebecca and Ramón look for Alex and Vincent in the park.
e. _____ Mr. Wang asks the boys whey they ran away.

10 What do they say? Use the words in the box to complete the sentences.

| child | father | ✓ friend |

1. "This is my worst nightmare — not knowing where your _____ is."

2. "Alex is my best __friend.__ We just wanted to do something special."

3. "Your _____ will go to Taiwan for one year."

Watch PART 2.

WHILE You Watch

11 Who is speaking? Write **RM** for *Ramón*, or **RC** for *Rebecca*.

1. __RM__ "I've got to do what's right for Alex."
2. _____ "You are doing what's right."
3. _____ "No, I've put him in a terrible situation."
4. _____ "Everybody says that a child should be with his mother."
5. _____ "You love your son. It's obvious."
6. _____ "Stop this right now!"

AFTER You Watch

12 How much do you remember about the story? Check (✓) the sentences that *are not* true.

1. _____ Ramón is upset.
2. ___✓___ Rebecca and Ramón decide to move to Los Angeles.
3. _____ Rebecca thinks Ramón is a bad father.
4. _____ Kevin tells Ramón where Vincent and Alex are.
5. _____ Rebecca meets Monica.

13 What does Ramón think? Complete the sentences. Choose the answers.

1. __b__ Ramón thinks it's ___hard___ to have a child, a restaurant, and a personal life.
   a. easy   b. hard   c. bad

2. _____ Ramón thinks he should _____.
   a. pay more attention to Alex   b. yell at Alex   c. send Alex to Los Angeles

3. _____ Ramón thinks he makes Alex feel _____.
   a. happy   b. confused   c. bored

4. _____ Ramón thinks he _____ what's right for Alex.
   a. is doing   b. isn't doing   c. shouldn't do

What About you? What is your opinion? Check (✓) *True* or *False*.

	True	False
1. A child should be with his or her mother.	_____	_____
2. A father can raise a child without a mother.	_____	_____

Watch PART 3.

WHILE You Watch

 Listen to Ramón talk to Alex. Check (✓) the sentences he says.

1. __✓__ "Listen carefully to what I'm going to say."
2. _____ "You don't have to worry about who you're going to live with."
3. _____ "I promise that you can stay with me."
4. _____ "And I promise that your happiness will be our first priority."
5. _____ "I don't want you to go to the restaurant."

AFTER You Watch

 How much do you remember about the story? Put the photos in order from 1 to 5.

a. _____
b. _____
c. _____
d. __1__
e. _____

a. "Happy New Year!"

b. "You know you're grounded, right?"

c. "At least you're home now."

d. "Are you all right?"

e. "I should go home. Good night."

What About you? What is your opinion? Check (✓) *I agree* or *I disagree*.

	I agree	I disagree
1. Alex needs to be punished.	_____	_____
2. Alex shouldn't be punished.	_____	_____
3. Punishing Alex will teach him a lesson.	_____	_____

HIGHLIGHTS

CULTURE

New Year's Eve is an exciting holiday in the United States and Canada. People usually do these things on New Year's Eve.

count down to midnight

kiss at midnight

wear funny hats

make resolutions

1. How do you celebrate New Year's?
   _____ I count down to midnight.   _____ I make resolutions.
   _____ I kiss someone at midnight.   _____ other _____
   _____ I wear a funny hat.

2. What resolutions will you have for next year?
   Next year I will. . .
   1. _____
   2. _____
   3. _____

EXPRESSIONS

16 Match the underlined words from the story with their meanings.

a. be very angry   c. forgot about the
b. faster way   ✓ d. get good

1. _____ Rebecca: "Maybe they <u>lost track of</u> time."
2. _____ Alex: "My dad will <u>have a fit</u>."
3. _____ Ramón: "There is a <u>short cut</u> through the park."
4. ___d___ Mr. Wang: "I expect you to <u>keep up your</u> grades."

EPISODE **48** page **7**

REVIEW AND DISCUSS

STORY SUMMARY

 17 Use the words in the box to complete the story summary for Episode 48.

angry	baby-sitter	call	find	happy	hospital	house
move	✓park	party	ran	restaurant	says	spend

Rebecca and Ramón look for the boys in the ___park___ (1). They can't _____ (2) them and decide to _____ (3) home. The Wangs pick up the boys at the _____ (4). Mr. Wang is very _____ (5). He wants to know why the boys _____ (6) away. Vincent says he doesn't want to _____ (7) to Taiwan. He wanted to _____ (8) New Year's Eve with Alex. Mrs. Wang _____ (9) that only Mr. Wang will move to Taiwan. They return to Ramón's _____ (10). Kevin and the _____ (11) are there. Ramón is _____ (12) to see Alex. He grounds him but lets him go to the _____ (13) for the _____ (14). Everyone celebrates the New Year.

VIEWPOINTS

 18 What do you think will happen? Check (✓) all your answers.

1. _____ Ramón and Rebecca will get married and be happy together.
2. _____ Rebecca will be a famous singer.
3. _____ Alberto will find a new girlfriend soon.
4. _____ Alberto will move to a different city.
5. _____ Vincent and Alex will always be friends.
6. _____ Kevin will move to San Francisco.

Discussion Group Index

To find the students for the Discussion Group, signs about the CONNECT WITH ENGLISH television program were placed in universities and community centers in the Boston area. More than 100 people offered to participate. From this group, about 40 people auditioned on tape. They were asked questions like, "Where do you come from?" and, "How did you get to the United States?" The final 16 people were chosen because they told the most interesting stories, felt comfortable in front of the camera, and had clear speaking voices. The students did not have a script to read from. All of their stories are true, and they did not practice their lines.

**Roberto Arévalo
Colombia**

Roberto moved to the United States because he wanted to see more of the world. He arrived in 1981 and now works as a video producer. His wife is a doctor.

**Olga Baloueff
Belgium**

Olga lived in Belgium and in Zaire before she moved to the United States. She is currently going to graduate school in the Boston area, and she has a husband and a son.

**Nina Chen
China**

Nina was a teacher before she came to the United States in 1982. Nina thinks education is very important and is proud that both of her daughters have finished college.

**Ventha Danapalan
India**

Ventha came to the United States in 1992. Before he moved to Boston, he studied electrical engineering in Arizona.

**Laura Eastment
Argentina**

Laura moved to the United States from Argentina in 1969. She came to the United States to study agricultural engineering.

**Nisenat Gabrezgi
Eritrea**

Nisenat came to the United States in 1992. She says that her experiences in her new home are a lot like Rebecca's—except that Nisenat has the extra job of learning English!

DISCUSSION GROUP INDEX

Patrick Jerome
Haiti

Patrick was a filmmaker in Haiti before he moved to the United States in 1993. He attends college in the Boston area.

Nela Hosic
Bosnia

Nela had been in the United States only two months before she became a part of the Discussion Group. Her husband and two children moved with her, but her parents still live in Bosnia.

Abdul Khushafah
Yemen

Abdul left his home country of Yemen in 1984, where he worked as a carpenter. He is glad he made the decision to move. He now works as a designer.

Boris Levitin
Russia

Boris was born in Moscow, Russia. He lived in Israel before he moved to the United States in 1979 at the age of fifteen.

Lan Ma
China

Lan is from Beijing, China, and came to the United States in 1990 to continue her education. When she arrived in Boston she didn't know anybody, but now she is very happy to live there.

Raúl Méndez
Puerto Rico

Raúl is a developmental psychologist at a hospital in Boston. He still works in Puerto Rico three months a year, and he has two grandchildren who live there.

Casilda Nunes
Brazil

Casilda is in the United States to study English. She only planned to stay for six months, but when the Discussion Group was filmed, she had been in the U.S. for almost two years.

Yukiyoshi Ozawa
Japan

Yukiyoshi was actually born in San Francisco, California, but he was raised in Japan. He is now a college student in Boston. He came to live in the United States in 1995.

Hai B. Pho
Vietnam

Hai arrived in the United States over forty years ago. His family wanted him to continue his education in the U.S. He moved back to Vietnam in the 1970s, but now he lives near Boston.

Rosalba Solís
Mexico

Rosalba came from Mexico in 1978 to pursue her dream of becoming a jazz musician. Like Rebecca, she wanted to go to music school, and today she is a music teacher in Boston.

DISCUSSION GROUP INDEX

Character Index

This index includes the names of most of the characters who appear in CONNECT WITH ENGLISH, alphabetized by their first names.

Alberto Mendoza
San Francisco, California.
An architect who meets Rebecca in the desert.

Alex Mendoza
San Francisco, California.
Ramón's son and a student at the after-school program.

Angela Calud
San Francisco, California.
A nursing student. She lives at Nancy Shaw's house.

Bill Ellis
San Francisco, California.
A student at the San Francisco College of Music and Rebecca's friend.

Brendan & Anne Casey
Aurora, Illinois.
Rebecca and Kevin's uncle and aunt.

Carmen & Enrique Mendoza
San Francisco, California.
Alberto and Ramón's parents. They own the Casa Mendoza restaurant.

Edward Shaw
San Francisco, California.
A retired musician, he is Nancy Shaw's uncle. He lives in a nursing home.

Emma Washington
San Francisco, California.
The director of the after-school program where Rebecca works.

Frank Wells
Boston, Massachusetts.
Patrick Casey's friend.

Jack Sullivan
Boston, Massachusetts.
Sandy's boyfriend.

Kevin Casey
Boston, Massachusetts.
Patrick Casey's son and Rebecca's younger brother.

María Gómez
San Francisco, California.
The financial aid counselor at the San Francisco College of Music.

Matt Carlson
Boston, Massachusetts. Rebecca's boyfriend in Boston.

Melaku Tadesse
San Francisco, California. A business student. He lives at Nancy Shaw's house.

Molly Kelly
Boston, Massachusetts. Margaret Casey's sister, and Rebecca and Kevin's aunt.

Nancy Shaw
San Francisco, California. Rebecca's godmother. She runs a boarding house for students. Rebecca lives with her in San Francisco.

Patrick Casey
Boston, Massachusetts. Rebecca and Kevin's father. He is a retired firefighter.

Ramón Mendoza
San Francisco, California. Alex's father and Alberto's brother. He works at his parents' restaurant.

Rebecca Casey
Boston, Massachusetts and San Francisco, California. A music student with a dream. She moves from Boston to San Francisco to study music. She is Patrick's daughter and Kevin's older sister.

Sandy Dawson
Boston, Massachusetts. Rebecca's best friend and Jack's girlfriend.

Professor Thomas
San Francisco, California. One of Rebecca's professors at the San Francisco College of Music.

Mr. & Mrs. Wang
San Francisco, California. Vincent's parents. Mr. Wang owns a store in Chinatown.

Vincent Wang
San Francisco, California. Alex's best friend at the after-school program. He is the son of Mr. and Mrs. Wang.

CHARACTER INDEX